MAINLAND SOUTHEAST ASIA: AN ANTHROPOLOGICAL PERSPECTIVE

MAINLAND SOUTHEAST ASIA

MAINLAND SOUTHEAST ASIA: AN ANTHROPOLOGICAL PERSPECTIVE

RONALD PROVENCHER

NORTHERN ILLINOIS UNIVERSITY

GOODYEAR PUBLISHING COMPANY, INC.
Pacific Palisades, California

FOR BARBARA AND HASNAH,
THEIR FAMILIES, AND THEIR FRIENDS

Library of Congress Catalog Card Number: 74-19947

Provencher, Ronald
  Mainland southeast Asia.
California   Goodyear Publishing Co., Inc.
April 1975
(Anthropology) 9-18-74

Library of Congress
Catalog Card Number:
74-19947
(Paper) Y-5376-2
(Cloth) Y-5384-6
ISBN: 0-87620-537-6
        (Paper)
        0-87620-538-4
        (cloth)

Current printing (last
digit):

10 9 8 7 6 5 4 3 2 1

Printed in the
United States of America

GOODYEAR REGIONAL ANTHROPOLOGY SERIES

Edward Norbeck, Editor

ANTHROPOLOGICAL PERSPECTIVES OF:

MODERN EUROPE
Robert T. Anderson

INDIA
Stephen A. Tyler

INDONESIA
James L. Peacock

CIRCUMPOLAR PEOPLES
Nelson H. Graburn and Barry S. Strong

NORTH AMERICAN INDIANS
William W. Newcomb, Jr.

SOUTHEAST ASIA
Ronald Provencher

Additional Volumes Forthcoming:

China

Africa

Philippines

Polynesia and Micronesia

Middle East

Latin America

CONTENTS

ACKNOWLEDGMENTS

The subject of this small book is very broad and complex. Obviously, I owe a debt of gratitude and recognition to hundreds of authors whose contributions to knowledge of the subject are here masked by generalizations that are necessary for brevity. Also, the best interpretations in the book owe much to the freely dispensed wisdom of my professors and other colleagues, especially Abdul Maulud Yusof, James Anderson, Milton Barnett, Gerald Berreman, William Davis, Frederick Dunn, May Ebihara, Delmos Jones, Henry Lewis, Lie Kian Joe, Theodore McCown, Robert McKinley, Frederick von der Mehden, Herbert Phillips, James Scott, Lauriston Sharp, Joseph Silverstein, Robert Spier, Syed Husin Ali, Teuku Jakob, and Paul Wheatley. Southeast Asian philosophers — Malay shamans and holy men, Thai priests, and Burmese monks — whose names are not recorded here, gave hours of time interpreting their cultures for an interested, but not always astute, stranger, and I thank them. I wish also to thank my wife, Barbara, for typing and editing drafts of the manuscript, and Edward Norbeck for trying to smooth my writing style. Finally, I owe the greatest debt of gratitude to Jasper Ingersoll for a careful reading of the manuscript and for his many insightful suggestions for improving it.

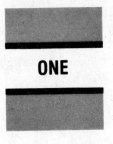

ONE

THE BEGINNING OF SOUTHEAST ASIA

Mainland Southeast Asia is a peninsula that lies east of India and south of China. The Naga Hills mark its boundary with the Indian realm on the west. Mountain ranges form the northern border with China. Three tines of the peninsula—Burma, Malaya, and Indochina—plunge southward. Malaya, the central tine, almost reaches the equator as it enters the island world of Indonesia. With the islands of Indonesia and the Philippines, it is a bridge between Asia and Australia that separates the Indian and Pacific oceans.

The peninsula and the islands seem to form a unit in many ways. Their flora, fauna, and cultural communities have much in common. The islands are often included as a part of Southeast Asia.[1] For similar reasons, Taiwan, Hainan, the Andaman Islands, Sri Lanka (Ceylon), and Assam are sometimes added. The task of describing the diversity that results from these additions is too great. This volume is focused on the peninsula of Southeast Asia.

The peninsula of Southeast Asia, hereafter referred to simply as mainland Southeast Asia, consists of Burma, Thailand, Laos, Cambodia, North Vietnam, South Vietnam, and the western portion of Malaysia (formerly Malaya). Brief reports of Singapore and the eastern portion of Malaysia are included. This area has about the same amount of land and about the same number of people as that part of the United States that lies east of the Mississippi River. It is neither an empty nor a crowded land.

It is an important area because of its location, resources, and people. It lies across trade routes between more politically powerful and more densely populated regions. Its mineral resources include petroleum, tin, iron, tungsten, and other metals. Its commercial agriculture produces large amounts of raw material and food for export. And it is an important market for goods manufactured in Japan, Europe, China, and the United States.

The saying that Southeast Asia is a land of diversity is both familiar and true. It is a land of mountains, hills, river valleys, coastal plains, and seashores. The natural landscapes of rain forest, jungle, bamboo thicket, scrub, and mangrove swamp are as varied as the commercial plantations of rubber, coconut, tea, oil palm, coffee, pineapple, and rice. Temperatures range from cold to hot, depending on altitude, latitude, and the time of the year. It may be dry as dust one season and muddy the next, or it may be wet the year around, depending on the place.[2]

Human beings who live there are a diverse lot, too. A very few make their living by hunting and by gathering wild products of the forest. A few others are slash-and-burn horticulturalists. Some are fishermen. Others are businessmen, clerks, soldiers, plantation workers, servants, or factory workers. Many are wet-rice farmers.

Physical types are diverse. Pygmies inhabit isolated forests in Malaya and southern Thailand. Their appearance is not the same as that of the Pygmies of Africa. On the average they are taller, have lighter skin and broader faces, and less frequently have kinky hair. The pygmy population is small—no more than two or three thousand. However, several traits usually attributed to them —short stature, dark skin, and kinky hair—occasionally appear in other populations. Among some hill peoples, a few individuals resemble Veddas of Sri Lanka (Ceylon). And some lowlanders, especially among the Khmers of Cambodia, resemble Dravidians of India. A majority of the people of mainland Southeast Asia look like the people of southern China, except that they have slightly darker skins, noses with higher bridges, and eyes with less noticeable epicanthic folds. Recent immigrants have increased the original diversity. Chinese, Tamils, Bengalis, Sikhs, Arabs, and Europeans have contributed to the diversity of physical types. All sorts of mixtures have occurred.[3]

The histories and customs of these peoples are so varied as to require most of this volume merely to sketch an outline of them. The broad dimensions of this variation—language, religion, social structure, and technology—intertwine, forming a mosaic of the most disparate combinations. Aboriginally, there were several hundred distinct languages belonging to six major language families. Languages of recent immigrants from China, India, and Europe have added variety. Buddhism, Islam, Christianity, and Hinduism, each with several sects, have many adherents in mainland Southeast Asia. Confucianism and Taoism are part of the religious tradition of millions of overseas Chinese in the area and have deeply affected the religious practices of the Vietnamese. Native religions, some very old and others recently synthesized from native and foreign elements, add variety. Bands, tribes, chiefdoms, kingdoms, and empires have been superficially transformed into models of Western states. Subsistence agriculture and modern industry exist side by side. These dimensions of cultural variety do not fit together precisely. The mosaic has many irregularities in its pattern.

Mainland Southeast Asia lies between India and China, but it is not merely a blend of the two. It is a distinctive, if complex, culture area. Diversity is one of its major characteristics, but there are regularities, which I shall attempt to describe.

OLD LAMPS AND NEW

Southeast Asian cultures are changing. However, details have changed much more rapidly than large patterns, insuring a relationship of continuity between cultural history and modern events in Southeast Asia. Government officials appreciate cultural history. It has become a part of building new nations in the region. Past achievements help support the national and cultural pride of modern political regimes. The people—urban workers, rural farmers, and horticulturalists—have, in their own way, shown great loyalty to their own particular cultural identities. When they have accepted certain portions of Western technology, they have usually viewed them as modern rather than as particularly Western. Their point of view is reasonable.

Changes in the cultures of Southeast Asia have accompanied close contacts with Western cultures that began more than four hundred years ago. These changes are comparable to those in European cultures during the same period of time, and they may be attributed to the same cause—participation in the Industrial Revolution. Indeed, Southeast Asians contributed as much as Europeans to the Industrial Revolution, which developed out of the ancient East-West sea trade in luxury goods. Initially, Southeast Asians controlled the trade route. Eventually, Europeans gained control. Later, as trade flourished beyond its original scope, the ancient capitalism of luxury goods gave way to the new capitalism of common goods. As producers of vast quantities of raw material and as consumers of large quantities of processed goods, Southeast Asians supported Western factories. The major organizational features of the Industrial Revolution, specialization and mass production, affected Southeast Asian cultures almost as much as they did European cultures.[4]

In spite of a common experience with the Industrial Revolution, the cultures of Southeast Asia have retained separate identities. No single Western nation ever controlled the whole area. The Americans, French, English, Dutch, Spanish, and Portuguese each controlled different areas, imparting different versions of Western culture. Often too, artifacts and behaviors that came from European culture have lost some of their original meanings and have acquired new meanings that are more compatible with the major perspectives and values, the patterns, of particular Southeast Asian cultures. These cultural patterns are not static. They are changing as they accommodate to artifacts and behaviors of Western culture. Changed, they differ from both the modern European and the traditional Southeast Asian patterns of culture. These several systems of artifacts, behaviors, values, and perspectives are contributing to the birth of a new civilization. We can best understand the nature of this new civilization and appreciate the character of its debt to the Industrial Revolution and to modern European culture by reviewing the ancient patterns of culture upon which it is based and by noting the earlier influences of Indian, Chinese, and Arabic cultures.

THE FIRST SOUTHEAST ASIANS

Members of our zoological family (Hominidae) have lived in Southeast Asia for more than a million years. Possibly, their occupation of Southeast Asia began several millions of years earlier, but no evidence supports such a claim. Indeed, fossil hominids have not been discovered in mainland Southeast Asia. The pertinent evidence is from China to the north and from Indonesia to the south. Between these two areas, mainland Southeast Asia must have been occupied, too. More archaeological research will probably produce the evidence. In any case, we cannot dismiss the possibility of discoveries that might parallel those of East Africa, where the search for hominid fossils has been much more thorough.[5]

The East African fossils together with Asian fossils indicate a succession of three hominid genera as follows: from fifteen million until ten million years ago, *Ramapithecus;* from about five million until two million years ago, *Australopithecus;* from about two million years ago until the present, *Homo.* Evidences of a species of *Australopithecus (A. robustus)* and several species of *Homo* occur among the fossils of Indonesia and China that represent the early hominid populations of Southeast Asia. *Australopithecus*, a four-foot-tall bipedal tool-user that is well known from numerous fossils in East Africa, is represented by only two very incomplete fossil specimens *(Meganthropus)* in Java and in southern China.[6] However, an early species of our own genus, *Homo erectus*, is well represented in the fossils of central Java and of southern and northern China.

Until the early 1960s, physical anthropologists usually placed *Homo erectus* in a separate genus, *Pithecanthropus*, which was thought to have been confined to Asia. More recent finds in Africa and further analyses of previous African and European finds have demonstrated that *Pithecanthropus* had a much wider geographical range. Also, a much needed reform of taxonomy now includes these fossils in our own genus, *Homo*.

Homo erectus was short by modern standards—about five feet tall. His postcranial anatomy (from the neck down) was probably very similar to that of modern man. The cranium (head) was different. The braincase was smaller (by one-third) and the jaws larger than ours. An extremely low forehead, heavy brow ridge, great width between the cheekbones, large teeth, and virtually no chin eminence gave *Homo erectus* a remarkably primitive appearance. Populations that lived in China, Southeast Asia, Africa, and Europe differed somewhat in appearance, and there were differences between early and late varieties. Those living in mainland Southeast Asia undoubtedly resembled the Javanese variety because Java was then geographically a part of mainland Southeast Asia. Rising seas, deepened by the melting of ice in temperate and arctic areas at the end of the Pleistocene era, caused the present separation of the Indonesian islands from the mainland.

No tools have been found in direct association with *Homo erectus* in Java or southern China. Fossils of a later race of *Homo erectus*, found in northern China, are associated with the earliest evidence of man's use of fire and with stone tools of a "chopper-chopping tool" tradition (Choukoutienian). Similar tools (Pajitanian tradition) have been discovered in a layer of earth that lies above some of the finds in central Java. Chopper-chopping tool traditions in mainland Southeast Asia include the Tampanian of Malaya, the Fingoian of Thailand, and the Anyathian of Burma.

Chopper-chopping tools were the most common kind of stone tools in Southeast Asia for more than half a million years. They are crude, consisting of large pebbles or flakes from which a few chips have been removed to form a rough cutting edge. Usually, the chips have been removed from only one side of the cutting edge, giving the tool an asymmetrical, unifacial appearance. Such tools are among the earliest known in East Africa. There, *Australopithecus* used them.

In Africa, Europe, and western Asia, tools that have chips removed from both sides of their cutting edges, bifacial tools, soon replaced the unifacial chopper-chopping tools. Eventually, tools of the Lower Palaeolithic were chipped and shaped over their entire surfaces, and tools with different uses acquired distinctive shapes. In Africa, Europe, and western Asia, *Homo erectus* and early varieties of *Homo sapiens* used such tools. During the Middle Palaeolothic (from one hundred fifty thousand years ago until thirty-five thousand years ago), Western varieties of *Homo sapiens* made some of their tools from flakes that were shaped before being struck from stone cores. They made core tools that were small and finely shaped. They developed special tools for particular uses.

Later, in the Upper Palaeolithic, they developed blade tools that were struck in succession from specially prepared cores. Many stone tool types for particular purposes were developed.

These cultural changes did not occur in Asia east of India although hominid evolution proceeded at the same pace as in the West.[7] Early Asian varieties of Homo sapiens were as advanced morphologically as Homo sapiens in the West. But the hominids of Southeast Asia did not develop advanced techniques for making chipped stone tools, and they seem to have been reluctant to borrow such techniques from their Western neighbors.

Bifacial handaxes that are similar to those of the Lower Palaeolithic in the West occur rarely in the Tampanian of Malaya and in the Pajitanian of Java, and a few bifacial flake tools have been found in Vietnam. These bifacial tools may have evolved separately, or the idea of making them may have come from the West. In any case, they were never very popular. Most stone tools continued to be unifacial.

Stone tool traditions of the Middle and Upper Palaeolithic of the West do not closely resemble any of those of Southeast Asia. During the time usually allotted to the Middle Palaeolithic of the West, the chopper-chopping tool traditions of Southeast Asia continued as before, little changed. Human beings changed, gradually assuming characteristics of early varieties of Homo sapiens. Fossil finds in southern China and in central Java signal their morphological progress.

Why did their stone tool traditions not progress? Perhaps appropriate kinds of stone for making finely chipped stone tools were not easily available. In fact, very few of the chopper-chopping tools are made from stone that has the proper kind of fracture (conchoidal) for making finely chipped tools. Also, other kinds of excellent, but perishable, material for making tools, such as bamboo, may have been so easily available that the possibilities of developing chipped stone tools were ignored. Another possibility is that the evolution of chipped stone tools in the West represents an increasing specialization in hunting large game animals for subsistence—a specialization that may not have been especially rewarding in most environments of Southeast Asia.

At the time of the Upper Palaeolithic in Europe (from thirty-five thousand years ago until twelve thousand years ago), an important change occurred in some of the chopper-chopping tool traditions of Southeast Asia. The most significant archaeological finds concerning this change are from the Palawan Caves in the Philippines and Niah Cave in Sarawak, both in island Southeast Asia.[8] However, the archaeological materials from these caves closely resemble finds in mainland Southeast Asia (North Vietnam, Malaya, and Thailand). The finds in the islands offer more information because their stratigraphic positions were not disturbed and because their age could be assessed by the radiocarbon method. Initially, the change included: (1) a gradual increase in the number of tools made from stone flakes rather than from cores; and (2) a gradual decrease in the size of stone tools. With this change, the Soan flake tradition, reflecting a generalized gathering economy in which mollusks and fish were important, developed.

About fourteen thousand years ago, two other tool-making traditions developed from the Soan flake tradition of Southeast Asia. In the islands of Indonesia and the Philippines, some communities adopted the techniques of striking several blades from a single prepared core, a technique employed thousands of years earlier in Europe. But the finished tools differed from those of the Upper Palaeolithic of the West. Other communities, especially in mainland Southeast Asia, developed the technique of shaping the cutting edges of flake tools by grinding several thousand years before the technique was employed in the West. What is even more surprising is that pottery making and plant domestication were a part of this same culture and were known much earlier in Southeast Asia than elsewhere.

This prodigious culture, the Hoabinhian, with its associated ground stone tools, pottery, and domesticated plants did not entirely replace other traditions. Chopper-chopping, small flake, and blade tool traditions continued. Probably, each tradition represents a different subsistence economy that was effective in some environments but not in others. Perhaps, chopper-chopping tools were efficient in generalized environments where hunting small animals, gathering plant food, and gathering mollusks were all necessary for subsistence. Small flake tools may have fitted into environments where specializing in the collecting of mollusks and fish was possible. Blade tools may have been part of an emphasis on hunting large animals. Edge-ground tools seem to have been associated with environments where a combination of mollusk collecting and horticulture was most important. The environments that were appropriate to each of the other kinds of subsistence techniques gradually contracted, but the techniques continued to be important for thousands of years.

These human developments that began more than a million years ago and lasted until about fourteen thousand years ago do not fit easily into Western notions about progress. At best, cultural progress seems to have been discontinuous during this period in Southeast Asia. How could people who made such crudely chipped stone tools for so long so quickly discover grinding techniques for making stone tools, invent pottery, or domesticate plants? Surely, such progress ought to be based on a foundation of earlier achievement.

Stone grinding techniques, pottery, and domestication of plants were undoubtedly based on earlier experiences. Probably, these included: (1) familiarity with mollusk shells and the ease with which they could be modified into tools and ornaments by grinding and polishing; (2) long familiarity with fire and its effect on heavy clay soils; and (3) familiarity with food plants that reproduced themselves obviously and quickly, that is, asexually. None of these experiences is related to the development of finely chipped stone tools that are used for killing large game animals and for using their remains. Experiences that did encourage development of finely chipped stone tools probably had little connection with Neolithic developments. Hunting and horticulture probably were distinct logical domains.

The law of evolutionary potential and the closely related concept of involution show the importance of this systemic or logical difference between hunting and horticulture.[9] Both concepts are attempts to explain the fact that long-term progress in organic and cultural evolution is not always continuous. That is, they are concepts that explain why dinosaurs did not become the ancestors of eutherian mammals and why England was not the first country to suffer (or enjoy) a socialistic revolution at the hands of industrial workers. Briefly, the law of evolutionary potential states that the form that has become most efficient (progressed the most) in one environment is least likely to give rise to the most efficient form in a new environment. Some less specialized form is more likely to be the basis of a new form. Thus, the lowly theriodontia gave rise to mammals, industrially backward Russia gave rise to the first successful socialistic revolution, and the chopper-chopping tool tradition of Southeast Asia gave rise to the horticultural Neolithic.

The concept of involution resembles the law of evolutionary potential. It has been used to explain periods of stagnation in histories of art styles and of economic development. In its infancy, an art style or an economic system has only a few very general patterns. Gradually, these patterns are interpreted more precisely and logically. Alternatives are narrowed. In the end, further interpretation becomes impossible. The pattern is set. The art style or economic system has become saturated, and there are no more implications of its basic patterns to be worked out. As its social context changes, it will become obsolete. It will survive only in those diminished areas where the old context remains or where newer styles and systems do not compete. The fact of its systematic completeness makes change difficult. Change one part and it no longer fits. Or, change one part and the whole system collapses.

In this light, the early development in mainland Southeast Asia of polished stone implements, pottery, and horticulture is not surprising. And that the food-producing revolution did not originate in Western Europe, the home of highly specialized hunting cultures, is understandable.

The Southeast Asian horticultural Neolithic was characterized by garden crops and fruit trees that were cultivated by hand labor, and it differed from the later agricultural Neolithic, which was characterized by cereal grain crops and the use of draft animals. The horticultural Neolithic developed and spread to China, India, East Africa, and most of the islands of the Pacific Ocean. In the Pacific, it was the basis of the horticultural technology of Papuans, Micronesians, Melanesians, and Polynesians.[10] In China and India, it was the first phase of Neolithic development towards civilization. Also, it was an important late addition to the Neolithic of Madagascar and East Africa.

Ethnology has an advantage over archaeology in reconstructing details of the Southeast Asian horticultural Neolithic. In the past, most Western scholars assumed that mainland Southeast Asia was not a likely center of cultural innovation. Only a few suspected that early Neolithic remains would be found there. No one sought Neolithic remains. Palaeolithic and early historical archaeology seemed more rewarding. Also, convincing evidence of early Neolithic remains depends heavily on preservation of organic materials. Neolithic dwelling sites were usually in the open and constructed of wood; therefore, their remains were less well protected than Palaeolithic remains, which are often found in caves, and more subject to rapid deterioration than the stone or brick architecture of many historical sites. The hot humid climate, seasonal fluctuations in the groundwater level, and acid soils typical of Southeast Asia quickly destroy artifacts and organic remains of domesticated animals and plants. That has been one of the excuses for not looking. Actually, the numerous caves and peat bogs of Southeast Asia provide excellent protection for organic and cultural remains.

Ethnologists, geographers, and botanists have described the horticultural Neolithic in much greater detail than archaeologists. Here, Linton's reconstruction, the most recent besides Solheim's, is supplemented with archaeological findings.[11] Linton did not use archaeological data at all, but the much more abundant ethnographical data of recent cultures of Southeast Asia, Madagascar, and the islands of the Pacific. He followed other ethnologists in assuming that culture traits diffuse outward from a nuclear point to other parts of a geographical area and that new traits are accepted first in the nearest communities and last in the most distant communities. Communities that are externally marginal to a center of cultural dispersal have traits that have already been replaced in more central communities. Also, Linton assumed that some communities close to the cultural center retain old traits because they fit special environmental circumstances. These internally marginal communities and the externally marginal communities mentioned above have traits that were common in the cultural center during a much earlier time. Thus the traits of the most primitive horticulturists in Southeast Asia and the traits of the peoples of the Pacific islands and of Madagascar figure prominently in Linton's reconstruction.

The basic postulate of this method of reconstructing cultural history is that differences in the spatial distribution of traits at the present time reflect differences in the time depth of the traits. There is no allowance for possible convergence or divergence of specific traits due to ecological circumstance. Additionally, the method tempts one to trace the distributions of whole cultures rather than just of individual traits. This leads to grandiose theories of migration and the confounding of race, language, and culture. Because archaeological data are incomplete, I accept the results of this ethnological method only as hypotheses that may be disproved or not according to archaeological evidence. In the next several paragraphs, I present Linton's ethnological reconstruction and indicate how it agrees with, or should be altered to agree with, present archaeological facts. Further changes in this reconstruction should occur as more archaeological data become available.

According to Linton, domesticated plants of the horticultural Neolithic included yam, taro, breadfruit, banana/plantain, paper mulberry, coconut, and dry rice. Bananas, breadfruit, and paper mulberry are seedless and depend on humans for propagation. This may indicate that they have been domesticated for a very long time. Archaeological evidence confirms an early date for the beginning of plant domestication. Analysis of pollen from different depths of soil indicates that the people of Taiwan practiced slash-and-burn cultivation as early as eleven thousand years ago. At that time Taiwan was, culturally speaking, very much a part of Southeast Asia. Other archaeological findings, in South Vietnam and Thailand, support the evidence from Taiwan. There is some evidence that people cultivated rice in South Vietnam as early as nine thousand years ago. There is good evidence that at that time people of Thailand cultivated beans, peas, water chestnuts, cucumbers, pepper, areca nuts, and bottle gourds. Archaeological evidence indicates that Linton's list of domesticated plants should be enlarged.

According to Linton, chickens and pigs were the major domesticated food animals. Chicken bones have not yet been reported in early Neolithic sites. However, there is no doubt that chickens are native to Southeast Asia. Pig bones are abundant in the remains of early Neolithic sites in North Vietnam and in Malaya and in Sarawak and Java. Once again the best evidence is from the islands rather than the mainland. Bones from a Neolithic site in eastern Java have been identified as *Sus vitatus*, the domesticated pig of

Southeast Asia. The bones from the other sites are of *Sus barbatus*, a wild species. Linton lists dogs as domesticates, too. They have been used as food in recent times in Southeast Asia, but in earlier periods, they probably had other uses. The domestication of dogs does not mark the beginning of food production. In any case, their bones have not been found in early Neolithic sites.

Linton stated that pottery was weakly developed or absent in the Southeast Asian Neolithic. Archaeological evidence shows this statement to be utterly false. Pottery is associated with the earliest evidence of plant domestication, and it was produced in Southeast Asia earlier than in any other area.[12] It was well-made pottery that evolved through several major types. Cordmarked, incised, and painted wares developed, in that order, and were dispersed with other elements of the Neolithic complex into nearby areas. Quite probably, the earliest pottery of China was from Southeast Asia. Millenia later, the easy availability of finely made Chinese trade wares depressed (but never entirely extinguished) manufacture of native wares in Southeast Asia. Pottery making spread to the Pacific islands, too, but had gradually declined in importance by the time Europeans first arrived. It is traits of this sort, traits that have nearly disappeared, that are apt to be overlooked in ethnological reconstructions of the past.

Linton described other artifacts of the Southeast Asian Neolithic. The manufacture of basketry was well developed. Bamboo tubes served as containers and as cooking vessels. Earth ovens were commonly used for cooking. Many varieties of matting were produced, and bark cloth was used for clothing, the loom being unknown. Woodworking was elaborate. Adzes and chisels were characterized by angularity and polishing of all surfaces. Chipping as a stone-tool-making technique was rarely used. Bamboo was used for making knives, scrapers, and projectile points. Weapons included clubs, spears, and slings. Shields were lacking, and the bow and arrow were hardly used. Water transport was well developed and included outrigger canoes and the use of sails. Houses were rectangular, had gabled roofs, and were upraised on posts or a platform.

Archaeological evidence confirms the existence of some of these traits in the Southeast Asian Neolithic. Impressions of basketry and matting on early pottery show that both were well-developed arts. Bark cloth has not been recovered from any archaeological site, but tools for making it have been. Finely made adzes and chisels are among the most common types of implements recovered from early Neolithic sites, suggesting both that they were important and that they were part of an elaborate woodworking technology. However, not all of the adzes are angular in form, rather some are lenticular or round in cross section. While these round adzes may represent a distinct culture, they appear to be as closely associated with the Southeast Asian Neolithic as the more angular or so-called quadrangular adzes. Finally, we might note that, like pottery, the bow and arrow may once have been much more important than when ethnographers first described the cultures in Linton's sample.

Eventually, archaeologists may be able to test Linton's ideas about social institutions that were common in Southeast Asian societies at the time of the horticultural Neolithic. So far, no archaeologist has attempted this, although similar kinds of archaeological research have been successful in other parts of the world. For now, I will merely repeat Linton's reconstruction of social institutions. The reader should realize the speculative nature of this list.

Political systems were weakly developed, with each village a separate political unit ruled by a village oligarchy. Each village was endogamous. That is, marriages were between members of the same village. Individual status was based on age, kinship, and wealth. Descent was bilateral. Daughters and sons had equal rights of inheritance. Each village had a separate house for bachelors. Marriage was monogamous and was considered consummated only upon pregnancy. Religion was a mélange of ancestor worship, nature deities, local spirits, *tabu,* and magic.

WAVES OF IMMIGRANTS:
RACE, LANGUAGE, AND CULTURE

Methods similar to the age-area method used by Linton in reconstructing traits of the horticultural Neolithic have also been used in analysing the racial history of Southeast Asia. Almost everyone who has commented on the cultural history of the area has commented on its racial history. Racial history has been constructed, usually, on the assumption that people living in isolated mountain and forest areas are descendants of the earliest racial types and that people living in coastal areas and easily accessible river valleys are racial types that arrived more recently. Several racial types are usually distinguished—Negritos, Veddoids, Palaeo-Mongoloids, and Southern Mongoloids.[13]

The first of these to arrive in Southeast Asia is supposed to have been a pygmy race—Negritos. The Semang (Jehai, Lanoh, and Mendrak) of Malaya, the Ngo (Ngok and Ngok Pa) of southern Thailand, and the Saoch (Samre and Pear) of southwestern Cambodia represent this racial type. In stature and general appearance, they resemble the Aeta of the Philippines and the Mincopi of the Andaman Islands. Perhaps they are related to the Pygmies of Africa, but this is even less certain than their relationship to the Aeta and the Mincopi.

Palaeontological and linguistic evidence of their origins, whether by migration into the area or by evolution from earlier hominid populations, is almost lacking. Such evidence as exists suggests only that they inhabited Southeast Asia before other racial types. At two archaeological sites, one in Vietnam and the other in Sarawak, what appear to be the skeletal remains of Negritos were found in deeper (earlier) strata than the skeletal remains of southern Mongoloids. Southern Mongoloids are the racial type that now inhabit most of the lowland areas in Southeast Asia. Linguistic evidence is poor. All Negritos speak dialects of the languages of other people in Southeast Asia. Languages spoken by the Negritos of Malaya, Thailand, and Cambodia are very closely related to the Mon-Khmer family of languages. Words of other languages have entered their vocabularies. Some authors believe that a few words of an unknown original Negrito language have persisted. This was possibly a Papuan language, as evidenced by the possible relationship of Andamanese to Papuan languages of New Guinea.

The idea that Negritos were the first of the present races to settle in Southeast Asia is based on the fact that they are mostly hunters and gatherers while members of other races have more advanced technologies. Also, they live in the most isolated areas, where they might have been pushed by the arrival of other peoples.

The name *Negritos* is not entirely appropriate. It means "little blacks." Their skin color is darker, on the average, than that of other people in the area, but it is not black. It is sepia to chocolate brown. They are of short stature, but other populations in the area are almost as short. The average height of adult male Negritos is about 150 (4 feet, 11 inches). Adult males in certain other populations, the Semai of Malaya for example, average only one or two centimeters taller, and some individual Negritos (particularly among the Jehai) reach a height of 168 centimeters (5 feet, 6 inches) or more. Females are usually ten or twelve centimeters shorter than males.

Most authors describing Negritos as a racial type have noted that the head hair is tightly curled or kinky. But only about one Negrito in twenty has truly kinky hair, and the others have deeply or moderately wavy hair. Body hair is usually sparse. A few old men have thin beards and mustaches. The bodies of Negritos are well proportioned and well muscled. Female breasts are usually pendulant. Negritos seem to age rapidly. Broad heads, where the width of the cranium is eighty percent or more of the length, are common. The face is broad with fairly massive cheekbones (malars and zygomatic arches) and bulging forehead. Noses vary in shape, but most are rather flat with depressed root and short low bridge. Lips are wide and full but not everted. Ears are small and set close to the head. Eye color is yellowish brown to dark brown. The inner epicanthic folds of the eyelids are rarely large enough to give a "slanted" appearance to the eyes.

The Negrito population is now very small, numbering only a few thousands of individuals. Perhaps they were more numerous in the past, before the beginning of the Neolithic period. They appear to have shared their genes with other populations since their distinctive physical characteristics are widely distributed among other peoples.

Some non-Negrito populations of Southeast Asia live in places that are nearly as isolated as those inhabited by Negritos. For the most part they are slash-and-burn horticulturists who only occasionally hunt or gather. Their technology thus appears to be more advanced, and some authors conclude that they are more recent than Negritos as immigrants to their present habitats. A major problem in designating them a wave of immigrants is that their physical appearance varies greatly from group to group and even from individual to individual within the same village.

In the Malay peninsula, some of these people are referred to as Senoi or Sakai. *Sakai* is a pejorative Malay word meaning "slave." Anthropologists usually use the term *Senoi*, a Mon-Khmer word meaning "people." In spite of the great variety of physical types referred to above, some authors have thought the Senoi constitute a single racial type that arrived in Southeast Asia after the Negritos. The great variety of physical types is explained as the result of interbreeding with other populations—Negritos, Malays, Chinese, and Indians. The "pure" Senoi are said to be similar to the Vedda of Sri Lanka and for that reason are called Veddoids.

Authors who speak synonymously of "Australoid," "Papuan," or "Melanesoid" elements in the racial history of Southeast Asia are usually referring to ancestors of the Senoi population. Characteristics of its members are long heads with breadth less than seventy-five percent of the length, and strong development of supraorbital ("brow") ridges. The cranial features of skeletons found in the context of Soan (late pre-Neolithic) and Hoabinhian (early Neolithic) archaeological sites in Vietnam and Malaya are those of this racial type.

The Senoi are slightly taller than Negritos, and they have somewhat lighter skin color. Body build tends to be slender. Head hair is deeply waved to straight. Occasional individuals have strongly developed beards and mustaches. Some individuals have noticeable inner epicanthic eye folds. Eyes are dark brown in color. Typically, the bridge of the nose is low and medium in width. Lips are thick but not everted.

Variations away from the "pure" type of Senoi usually resemble Negrito or aboriginal Malay types. Indeed, these variants are so common that it has been suggested the Senoi are merely a hybrid population resulting from Negrito and aboriginal Malay interbreeding. The problem with this interpretation is that some Senoi have characteristics—long narrow head, heavy beard, and light-colored skin—that are not intermediate between those of Negritos and aboriginal Malays.

Aboriginal Malays sometimes live in fairly isolated places, too. Like the Senoi, some groups (for example, Jakun and Temuan) are slash-and-burn agriculturists, but they less frequently rely on hunting and gathering. Other groups (for example, Orang Laut and Moken) are coastal boat people. The aboriginal Malays are similar in racial type to many of the hill people of Indochina, Thailand, Burma, and Assam. They are also similar to many of the people of Indonesia and the Philippines. All of these people are basically Palaeo-Mongoloids; that is, they are an ancient and generalized type of Mongoloid. Most authors have referred to them as "Proto-Malay" or "Indonesian." But these terms are not entirely appropriate since many of the people to whom they apply are not ethnically or linguistically related to Malays or Indonesians. In Southeast Asia, many of the people of this racial type speak Mon-Khmer languages. Even in Malaya, some of the Palaeo-Mongoloids speak Mon-Khmer rather than Malayo-Polynesian languages.

The Palaeo-Mongoloids are taller than the so-called Veddoids, with adult males averaging about one hundred fifty-eight centimeters. Body build is often quite stout and muscular. They have broad heads with wavy to straight head hair. Facial hair is sparse and body hair scanty. Eye color is brown, and some individuals have noticeable inner epicanthic eye folds. The nose is low to medium in height and medium or occasionally narrow in width. Lips are medium to thin. Some individuals have facial features that are similar to those of southern Europeans. Probably, these similarities are more the remnant features of an ancient and generalized *Homo sapiens* type than the result of recent interbreeding.

Racial historians have usually credited the Palaeo-Mongoloid racial type with the spread, if not the invention, of the Southeast Asian horticultural Neolithic and with the spread of Malayo-Polynesian languages. It is true that speakers of Malayo-Polynesian languages in such distant places as Madagascar and eastern Polynesia are physically somewhat similar. But there are striking differences, too. Many speakers of languages of the Melanesian branch of Malayo-Polynesian are oceanic Negroid in racial type. In the past, it was more the coincidence of horticultural Neolithic traits and Malayo-Polynesian languages than the coincidence of similar racial types that led cultural and racial historians to write about a Proto-Malay race that brought the horticultural Neolithic from China to Southeast Asia and carried it with them in their further travels to Madagascar and to the islands of the Pacific.

The distribution of Malayo-Polynesian languages may support this idea. There are none in mainland China and only a few in mainland Southeast Asia. However, the Kadai languages of northern Vietnam and southern China may be related to Malayo-Polynesian and may represent a remnant from ancient times. The possible further relationship of Kadai and Tai languages would support this point. To the south, in the Philippines and in Indonesia (with the exception of Papuan languages of New Guinea), all of the native languages are Malayo-Polynesian. The same is true in the islands of the Pacific. And, of course, the Malagasy language of Madagascar is also a Malayo-Polynesian language. This distribution might suggest that Malayo-Polynesian languages originated in China and later diffused into Southeast Asia, Indonesia, the Philippines, the Pacific islands, and Madagascar. However, other linguistic evidence seems contradictory.[14]

Malayo-Polynesian languages may be divided into two subgroups—a western and an eastern branch. The western branch consists of all of the Malayo-Polynesian languages in mainland Southeast Asia, Indonesia, the Philippines, the Marianas, and Madagascar. The eastern branch consists of languages spoken in Melanesia, Micronesia (except the Marianas), and Polynesia. Melanesian languages, especially Fijian, appear to be central in the development of the eastern languages. In effect, Polynesian languages appear to have developed from Melanesian languages like Fijian, Rotuman, and northern New Hebridean. Moreover, it has been suggested that the western or "Indonesian" branch has diverged farther from earlier forms of Malayo-Polynesian than has Fijian. Languages of the western branch may have developed from Melanesian languages, too. Does this mean that modern speakers of Malayo-Polynesian languages have immigrated to Southeast Asia from the islands of the east rather than from the mainland of Asia? This last possibility is not easily refuted.

Cham and Malay are the principal Malayo-Polynesian languages of mainland Southeast Asia. Cham and related dialects (Bih, Churu, Hroy, Jarai, Krung, Noang, Raglai, Rai, Rhade) that are spoken in South Vietnam and Cambodia are closely linked to Achehnese, which is spoken in northern Sumatra. According to their own traditions, Cham speakers came to the mainland from an island homeland. And before the breakup of the kingdom of Champa in the fifteenth century, almost all Cham speakers lived along the coast of Vietnam. Malay speakers are no more certainly an ancient population of mainland Southeast Asia than are the Cham. Chinese sources mentioned the Cham kingdom of the Annamite coast and the Malay kingdoms of the Malay Peninsula at about the same time (second century), and the migrations of Malays from Indonesia (mentioned in their own traditions from the fourteenth century) have continued to the present day. Like the hill dialects of Cham, the dialects of Malay spoken by inhabitants of isolated hill and forest areas may be the result of linguistic acculturation during the heyday of Malay kingdoms, or they may reflect recent migration from coastal areas. The Malays and Chams speak Malayo-Polynesian languages, but they cannot properly be described as

Palaeo-Mongoloids. Usually they are taller and have straighter head hair. Like other natives of Southeast Asia's lowlands, they are southern Mongoloids. Their physical characteristics differ from those of Palaeo-Mongoloid and oceanic Negroid peoples who speak Malayo-Polynesian languages and have culture traits that derive from the horticultural Neolithic.

Evidence in the form of fossil hominids suggests that Southeast Asia has been inhabited continuously for more than two million years. Some of its present day population must have evolved in place. It would be easier and more consistent with evolutionary theory to view the highly variable populations in the hills as ancient and generalized rather than as the result of hybridization between specialized "pure" races. The early development of a Neolithic technology indicates that the impetus for culture change need not always be attributed to outsiders who have migrated into the area from the north. Relationships between race, language, and culture in the area cannot be explained satisfactorily by simple notions about waves of immigrants.

BRONZE, IRON, AND WET-RICE CULTIVATION

Before turning to a description of early states, I must remark on the importance of metals in the prehistoric technologies of Southeast Asia. The people of Southeast Asia, if not inventors of bronze, were quick to learn how to make and use it. Four thousand years ago, probably more, they were making bronze weapons and tools in Thailand and South Vietnam. They used local deposits of copper and tin to make the metal and implements were cast in double molds.[15]

At that time, many traits of the Southeast Asian Neolithic that had spread to India and China were being superseded there by technological traits developed locally or coming from farther west. The outward expansion of Southeast Asian culture to the west and north had slowed. Elements of Indian and Chinese cultures were about to begin flowing into Southeast Asia. Bronze metallurgy may have been among the first of these culture traits to arrive. Or it may have been invented independently in Southeast Asia.

Until the first discoveries of these early bronze artifacts were reported in 1968, most prehistorians believed that bronze was not used in Southeast Asia earlier than about twenty-five hundred years ago. It is commonly supposed that at that time the so-called Dongson Culture first came into the area from the north.[16] The diagnostic artifacts of this "culture" are large bronze drums decorated with figures of people and animals and with geometric designs of scrolls and triangles. A few prehistorians have accepted the idea that the drums represent Scythian influences in southern

China. The drums have been found throughout the mainland and islands of Southeast Asia. Some are still prized heirlooms. Their decorations may provide information about the first makers of the drums. Presently they are closely integrated with the cosmological beliefs of their owners, and they probably reflect the cosmology of their owners' ancestors.

The Dongson drums were not the first objects of bronze in Southeast Asia, but it has been said that their first appearance coincided with the expansion of southern Mongoloids into the area. According to Frederick Barth, southern Mongoloids first migrated into Southeast Asia between twenty-five hundred and two thousand years ago.[17] He says that they brought the first wet-rice cultivation and implements of bronze and iron. He argues that the earliest evidences of irrigation and metal implements are associated with the skeletal remains of southern Mongoloids, whereas earlier Neolithic remains which lack these technological refinements are associated with the skeletal remains of Negritos, Papuans, Melanesians, or Indonesians.

The interesting part of Barth's story is his explanation of the late arrival of southern Mongoloid technology in Southeast Asia. He speculates that the ecological boundary between dry temperate and wet tropical climates was a threshold that the Mongoloids could not easily cross until they knew how to cultivate wet rice. Their wheat could not be grown in the wet tropics. When they either invented or learned wet-rice cultivation, they left their wheat fields and crossed over into the wet tropics, bringing bronze and iron implements with them.

The flaw in this interesting idea, of course, is that bronze implements were made in Southeast Asia well before twenty-five hundred years ago. Perhaps iron was known earlier, too, even though there is no direct evidence of it. The methods and equipment used by Southeast Asians to make implements of iron are not like those used in China. They most closely resemble those of East Africa. At present, it seems more likely that the East Africans learned iron smithing from Southeast Asians than vice versa. The earliest evidence of direct contact between Southeast Asians and East Africans, however, is rather late—about two thousand years ago. Iron-working techniques could have been learned from the Chinese or Indians, transformed by Southeast Asians, and then passed along to East Africans. In any case, tools of iron were an essential part of technology in every part of Southeast Asia centuries before the beginning of the historical period.

Large numbers of southern Mongoloids may not have moved into Southeast Asia before twenty-five hundred years ago. Chinese civilization did not cross the Yangtze until the second century B.C., and the Siamese entered Southeast Asia less than a thousand years

Other southern Mongoloids moved south before the Siamese, **19**
under pressure from Chinese conquests. They learned the techniques for growing wet rice as they moved southward into Southeast Asia.

SUMMARY

Human beings have inhabited Southeast Asia about two million years. The evidence of hominid fossils of nearby areas indicates that the biological evolution of the genus *Homo* proceeded at the same rate in Southeast Asia as in Africa, Europe, and the Middle East. *Homo sapiens* of Southeast Asia probably began to diverge into three local races—Palaeo-Mongoloids, Veddoids, and Pygmies—before fifty thousand years ago. Another racial type, southern Mongoloids, may have evolved in southern China. Archaeological and historical evidence suggests that southern Mongoloids have migrated southward into Southeast Asia during the past two or three thousand years.

The evolution of stone tools proceeded more slowly in Southeast Asia than in western regions of the Old World until about fourteen thousand years ago. At that time, some Southeast Asians began making stone tools by grinding rather than by percussion techniques. They also made pottery and domesticated plants and animals. They became food producers several thousand years before the peoples of other regions. Their Neolithic innovations diffused to other regions—China, the islands of the Pacific, India, and East Africa. That Southeast Asia continued to be a center of cultural innovation for several thousand years is suggested by evidence of early bronze metallurgy in Thailand.

The linguistic affiliation and the racial type of people who participated in developing the horticultural Neolithic of Southeast Asia are not known. Mon-Khmer languages and Malayo-Polynesian languages were spoken in the earliest historical kingdoms. Sinitic languages were spoken in kingdoms that developed later. Hill tribes speak Mon-Khmer, Malayo-Polynesian, and Sinitic languages. Mon-Khmer languages predominate among hill tribes. Malayo-Polynesian languages are associated with the most distant diffusion of Southeast Asian culture, and like Mon-Khmer languages, they are spoken by a wide range of racial types.

REFERENCES

[1] Two syntheses of the cultures of Malaysia, Indonesia, and the Philippines are Fay-Cooper Cole, *The Peoples of Malaysia* (New York: D. Van Nostrand Company, 1945); and Ben J. Wallace, *Island Peoples of Southeast Asia* (Boston: Little, Brown & Company, 1972).

[2] E. H. G. Dobby, *Southeast Asia,* 7th ed. (London: University of London Press, 1960), is one of the more complete works on the geography of Southeast Asia.

[3] For a general perspective on races of Southeast Asia see Carlton Coon, *The Living Races of Man* (New York: Alfred A. Knopf, 1965).

[4] The best exposition in English on ancient and modern capitalism is J. C. van Leur, *Indonesian Trade and Society* (The Hague: Van Hoeve, 1955).

[5] See chapters 8–10 of John Buettner-Janusch, *Physical Anthropology: A Perspective* (New York: John Wiley & Sons, 1972); and chapters 6–7 of C. L. Brace and M. F. Ashley Montagu, *Man's Evolution: An Introduction to Physical Anthropology* (New York: Macmillan Company, 1965).

[6] J. T. Robinson, "*Meganthropus, Australopithecus;* and Hominids," *American Journal of Physical Anthropology* 11 (1953): 1–38.

[7] H. L. Movius, "The Lower Palaeolithic Cultures of Southern and Eastern Asia," *Transactions of the American Philosophical Society,* n.s., vol. 38, pt. 4 (Philadelphia, 1948).

[8] T. Harrisson, "New Archaeological Results from Niah Caves, Sarawak," *Man* 59 (1959): 1–8; and R. B. Fox, "Excavations in the Tabon Caves and Some Problems in Philippine Chronology," in Mario D. Zamora, ed., *Studies in Philippine Anthropology* (Manila: Alemar, 1967).

[9] M. D. Sahlins and E. R. Service, eds., *Evolution and Culture* (Ann Arbor: University of Michigan Press, 1960); and C. R. Geertz, *Agricultural Involution: The Processes of Ecological Change in Indonesia* (Berkeley and Los Angeles: University of California Press, 1963).

[10] R. C. Suggs, *The Island Civilizations of Polynesia* (New York: Mentor Books, 1960).

[11] R. Linton, "The Southeast Asia Complex," in *The Tree of Culture* (New York: Alfred A. Knopf, 1961); P. Sarasin and F. Sarasin, *Reisen in Celebes* (Wiesbaden, 1905); C. O. Sauer, *Agricultural Origins and Dispersals* (New York: American Geographical Society, 1952); W. G. Solheim II, "Reworking Southeast Asian Prehistory," Social Science Research Institute, Reprint no. 34 (Honolulu: University of Hawaii, 1970).

[12] K. C. Chang and Minze Stuiver, "Recent Advances in the Prehistoric Archaeology of Formosa," *Proceedings of the National Academy of Sciences* 55 (1966): 539–43.

[13] See, for example, page 17 of Norton Ginsburg and Chester F. Roberts, Jr., *Malaya* (Seattle: University of Washington Press, 1958).

[14] See I. Dyen, *Proto-Malayo-Polynesian Laryngeals* (Baltimore: Johns Hopkins Press, 1953); and G. W. Grace, "The Position of the Polynesian

Languages within the Austronesian (Malayo-Polynesian) Language Family," *International Journal of American Linguistics,* Memoir 16, 1959.

[15] W. G. Solheim II, "Early Bronze in Northeastern Thailand," *Current Anthropology* 9, no. 1 (1968): 59–62.

[16] V. Goloubew, "L'Age du Bronze au Tonkin et dans le Nord-Annam," *Bulletin de l'Ecole Française d'Extrême-Orient* 29 (1929):1–46.

[17] F. Barth, "The Southern Mongoloid Migrations," *Man* 52 (1952): 5–8.

ANCIENT CAPITALS AND PORTS

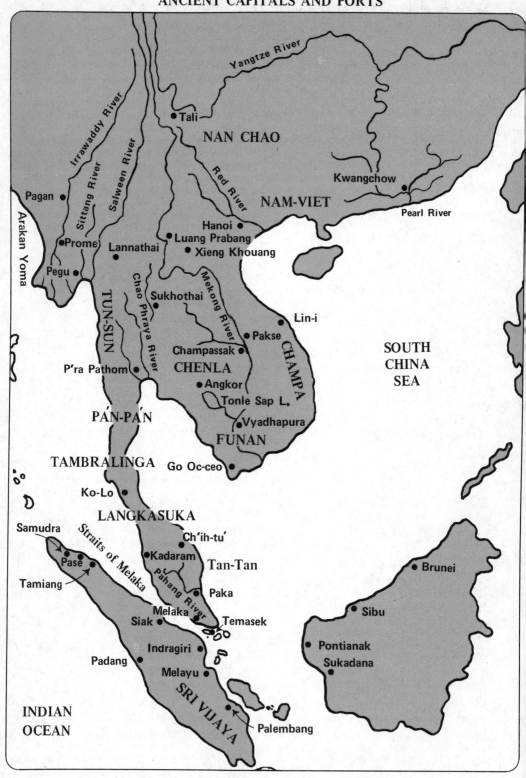

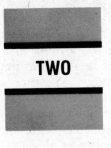

TWO

NATIVE CITIES, KINGDOMS, EMPIRES
OF THE PAST

Precocious in the development of a food-producing technology, Southeast Asians were slow in developing cities and states. An urban revolution did not follow the food-producing revolution as it had in the Middle East. Cities and states seem to have become common only about two thousand years ago.[1] This coincided with a time of strong influence from India and China.

Why? Was the horticultural technology of Southeast Asia not appropriate for developing urban centers? Did native social structural arrangements deter urban development? Is it only that evidence of early urbanism still awaits discovery?

Historical evidence of urbanism is late, but it appears in the first coherent accounts of Southeast Asia. Indian and Greek writers of the first and second centuries A.D. mentioned the area, saying that it was a great source of gold and silver.[2] Place names in the accounts refer to these important resources and show that writers in the West had only heard rumors of Southeast Asia. Chinese accounts from the second and third centuries A.D. contain actual place names and give brief descriptions of the people and their customs. The Chinese had firsthand knowledge because of their proximity. They had annexed northern Vietnam into the Chinese empire during the second century B.C. Their first recorded stories of Southeast Asia mention kingdoms and cities and contain internal evidence that suggests that these had existed since several centuries earlier.

Funan may have been the earliest kingdom and certainly it was the most important of early states. It had two large cities—an inland capital and a sea port. A great wall encircled the capital, Vyadhapura. Its buildings were constructed of brick and covered with plaster. This "City of the Hunters" was north of the Mekong delta, next to the hill called Ba Phnom near the confluence of the Mekong and the Tonle Sap rivers. Its legendary first ruler, the first

Kaundinya, was literally the "King of the Mountain." His title had
double significance because of the strong contrast and complemen-
tarity of hill people and riverine people in local mythology and
political structure and because of the importance of Mount Meru
as the center of the universe in Hindu and Buddhist cosmology.
Hindus and Buddhists were important foreigners, politically and
economically speaking. The King of the Mountain claimed a powerful position as chief sorcerer of fire and lightning in the native
cosmology and as controller of the pivot of the universe in the
cosmology of a powerful foreign people. His capital may have derived much of its support from the wet-rice lands around the edge
of Tonle Sap lake, but the capital relied on its port, Go Oc-ceo, for
much wealth, too. Go Oc-ceo was 120 miles away, on the coast at
the western edge of the Mekong delta.[3] It was a link in the trade
route that reached from the Spice Islands and China to India,
Arabia, and Rome.

Funan was the head of a confederation of Cham, Khmer, Mon,
and Malay states that lay across the trade route between India and
the East. The ethnic identity of the people of Funan is lost. There
are no Funanese, now. Various clues suggest in turn that they were
one or the other, or were closely related to one, of the surviving
ethnic identities—Chams, Khmers, Mons, and Malays. Next to
Funan, the most important state in the confederation was Chenla,
a Khmer state that occupied the middle Mekong valley and the
area around Tonle Sap lake. To the east, along the southern two-
thirds of the Vietnamese coast, lay the Cham kingdom, Champa. A
Mon kingdom, Tun-sun, occupied the lower Salween and Chao
Phraya river valleys and the upper reaches of the Malay Peninsula.
Various Malay states—Kolo, P'an P'an, Tambralinga, Langkasuka,
Kadaram, and Tan-Tan—controlled the rest of the Malay Peninsula. Until the fifth or sixth century A.D., most of the sea trade
with the West did not pass through the Straits of Malacca; rather,
it came to land at the western shores of lower Burma or the Malay
Peninsula. The most northern route began at the Arakan Yoma,
passed northward through the Irrawaddy valley and overland into
the heart of China—a difficult, mountainous trail and one controlled at its origins by Pyus, Tibeto-Burmans who were not part of the
confederation. The easier southern routes crossed the narrow
Malay isthmus to the western shores of the Gulf of Siam. Mons
controlled the northern portages and Malays the southern.
Some traders did not use the portages but coasted through the
Straits of Malacca and around to the east coast of Malaya. From the
western shores of the Gulf of Siam, traders sailed north along the
coast and then east to Go Oc-ceo. Some continued along the coasts
of Vietnam, stopping occasionally at Cham ports, then sailing to
the Pearl River. Others sailed across Funan and up the Mekong
until traveling by boat was no longer easy. Then they followed a

land route along the coast into southern China. In any instance, the south China coast was the end of the trail. The return routes were the same, and even with the possible variations required by the season of travel, the easiest routes kept traders within the realm of the Funanese confederation.

Monsoons imposed a temporal regime on travel by sea. The summer monsoon blows from the southwest and the winter monsoon from the northeast. During the doldrums of spring and fall, the direction of winds varies or the winds do not blow at all. Traders did not complete sea journeys between India and China in a single season. Even with good fortune, a return journey required most of a year, going with one monsoon, resting during the doldrums, and returning on the other monsoon. Probably, very few traders travelled the whole distance between India and China. Southeast Asian ports served as terminal points of trade from India and from China. Traders sailed with the monsoon to Southeast Asia, traded their goods during the doldrums, and returned on the next monsoon. The ports were entrepôts with facilities for storing goods and for housing and feeding weary travellers. Foreigners were an important part of the population of Southeast Asian cities from early times.

Obviously, the port towns and coastal kingdoms owed their existence to trade and contact with foreigners. But what of inland cities such as the capital of Funan? Did they develop before the trade routes across Southeast Asia became important? The answer depends on whether or not root-fruit crop horticulture was a good technological basis for urban development and, if not, whether wet-rice agriculture developed early as a part of the horticultural Neolithic or much later as a part of a movement of agricultural people from the temperate lands of China into the tropical lands of Southeast Asia.

Pacific islanders knew nothing of rice until after the arrival of Europeans in the sixteenth century.[4] But their horticultural technology included most of the root and fruit crops and three of the domesticated animals (pig, chicken, and dog) of the Southeast Asian horticultural Neolithic. Rice must not have been a very important part of the Neolithic when the islanders emigrated from Southeast Asia. Archaeological and lexicostatistical evidence shows that the peopling of the Pacific did not begin before three thousand years ago.[5] While rice may have been one of the available cultigens, it could not have been very important for the islanders not to have carried it with them in their travels. Rice is much less delicate than some of the root crops and could easily have survived journeys at sea. Also, the Pacific island cultures, based on root and fruit crops, did not develop urban centers or states. The root and fruit crops of the Southeast Asian Neolithic may not have supported very dense populations. Dry-rice farming does not support dense populations, either. Wet-rice agriculture requires more labor and will support very dense populations. It seems an excellent basis for urban development. Archaeological evidences of wet-rice agriculture, faint traces of a vast network of canals in the area of old Funan and a system of water reservoirs in the old Champa area, have not been precisely dated, but they indicate that the inhabitants practiced wet-rice agriculture before the arrival of the Vietnamese and before the beginning of Chinese or Indian influence.

Wet-rice agriculture increased the possibility of urbanism. It led to increases in the density of rural populations through its requirement for high labor input and its high productivity. Surpluses could pay for higher and higher levels of ritual redistribution and for increasing numbers of ritual, military, and commercial specialists. Small-scale kingdoms probably developed in the alluvial areas most favored for wet-rice agriculture before the first contacts with Chinese and Indian civilization. Given the superior navigational skills and maritime supremacy of Southeast Asians in the Indian Ocean and the South China Sea, they probably made the first contacts. Later, as the intensity of contact increased with trade, Southeast Asian rulers adopted aspects of Chinese and Indian civilization that strengthened their hold on their own kingdoms and on their position in international trade. Also, new kingdoms developed that were wholly dependent on international trade. They even bought their supplies of rice from other kingdoms nearby that had a surplus.

FUNAN

The earliest eyewitness accounts of Funan (Chinese transcription of Mon-Khmer *Bnom*, "mountain") are by the senior secretary and the cultural affairs officer of the third century embassy from the state of Wu, reciprocating an earlier Funanese mission to China.[6] The account seems to confound descriptions of urban and rural life, speaking in one utterance of walled towns and palaces and also of inhabitants who went naked and barefoot and had black skin and kinky hair and who sowed one year and harvested three. The inhabitants, by this description, were more like the Pear than like the Khmer. Also, sowing one year and harvesting for three may be an imperceptive description of slash-and-burn agriculture rather than of the occasional practice among wet-rice agriculturists of harvesting a field a second time after the roots of harvested rice sprout leaves again, flower, and produce another crop. On the other hand, the account may be accurate. Perhaps the ancestors of the Pear were the Funanese inhabitants of the "City of the Hunters."

Fifth-, eighth-, and tenth-century sources describe the same third-century expedition but with more detail, which may have been added later. According to these sources, the merchandise of

Funan included rings and bracelets of gold, vases of silver, and silk. There were books written with an Indian type of orthography and book depositories. All of the people wore sarongs of cloth. The sarongs of noble men were brocade. Women wrapped their heads in cloth. Houses were of wood and had roofs of woven palm leaves. They were built on pilings and enclosed within wooden palisades. Several dozen families shared a single well. The Funanese built large boats up to ninety feet long with bow and stern shaped like the head and tail of a fish. For amusement the people watched cock fights and pig fights. They paid their taxes in gold, silver, pearls, and perfume. Slavery was important, and the military were constantly raiding the territories of other states to get slaves. The king lived in a many-storied pavilion. He travelled with his concubines and courtiers, all riding on elephants. There were no prisons, but there was trial by ordeal to test the innocence or guilt of contending parties. The Funanese worshiped bronze images of the spirits of the sky. Shaving the beard and head was a sign of mourning. Corpses were submerged in the river, cremated, buried, or exposed to vultures.

The same officers of the embassy from the state of Wu, while at the court of the king of Funan, met an envoy from the king of Murunda, in India. They questioned him very carefully, acquiring information about dozens of kingdoms in Southeast Asia and the southern seas. Most of the kingdoms cannot be located with precision, and there is little ethnographic detail. But the Mon kingdom of Tun-sun is described more fully than even Funan.

TUN-SUN = Dvaravati

Tun-sun consisted of five subkingdoms, each with its own king. All acknowledged themselves vassals of Funan. Fan-man (third-century king of Funan) conquered them. The eastern part of Tun-sun was in communication with Tong-king (North Vietnam), and the western part was in communication with India and Parthia. People from the East and the West met daily in the city and traded rare and precious merchandise of all kinds (". . . there is nothing which is not there."). Patchouli, an herb highly valued in ancient times for perfuming and preserving clothing, grew in abundance there. In the third century, five hundred families of Indian traders lived in the country. There were several resident Buddhist monks and a thousand Indian Brahmans, according to the Chinese reports. The people of Tun-sun followed the doctrine of the Brahmans and gave their daughters to the Brahmans in marriage so that the Brahmans would not want to leave. Studying the sacred canon, bathing themselves with scents and flowers, and practicing piety were the only activities of the Brahmans. Exposure and cremation were the common ways of disposing of corpses. Exposure was thought to be an act of piety. In times of sickness, some people would vow a bird burial (exposure of the corpse to vultures). They were escorted with singing and dancing outside the town where the birds devoured them. The remaining bones were burned, placed in an urn, and sunk in the sea. If the birds refused to eat a man, he knew he was impure and his only recourse was to cremate himself by rushing into the flames. If he could not do that, he was thought to lack good character. There is no report of amusements in third-century Tun-sun, but a native wine received regular notice. It was said to come from a wine tree that was rather like a pomegranate, and the wine was fermented from the flowers. Probably, the wine was toddy, the fermented sap that is tapped from the blossom stalk of the nipah palm.

The author of one of the notices on Tun-sun notes that the Gulf of Siam is very great in extent and that, in the third century, oceangoing junks had not crossed it directly. Sailing along the eastern coast of the Malay Peninsula along the northern shore of the Gulf of Siam and around the tip of Indochina and along the Annamese coast into southern China must have been very time consuming, and it probably discouraged traders from extending an already long journey by sailing south through the straits of Malacca. However, by the fifth century, Malays were sailing directly across the Gulf of Siam and also directly across the South China Sea.[7] By shortening the sailing time from the Malay Peninsula to southern China, the Malays made the journey through the straits more attractive. This discovery of an easier route eventually undermined the prosperity and political power of the Funanese confederation.

There are descriptions of other states in the Chinese records at an early time, that is, before the fall of Funan, but present-day scholars cannot agree on the geographical location of many of them. Only the most important dependencies of Funan can be located precisely. One of these, the Mon kingdom of Tun-sun (later known as Dvaravati), I have already mentioned. It lay to the west and south of Funan. Chenla, a Khmer kingdom, lay to the north of Funan, and Champa, a Malayo-Polynesian kingdom, lay to the east. All of these states were approximately as ancient as Funan.

CHENLA

No explanation for the name *Chen-la* exists, but from the very beginning the Chinese used it in referring to a Khmer state on the middle course of the Mekong which eventually became Cambodia. The customs of the people of Chenla were like those of the Funanese, and Chenla was the successor state of Funan, showing that the Funanese were probably Khmers, too. Shreshthapura, the most important city of Chenla, was built on the site of a former Cham city, Champassak, which may once have been the capital of the Cham world. A natural linga, a great spire of stone, dominates the hill nearby, and it was the site of a cult of human sacrifice. Even the cult seems to have been started by the Chams. One night each year, the king sacrificed a human life in a temple at the summit of the hill. For the Khmers, the ritual was probably an act of celebration for victory over the Chams and also, as for the Chams, an act of worship of Siva, the destroyer god of the Hindu pantheon, and a mode of ritual identification of the king with Siva.

CHAMPA

According to Chinese records, the Chams founded the kingdom of Lin-i in the area of the modern city of Hue in 192 A.D. The Chinese name has no particular meaning, and it is not similar to any of the ethnic or place names in the area. Sanscrit inscriptions dating from the fourth century, however, bear the name of Champa, and at that time, the Chinese still referred to the kingdom as Lin-i. Champa was given the same name as a region in the delta of the Ganges River.

In Champa, according to Chinese sources, houses were built of fired brick, plastered with lime, and were surmounted by a platform terrace. The people had deeply set eyes, straight and prominent noses, and black frizzy hair. The women wore their hair in a knot on top of the head. Both men and women wore cotton sarongs. They pierced their ears and wore ear rings. The upper classes wore leather shoes, and the common people went barefoot. The king's crown was a tall cap with flower designs embroidered in gold and topped with a silk tassel. On his journeys, he rode under a parasol on an elephant and was accompanied by a large retinue. Musical instruments included the zither, five-stringed fiddle, and flute. Chinese considered the Chams a cruel and warlike people. Their weapons were bows and arrows, lances, sabers, and crossbows. They used conches and drums as warning signals. Burials varied according to class. After death, the burial of a king took place in seven days, the burial of a high official in three days, and the burial of an ordinary person the following day. In any case, the body was carefully shrouded and carried to the seashore or the bank of a river. There, amidst dancing and to the sound of drums, the corpse was cremated on a flaming pyre. The remaining bones of a king were placed in a golden vase and thrown into the sea, those of an official were placed in a silver vase and thrown into an estuary, and those of a commoner were put into a ceramic jar and thrown into the river. The parents of the dead person cut their hair as a sign of mourning.

ARCHAEOLOGICAL EVIDENCES

The Chinese historical sources that are the basis of these ethnographical accounts, although meager, provide most of our knowledge of the early states of Southeast Asia. Archaeological finds have added little, but they have confirmed the general outline of historical records. We are fortunate in not having to rely entirely on archaeology. Vyadhapura, for example, left no ruins or at least none that have been discovered, even though it was undoubtedly one of the largest cities and its precise location is known. Ruins of Vyadhapura's port, Go Oc-ceo, have been discovered. Slight traces of the foundations of buildings and canals survived along with a few Roman coins and a few shards of Greek vases. The ruined foundations of settlements in Tun-sun have been discovered at P'ong-Tuk and P'ra Pathom in the Mekong River valley of Thailand. Foundation stones of temples of ancient Kadaram have been discovered along the banks of the Merbok and Muda rivers in the state of Kedah in northwestern Malaya. These archaeological finds date from the second to the sixth century A.D. The most ancient remains of Cham civilization are in the form of rock inscriptions that were written in an Indian orthography but in Cham language. Dating from the fourth century, they comprise the oldest texts in any Malayo-Polynesian language. Most of these earliest archaeological evidences of urbanism date from the fourth and fifth centuries—the heyday of Funanese power. An archaeological lacuna of several centuries follows that probably indicates a period of relative anarchy in which the old economic, religious, and political relationships between states changed.

THE FALL OF FUNAN

Malay shipping became increasingly important in the sea trade between the northwestern ports of India and the southern ports of China. Not only did Malay traders sail directly across the South China Sea, they also sailed directly across the Indian Ocean, resting briefly at Sri Lanka or the southern part of the Coromandel coast before sailing northward along the western coast of India. In Southeast Asia, the trade route shifted southward. Portages across the Malay Peninsula became less frequent as traffic through the Straits of Malacca increased. The coasts of Funan and the Mekong River became less important as the Annamite coasts of Champa increased in importance. Economic and political power may have begun to shift towards the Malay world as early as the fifth century, when a former king of the Malay kingdom of Tan-Tan ruled as the second Kaundinya of Funan. He had studied at Brahman courts in India, and he introduced many new Hindu customs at the royal court of Funan. In effect, a Malay kingdom, Tan-Tan, appears to have had more direct acquaintance with Hindu culture than Funan, and perhaps it even outranked Funan in cultural prestige.

In the sixth century A.D., Funan lost control of the confederation. For a few years, the Khmer kingdom of Chenla claimed control over the confederation, but then it retreated to its lands in the middle Mekong and around the Tonle Sap. Several small kingdoms along the old Funanese coast, the Mon kingdom of Dvaravati in the middle Chao Phraya valley (central Thailand), and the Malay kingdoms of the peninsula all became independent. The confederation had shattered. Undoubtedly, one of the underlying causes was economic—loss of control over the East-West trade. Another may have been a shift in cosmological beliefs that affected kingship.

COSMOLOGY AND RELIGION

Hindu and Buddhist sects existed side by side from the time of the earliest kingdoms. The Buddhists proselytized more actively, but the royal courts usually favored the Hindu sects because they provided a more thorough and clear rationalization for kingship. Brahman priests were officials of the royal court. They were responsible for maintaining the god-king cult. In these cults, the king was an incarnation of the chief deity—Siva, Vishnu, or Indra.[8] The king was literally god. Moreover, his court was constituted in the image of the court of a Hindu god, and his city was a magical model of the universe that was ruled by the god. An image of Mahameru, the sacred mountain, was at its center. This image was a natural or man-made hill. The palace was near the center, too. Around it in ever larger perimeters were other sacred buildings—4, 8, 16, and 32 buildings, the magical numbers of Hindu cosmology. Around it all was a wall and a moat. But the city did not end there. It was a model of the whole kingdom as well as a model of Paradise. The city was a sacred place, carefully chosen and planned, that was the point of contact between the material and spiritual universes. But the god-king was usually more important than the city. At any time he might leave his old city and build a new one. He was a god-king.

Siva, the destroyer and restorer, was especially popular as the royal deity. His sign was a phallus, a solid stone cylinder mounted on a circular base, called a linga. It resembled, in a general way, the megaliths that some Southeast Asian people placed on the graves of their chiefs in earlier times, before the arrival of the Hindu priests. Other characteristics of Siva must have struck a familiar note. For example, Brahman priests identified Siva with Rudra, the Vedic god of thunder, and many of the natives of Southeast Asia worshipped a god of storms and honored sorcerers who claimed to have control over lightning. The importance of Parvati, the consort of Siva, complemented native social organization, in which women enjoyed fairly high status. Even Siva's mount, a bull called Nandi, fitted in well with the usual experience of Southeast Asians who rode water buffalo. But what must have been most important to the native chiefs who adopted the worship of Siva and thereby became kings was the character of Siva—a strong personality who took and gave as he willed and who ruled absolutely.

Vishnu worship made strong inroads during the sixth century into the position of Siva worship in the royal court of Funan. It may have paved the way for a brief period, just before the end, when Theravada Buddhism predominated. Vishnu worship allowed the blending of Buddhist and Hindu belief through the belief that Buddha was one of the manifestations of Vishnu, the preserver. Vishnu was known to have many avatara (aspects, manifestations, personalities, or incarnations), including not only Buddha, but also a fish, a turtle, a boar, a lion, a dwarf, Rama (of the Ramayana epic), and Krishna (of the Mahabharata epic). He, too, had a consort whose avatara—good fortune, Sita (wife of Rama), and Radha (wife of Krishna)—were worthy of worship. His mount, an eagle (garuda), was probably well regarded by natives in pre-Hindu times. Birds were alter-images of "personal soul substance" (Malay semangat), which was an important concept in native beliefs that paralleled Hindu conceptions of reincarnation and Nirvana. With Indra, king of the gods, Vishnu was supposed to be concerned with preventing drought and with fighting black savages. Indra was even more closely identified with the native god of storms than was Siva. Siva was usually favored over Indra and Vishnu by the early rulers of Funan. Long after the fall of Funan, Theravada Buddhism became the predominant religion in mainland Southeast Asia. Then, Indra and Vishnu cults flourished, and the cults of Siva were no longer important.

In the last half of the sixth century, the Siva cult lost favor in the Funanese court. First the Vishnu cult and then Theravada Buddhism held the attention of kings. The cosmological basis of universal kingship was temporarily lost. An heir to the kingdom was denied his claim by the Saivite king of Chenla. The Khmers of Chenla claimed and conquered Funan. Once broken, the confederation of Funan never rose. Even the god-kings of Chenla could not put Funan back together again. Chenla broke into two parts: Water Chenla, on the old Funanese coast, and Land Chenla, in the middle Mekong valley and around the lake of Tonle Sap. Khmers were very aggressive at this time. Their kings were firm supporters of Siva, the Destroyer. They claimed to be the rightful heirs of the royal Funanese and did not easily acquiesce to the breakup of empire. Champa, still firmly ruled by avatara of Siva, occupied some of the old Funanese territory in the Mekong delta, but they lost territory near Champassak to the Khmers. By this time, Theravada Buddhists were well established in the Mon courts. The Mons made no claim to the territory of Funan. They retreated to their cultural heartlands in the middle valley of the Menam Chao Phraya and the upper peninsula of Malaya. However, their reputation as scholars remained and grew. Possibly it was related to their former position in the court of Funan. In the centuries following the fall of Funan, their territories were absorbed into the kingdoms of new people who arrived from the north—Thais and Burmese. But they were the teachers of conquerors, including the Khmers, serving as scholars and advisers to the royal courts, and eventually they converted their masters and the citizens of the new kingdoms to Theravada Buddhism.

The cosmology of Buddhism is similar to that of Hinduism, but it lacks an all-powerful god who could be manifest in the strong personality of a universal king. Some kings did identify with Buddha. They had themselves declared an emergent Buddha (bodhisattva), or the courtesy of their court required that the prince who was to be the next king be referred to as "Bud of the Buddha" and that the king who had just died be referred to as "His Highness the Buddha." However, the personality of Buddha was not that of a strong king but rather that of a kindly prince who desired nothing, much less the power of ruling a kingdom. Usually, in fact, the god-king cult continued to play an important part in Buddhist kingdoms. Ritual aspects of the cult were subsumed into the rituals of coronation and funeral in the most orthodox Theravada Buddhist regimes, and in other regimes a god-king cult (Vishnu or Indra) was openly maintained in the royal court.

Theravada Buddhism was a more popular religion than Hinduism. It could be a more effective means of controlling large populations. This was important after the sixth century because of the loss of control over much of the international trade to Malay and Javanese kingdoms that bordered the Straits of Malacca. International trade had provided most of the economic support of the early kingdoms of the Funanese confederation. When international trade was reduced, more economic support for the royal court had to come from the surplus production of ordinary inhabitants. Their willingness to produce a surplus and give it up to the state either directly or in the form of nonfood-producing labor was ameliorated by the more comfortable yoke of Buddhism. In Buddhist doctrine there are no castes. Any person is worthy and can attain through merit a spirituality greater than that of a god. No pantheon of gods competed with the worship of local and ancestral spirits—the traditional religions were not interfered with as much as they had been under Hinduism. Moreover, local boys and men held the religious offices of local temples and were supported through acts of merit by other local inhabitants. Local bishops owed allegiance and obedience to a Buddhist primate appointed by the king. In this way the religious doctrine and belief of Buddhism reached from the most humble village to the royal court in a much more thorough fashion than Hinduism. Theravada Buddhism did not directly siphon the surpluses of peasants into the royal treasury. Indeed, the state supported the religion by assigning whole villages to the support of large temples or by allocating resources and labor for the construction of large temples. The primate, the bishops, and the monks accepted royal help and returned loyalty—supporting the king's taxes and conscriptions.

Theravada Buddhism did not sweep rapidly through Southeast Asia. It crept slowly eastward from its Mon base in the west. In the east, the Chams remained fiercely Hindu. And the Khmers, in the middle, vascillated between Buddhism and Hinduism. The suzerainty of a foreign Mahayana Buddhist power, the Sailendra regime of Java, over much of Water Chenla in the eighth century probably assured the predominance of Mahayana Buddhism in Cambodia at that time just as it gave impetus to a defiant shift to the predominance of the Hindu cult of Siva in the following century when Cambodia was liberated from Javanese imperialism.

ANGKOR: HEIR OF FUNAN

For the new rulers of Cambodia, the Javanese Sailendras were an important link with the glorious Cambodian past. They were also the beginning of a glorious Cambodian future. They claimed to be the heirs of Funan. At the least, this was a claim of inheritance of the political and spiritual leadership of the Funanese "Kings of the Mountain" (the Funanese and Sailendra royal titles had the same meaning). At the most, the Sailendras claimed to be descended from Funanese royalty. In any case, they were great kings who controlled much wealth and large labor forces. The economic power of the Sailendra kingdom in central Java was based on wet-rice agriculture. Through their development of extensive irrigation works, they had a strong claim on the food surpluses and labor of agriculturists. These builders of irrigation systems and the Borobudor in central Java strongly influenced the Khmer kings of Angkor, who after evicting the Sailendras from Cambodia, imitated them. The Khmer kings began by relying less on foreign trade and more on taxation of agriculturists and tribute from lesser states. They also followed the Javanese in the art and architecture of their monumental buildings.[9] None of this is very surprising when it is realized that the Khmer king who won independence for Angkor grew up in the Sailendra court in Java. But outcomes do not always replicate beginnings. In the ninth century, the Sailendra kingdom of Java merged with the Sumatran-based empire of Sri Vijaya and ceased to exist as a political entity, while the kingdom of Angkor outgrew its Javanese influences and became a great power in its own right.

The Javanese had attempted gaining suzerainty over Champa and Vietnam, too, in the eighth century. Their raids along the Cham and Tongking coast were successful but had no long-term effect. Vietnam, a province of China for a thousand years, gained its independence in the tenth century and began to press southward, encroaching upon the northern territories of Champa. At the same time, the Khmers pressed the Chams from the south and the west. Champa differed from its two adversaries in that its economy was based largely on foreign trade rather than wet-rice agriculture. The Javanese and Sumatran vessels that refitted in its ports on their way to south China supplied most of the surplus required for monumental architecture and the needs of the royal court. The Chams, themselves, were great sailing and trading masters who were respected in all of the port cities of Java, Sumatra, and Malaya. Indonesian states had very close relations with Champa, and the economic welfare of Champa depended upon their maintenance.

There were times of full-scale warfare, of course, but Champa lost most of its territory to wet-rice agriculturists who simply moved in and began farming. This was particularly true of Vietnamese expansion into Cham territory. On the relatively rare occasions when Chams attempted to move the Vietnamese farmers off the land, the peaceful conquest became more violent. The farmers requested help from the Vietnamese court but received it so seldom that they learned to rely on their own military skills. Usually, the Vietnamese failed in standing battles, but they succeeded in occupying territory and eventually learned to avoid battles that they would surely lose. In the meanwhile, Cham warriors successfully raided Khmer and Vietnamese coastal towns and cities, winning battles while they were losing territory. By the eleventh century, Champa had lost its northern territories to the Vietnamese, and in the first half of the twelfth century, the Khmer controlled the southern territories. Champa, in its classical style of warfare, destroyed the Khmer capital at Angkor Wat in retaliation but occupied the area for only a short time. The Khmers rebuilt their own capital (Angkor Thom) and annexed the Cham kingdom for the next 30 years (until 1220 A.D.).

The Khmers had been equally successful in the west during the tenth, eleventh, and twelfth centuries, conquering the Mon and extending their borders to Burma and the northern half of the Malay Peninsula. From the time of the breakup of the Funanese confederation at the end of the sixth century, Burmese had been moving south from their old homelands in eastern Tibet, conquering and absorbing their relatives, the Pyu, who lived in the Irrawaddy plain. They captured the Pyu capital of Prome in the eighth century and founded their own capital at Pagan in the following century. In the eleventh century, the Burmese overthrew the Mon kingdom in southern Burma and ruled the Mons until the end of the thirteenth century. But the Burmese did not come into direct conflict with the Khmers. The Khmers had reclaimed almost the whole of the old territory of the Funanese confederation.

The Thai people moved southward at a somewhat later time than the Burmese, and they caused the Khmers a great deal more trouble. They call themselves "Tai" or "Thai" but are known by other names in other languages. These other names, *Lao* in Chinese and *Shan* in Burmese, are well known even in Western countries where most persons assume that they refer to very different ethnic groups inhabiting different parts of a vast territory that includes Yunnan province in China, northern Burma, most of Thailand, and Laos. In the seventh century, the country of the Tai, Nan Chao, had its capital at Tali in Yunnan. From that time, under pressure from the Chinese, many of them drifted southward, following the great river valleys—the Irrawaddy, the Salween, the Chao Phraya, and the Mekong. They were established in northern Burma by the middle of the eighth century, in northern Thailand by the middle of the ninth century, and in Laos by the eleventh century. Like the western Khmer and Burmese before them, the Tai accepted the religious teachings of the Mon, becoming Theravada Buddhists. All that remained for the spread of the Tai and of Theravada Buddhism to be complete was Kublai Khan's conquest of Nan Chao (Yunnan) in 1254 and the invasion of Burma by his army in 1287, pushing speakers of Tai languages further southward, shattering the newly won empire of the Burmese, and crushing the western flank of the Khmer empire. Many Tai kingdoms—the Shan states of northern Burma, the Thai states of Lannathai and Sukhothai of northern and central Thailand, and the Lao states of Luang Prabang, Vientiane, Paks, and Xieng Khouang of Laos—gained large territories. Released from the overlordship of the Burmese, the Mon kingdom of Pegu flourished as a prestigious center of culture and Theravada Buddhism for the next two hundred years. The Central Thai of Sukhothai carried the religion to the very gates of Angkor Thom (abandoned in the fifteenth century) as they acquired suzerainty over the old Khmer kingdom.

A few Thais pushed southward into the Malay Peninsula at the end of the thirteenth century. Since the eighth century, the Malay states—Langkasuka, Saiburi, Kelantan, Trengganu, Nasor, Paka (Pekan), Muar Dungun, Temasek (Singapore), Johore, Sungei Ujong, Klang, Kedah, Jerai, and Kanjapiniran—had been part of the empire confederacy of Sri Vijaya that was headed by Palembang in Sumatra. Palembang had captured most of the foreign trade from Funan by the sixth century and proceeded to add all of the Malay states to her own empire. When Melayu (near modern Djambi in Sumatra) succeeded Palembang as the chief state of Sri Vijaya, at the end of the thirteenth century, the confederacy was at low ebb. The states in the peninsula broke away from the suzerainty of Melayu. Soon afterward, the Javanese state of Majapahit conquered the whole of Sumatra, more completely severing political ties between the peninsular and Sumatran states. The kingdom of Sukhothai, the ancestral state of the modern nation of Thailand, filled what is nowadays called a "power vacuum" by claiming suzerainty over all of the Malay states of the peninsula. Thai influence was strong in the northern Malay states during the fourteenth century but weak in the southern states. Some of the northern states exchanged their Mahayana Buddhism and Siva worship for Theravada Buddhism, while in the south, court ritual and religious belief were unaffected. Temasek (Singapore) in the extreme south was not within the Sukhothai realm but rather was the last outpost of the Javanese empire of Majapahit. Mahayana Buddhism and Hinduism were not wiped entirely from the Malay Peninsula.

THE RISE OF MELAKA

A former ruler of Temasek, who had defeated the Thais but lost to the Javanese, moved to the village of Malacca (or more properly, Melaka) near the end of the fourteenth century.[10] This village had the best anchorage in the narrowest part of the straits between the Malay Peninsula and the island of Sumatra. Moreover, an easy overland route that began at the village edge led to Pahang and the South China Sea. Within the lifetime and reign of its first ruler, Melaka became the most important of the peninsular states and obtained a guarantee from China that Thailand would respect its independence. By extending its suzerainty over all of the peninsular states and all of the Sumatran states along the shores of the straits, Melaka gained control of the sea trade between India and China. The first ruler converted to Islam, and this had political and economic consequences that were of enduring importance.

In Southeast Asia, the major religions—the various Hindu cults, Mahayana Buddhism, Theravada Buddhism, Islam, and the ethical codes of Confucius and Tao—had the same importance in the organization of economic and political affairs as religion in medieval Europe and political ideologies in the modern world. Before Sri Vijaya fell at the end of the thirteenth century, Indian shipping dominated the trade to the west.[11] This dominance came about in the eleventh and twelfth centuries in spite of Sri Vijaya's success at repulsing South Indian attempts to conquer parts of the confederacy. Indian traders became more numerous, and Gujaratis were the most numerous of Indian traders. They were Moslems. Theirs was the religion of a merchant, and they proselytized successfully among the leading Malay merchants and among Malay princes who depended upon trade for their wealth.

When the first ruler of Melaka, Parameswara, converted to Islam and became Iskandar Shah, he did so for two purposes. First, he sought a trading alliance with the Islamic kingdom of Pasai

(Pase) in Sumatra, which had previously converted to Islam and thereby gained the favor of Gujarati merchants, and second, he sought allies in his opposition to Thai control of the Malay Peninsula. He was successful on both counts, and his example and the support of the kingdom that he founded were instrumental in the speed with which Mahayana Buddhist and Hindu kingdoms of the Indonesian area became Islamic. Within a hundred years, Melaka gained suzerainty over most of the kingdoms on the Sumatran side of the straits and wrenched control of the kingdoms in the southern half of the Malay Peninsula from the Thai.

Two Chinese accounts, one by a junior officer and the other by a Muslim interpreter, indicate that the Ming sent the famous eunuch admiral, Cheng-Ho, to Melaka at least once and probably several times to insure its independence from the Sukhothai. According to these accounts, wet-rice agriculture was not developed in the region surrounding the city. Starchy pellets of flour made from the heart of the sago palm were imported from the interior and served as the staple food. Water buffalo, goats, chickens, and ducks were scarce and very expensive. However, vegetables and fruits were in good supply. Mangosteens, jackfruit, bananas, rambutans (a relative of the lichee), sugar cane, onions, ginger, leeks, mustard, gourds, and watermelons were offered for sale to foreign visitors. A wine made by fermenting the sap from blossom stalks of the coconut tree and the nipah palm was available, too. The inhabitants grew and exported a valuable herb, *Coptis teeta*, the rhizomes of which were used for medicine in both India and China. Mats made of palm leaves were also exported. But the major exports were ebony, dammar, and tin. Dammar (or more properly, *damar*, which is the Malay word from which the English word is derived) is resin from trees. Most of the trees that produce the resin belong to the Dipterocarpaceae family. Different species produce resins that are useful for different purposes—incense, gems, torches, paints, caulking, and medicine. The resin exudes from breaks in the bark caused by disease organisms, animals, or human beings. Until a very strong demand for the resins developed, collectors probably just searched for existing exudations on the trunks, branches, and roots of damaged trees. As demand increased, they made their own incisions in the bark, tapping resin just as their descendants would tap the latex of rubber trees centuries later. More than a dozen varieties of *damar* were recognized by the inhabitants of Melaka, but they probably were not the actual collectors of *damar* in the fifteenth century. Rather, they received it in trade with aboriginal collectors who lived in the interior and who subsisted by hunting, fishing, gathering, slash-and-burn horticulture, and collecting forest products for sale to traders. The local inhabitants of Melaka used the *damar* for torches and for waterproofing their boats. Chinese used it for caulking and painting their ships, and they valued one hard and clear variety as gemstone.

Tin was the principal export of Melaka. Even town dwellers panned for tin ore (tin dioxide is the most common form) in the local streams. Much more was shipped into the town from upstream areas. According to the Chinese accounts, there were two important tin-mining areas in the mountains behind Melaka that furnished most of its tin. Both areas were controlled by officials of the Melaka royal court. The tin ore was washed out in sieves, smelted, and cast into disk-shaped ingots of standard weight. Single ingots, bundles of 10 disks, and bundles of 40 disks were used as money in all of the trading transactions of the people of Melaka.

Trade was more than the lifeblood; it was the very bones of the Melaka state. River systems were the highways of the interior where forest products and tin were available in great abundance. The lowest ranking chiefs were farthest upstream. Their title, *penghulu*, means something like "one who is upstream." They were closest to the resources and were located where the resources had their least value—at a great distance from the market. *Penghulus* built their villages at the confluence of two streams so that they could control the movement of more of these resources downstream. Higher ranking chiefs located their villages or towns farther downstream and at the confluence of rivers so as to control the resources sent downstream by two or more *penghulus*. A prince or king built his town or city near the confluence of a large river and the sea, thus controlling all the chiefs and resources of the river's watershed. The king of Melaka controlled more than a dozen such watershed kingdoms through his monopoly of foreign trade in the straits. His was the final market. Many products that foreigners assumed came from the area of Melaka or from distant foreign lands were products from other river kingdoms that were controlled by Melaka. Gold and silver, for example, are mentioned as foreign trade goods along with the blue and white porcelain ware of the Ming and the colored taffetas of India. The Chinese did not realize that the gold and silver came to the market from Sumatran and peninsular states that were controlled by Melaka. Probably, much of the tin that found its way to Melaka was from these other states, too. The king made a profit in trade with the interior and with the minor kingdoms. He made a profit in trade with foreigners. It is known that his officers collected customs duties and harbor fees from foreigners. He claimed annual tribute in goods from the lesser kingdoms.

The Chinese mention the city plan and details of everyday behavior. These details—wearing sarongs, vests *(baju)*, and headkerchiefs, building houses on stilts with floors of split slats, sleeping and eating on mats placed directly on the floor, sitting cross-legged on the floor, and fearing were-tigers—match the details of everyday behavior among traditional Malays to this day. Melaka, according to these descriptions, had four gates in the city wall, each with watch and drum towers. A special pallisaded enclosure within the wall housed the sheds where goods and provisions were stored and loaded on ships and where ships were repaired. Booths for the marketing of goods were built on the bridge that crossed the river. At night, all of the districts of the city were patrolled by men with handbells.

We are told that the king wore a white turban of local cloth, a long robe of green calico, and leather shoes, but there is no clue to the organization of the royal court and of ritual beyond the observation that language, books, and marriage ceremonies resembled those of the Javanese. However, the details of court ritual and organization are preserved in Malay literature of that time. Many of the symbolic elements of Hinduism and Mahayana Buddhism were still important. Like Siva and the bodhisattvas or "emerging Buddhas," members of Malay royalty were thought to have "white blood." At his coronation, a king sat on a seven- or nine-tiered model of Mount Mahameru, and his palace, audience hall, and mosque were always in a special sacred district of the city on the highest local hill or at its base. The highest mountain in a kingdom was the source of its magical power and the focus of many royal legends. Such was Gunong Ledang, the highest of mountains near Melaka and the home of a queen-goddess who was much desired as a consort by the city's kings. In the legends, they courted her but failed because they refused to give her the wedding gift she most desired—human blood to drink. But they were willing to satisfy her other demands such as building a golden bridge from the top of Gunong Ledang to the center of the city. Probably, she was Kali or Durga, the blood-drinking consort of Siva. Officials of the kingdom reflected the magical numerology of Hinduism and Buddhism in their numbers—4 chief ministers, 8 chiefs of the first rank, 16 chiefs of the second rank, and 32 of the third rank. Brahman priests as such were no longer welcome at the Islamic courts of the Malays, but the royal magicians were steeped in Hindu lore and were in charge of court ritual just as Brahmans had been before. Moreover, the Moslem advisers of the kings were Indians, and they may have viewed much of Hindu and Buddhist symbolism as merely Indian.

Whatever the ritual similarities to Burmese, Mon, Thai, and Khmer kingship, Malay kingship differed because of its immediate political and economic alliance with the Islamic world and because of the distinctiveness of its underlying ethnicity. Malay kingdoms naturally rallied to the cause of Melaka against the Thais and, for that matter, against all of the other contending nation states. The one exception was the Chams. Their language and culture was similar to that of the Malays, and Champa was well placed for provisioning Malay ships on their trips to and from the ports of southern China. Much of that trade was accomplished in Cham ships anyway. Malay literature from the fifteenth century is full of references to Cham shipmasters and their high esteem in the eyes of Malay royalty. As a result of these close ties to the Malays, many Chams converted to Islam.

But Champa was at the end of its history. It had been conquered by the Angkor kingdom of the Khmers two centuries before. Then, Angkor had reeled under the impact of the Thais arriving from the north and the west. Weakened, the Khmers began to lose their hold on territories in the east to the Vietnamese. Champa was one of those territories but one that had been allowed the status of a dependent kingdom. In 1471, the Vietnamese conquered Champa. Some Chams fled into the mountains; others migrated to what was left of the Khmer kingdom in the area around the great lake (about this time Angkor Thom was abandoned by the Khmers); others moved to the least attractive lowlands in South Vietnam. Champa ceased to exist. Chams no longer had a homeland.

VIETNAMESE CIVILIZATION

The people who vanquished Champa had the most distinctive of all Southeast Asian civilizations. In contrast to the others, it owed almost nothing to India and almost everything to China. The Vietnamese state had been a part of China for a thousand years when it gained its independence in 939.[12] During that time, the Chinese had imposed their own political, social, and economic institutions on the Vietnamese people. But the Vietnamese never really acquiesced. They attempted to overthrow Chinese rule at every opportunity. At the end of a thousand years their culture was, however, strongly Sinicized. Only the culture of the Viets who had lived in areas that were distant from the towns, the culture of the Muong, remained much unaffected by Chinese civilization.

Many Chinese social and religious institutions were imposed willy-nilly. For example, officials in the second century decided that Vietnamese marriage rites were not proper and that unless Chinese ritual was used for this purpose, couples were not really married and their children were not legitimate. Similarly, native Vietnamese clothing was considered improper, and Chinese substitutions were made.

Much of the impact of Chinese civilization was through the mandarin type of administrative bureaucracy that the Chinese imposed on the Vietnamese. There were two branches of the administrative service—military and civil. Each branch had nine ranks. Examinations determined who would be admitted to positions in the service. Individuals studied for years to pass the examinations, which were on the subjects of writing, history, rhetoric, ethics, and poetry. Almost all of the knowledge that was expected of candidates was drawn from Chinese civilization. Successful candidates in the district and regional examinations became local officials or school teachers. Those who succeeded in national examinations became mandarins of the royal court. Anyone with intelligence and a good education could obtain a position in the service. Only the sons of the wealthy or of the educated could obtain a good education, however, so that bureaucrats were drawn only from an elite ruling class. Members of the elite became thoroughly familiar with the Chinese writing system, Chinese history, and ethical precepts of Confucian philosophy.

The administrative service did not interfere with the internal affairs of villages. Villagers paid taxes, contributed labor for public projects, and sent their sons to fight in the army. In return, the state provided some protection of villagers from outsiders, occasionally fought for and won new land for wet-rice cultivation, repaired old irrigation systems, and built new irrigation systems. Village scholars, who with the more wealthy landowners comprised the village leadership, were those who had been least successful in the regional examinations. Of all officials, they were the most Vietnamese and the least Chinese in their cultural orientations.

Villagers did not have very direct relationships with the administrative service, but they had none at all with the royal court. The emperor, Son of Heaven, fashioned his court after that of the Chinese emperor. He lived in a forbidden city that was closed to all except members of the royal family and the highest mandarins of the court. His power was more ritual than political. Only he could make the annual offering to heaven in behalf of the state. But the high mandarins of the military service held actual political power.

Although the emperor had the highest ritual duty of all persons, he was not the head of the Buddhist religion of the state. Vietnamese Buddhism was based on a Chinese version of Mahayana Buddhism. It did not resemble the Mahayana sects that were so closely related to Hinduism during earlier centuries, and it was very different from Theravada Buddhism. Very few of the male villagers entered the monkhood, and the few that did tended to remain monks all their lives. Vietnamese Buddhism, unlike Confucianism, was hardly related to the structure of the state.

Vietnamese, Chams, Khmers, Thais, Laotians, Shans, Burmese, Mons, and Malays continued to gain territory or to lose and scatter or assimilate to new ethnic identities after the beginning of the sixteenth century. But Europeans began to arrive in force after that time, and although they were hardly noticed at first, they eventually brought great changes to the cultures of all Southeast Asians. In the beginning, the fortunes of native empires waxed or waned as the partial effects of European intrigue. The actual competition was almost entirely between native states. European adventurers sought riches or even religious converts rather than empires. In the end, for riches and a few converts, Europeans gained empires in mainland Southeast Asia. Atypical to the end, only the Vietnamese, of all the great lowland peoples of mainland Southeast Asia, converted to Christianity in large numbers. Malays and Chams remained Moslems. Khmers, Thais, Laotians, Shans, Burmese, and Mons remained Theravada Buddhists. Alas, the Vietnamese were Confucianists, Taoists, and Mahayana Buddhists, and many were to become Catholics.

REFERENCES

[1] The best general source on early Southeast Asian states is G. Coedes, *The Making of Southeast Asia* (Berkeley and Los Angeles: University of California Press, 1966).

[2] A classical work on the early historical geography of the Malay Peninsula is Paul Wheatley, *The Golden Khersonese* (Kuala Lumpur: University of Malaya Press, 1961).

[3] L. Malleret, "Les Fouilles d'Oc-Eo (1944)," *Bulletin de l'Ecole Française d'Extrême-Orient* 16, no. 1 (1951).

[4] A. Spoehr, "Marianas Prehistory," *Fieldiana* 48 (1957).

[5] G. W. Grace, "Austronesian Linguistics and Culture History," *American Anthropologist* 63, no. 2 (1961): 359–368.

[6] Wheatley, *The Golden Khersonese*, pp. 14–15.

[7] See chapter 1 of O. W. Wolters, *The Fall of Srivijaya in Malay History* (Kuala Lumpur: Oxford University Press, 1970).

[8] R. Heine-Geldern, "Conceptions of State and Kingship in Southeast Asia," *The Far Eastern Quarterly* 2 (1942): 15–30.

[9] G. Coedes, *Angkor*, trans., E. F. Gardiner (London: Oxford University Press, 1963).

[10] *Malacca* and *Malaka* are English versions of the Malay word *Melaka*.

[11] See chapters 3–4 of O. W. Wolters, *The Fall of Srivijaya in Malay History*.

[12] L. Aurousseau, "La Première Conquête Chinoise des Pays Annamites: Origine du Peuple Annamite," *Bulletin de l'Ecole Française d'Extrême-Orient* 23 (1923): 137–264.

THREE

THE EUROPEAN PRESENCE

EARLY ROMANTICS: CRUSADERS, CONQUISTADORS, AND TRADERS

Maurice Collis, in the first pages of *The Land of the Great Image*, noted that Portuguese traders who came to Southeast Asia in the sixteenth century were very different from the English who arrived a century later.[1] The first were adventurers in the fullest sense while the latter were businessmen whose only purpose was making a profit. This judgment of early English traders seems harsh, but the comparative comment of which it is part is accurate. The Portuguese had a remarkable romantic sense of adventure. They believed that their discovery of the sea route to Asia and their subsequent establishment of fortresses from the Persian Gulf through the Straits of Melaka to the Molucca Islands was a continuation of their crusade against the Moors and that theirs was a heaven-decreed (and lonely) duty to thwart the spread of Islam in Asia. They saw themselves as more than just Portuguese, more than European; they were paladins of a universal state, the Holy See, and of its priest-emperor, Pope Alexander VI (the Borgia). It was in this light that a seventeenth-century Portuguese historian stated that "... the kings of Portugal, as the first who had shaken off themselves the burden of these barbarians, and the first who passed over to crush them in Africa (obeying the Decrees of Heaven which required it) undertook to be the first to stop their proceedings in Asia."[2] The Portuguese also recognized and grasped opportunities for profit as they attempted to wrest control of the East-West sea trade from the Moslems. Moreover, they were willing, even eager, to gain economic dominance over other European powers. Two of the more famous evidences of this are Tome Pires's phrase, "Whoever is lord of Malacca has his hand on the throat of Venice," and Albuquerque's statement that "if we take this trade of Malacca away out of their hands, Cairo and Mecca are entirely ruined, and to Venice will no spiceries be conveyed except that which her merchants go to buy in Portugal."[3]

In judging the level of the achievement of sixteenth-century Portuguese as the first Europeans to establish direct trade relations with Southeast Asians, members of modern Western society usually overrate the ingenuity and underrate the courage of the Portuguese. Their "discovery" of the sea route to Southeast Asia was a discovery only from the viewpoint of European civilization. Arab navigators knew the route around the Cape of Good Hope from West Africa, and even Indian navigators knew the route from there to India. An Indian navigator was thus employed by Vasco da Gama in 1498 for the first Portuguese voyage to India. Middle Eastern, Indian, and Southeast Asian ships had sailed the sea route between the Persian Gulf and Southeast Asia each year for centuries before Portuguese ships joined them. The ships of these other nations were usually well armed, often with cannons and muskets, and the knowledge of their captains about local conditions was infinitely greater than that of the Portuguese captains. In discipline, the Portugese excelled. Their expeditions were financed by the state. Crew members were in the national service of their country. Noblemen and aristocrats led them. The Portuguese succeeded because they believed fervently in their cause (the destruction of Islam) and they had excellent discipline and courage. Their ships were not as good as those of their adversaries. Their weapons were little or no better. And in the beginning their knowledge was much less. But they moved slowly, establishing fortresses as they went, gaining strategic advantage over the Moors, and gathering information about the places that they had not yet reached.

When Prince Henry the Navigator died in 1460, his ships had gone only as far as Sierra Leone on the western coast of Africa. Undoubtedly, the Moslems of West Africa slowed their progress considerably. Almost three more decades (1487) passed before the Portuguese had established West African fortresses and rounded the Cape of Good Hope. At the same time they were attacking the Moslems of North Africa, Turkey, and the Arabian Peninsula. They did not always win. Even Alfonso de Albuquerque ("the Great" or "the Portuguese Mars") lost occasionally. However, by 1509, the Portuguese had established fortresses in East Africa, at the entrances to the Red Sea and the Gulf of Persia, and at three strategic points along the western coast of India. They had won control of the Arabian Sea. Their greatest victory had been in April of 1508 when a large combined force of Egyptians and Indians was defeated at Diu, northwest of Cambay. The short Arabian routes between Venice and India had been blocked, and the seas between Lisbon and Cambay by way of the southern tip of Africa had been made safe for Portuguese ships. Lisbon began to replace Venice as the leading market of Eastern goods in Europe.

Thorough to the end, the Portuguese captains followed the spice route farther east. Lopes de Sequeira brought a squadron of ships to Melaka in 1509. Apparently, he was in the process of negotiating arrangements for trade or, perhaps, a Portuguese fortress when a quarrel occurred. His ships bombarded the town but were driven off by the Malays. Some of his men were taken prisoner. A return engagement was inevitable. It did not take place until 1511. This time Albuquerque was in charge. Fighting began only after the prisoners from the previous engagement had been returned to the Portuguese and further negotiations (a demand that Melaka submit to the king of Portugal) broke down. It began on 25 July and ended on 10 August with much destruction of life and property. Here, we have followed the Portuguese account. Malays recorded two encounters before the fall of Melaka. The first was very friendly. Malays marvelled at the "white Bengalis," playfully twisted their beards, and played with their hats. The Portuguese commander was adopted by the chief minister *(Bendahara)*, and in turn the chief minister was given a gold chain. The Portuguese stayed through the doldrum season and returned. The next two encounters described in the *Sejarah Melayu* are the same as the two recorded in Portuguese history and described here.[4]

The Malay king and his retinue fled from Melaka. He located his court at Johore Lama (near the tip of the peninsula) for a time until defeated again by the Portuguese. From there he fled to the Riau Islands south of Singapore, and finally he died, a guest in another kingdom, in Sumatra. But his royal line was not extinguished. His oldest son became the sultan of Perak, and his third son became the first sultan of Johore. The Malays continued fighting the Portuguese at every opportunity. So did the Sumatran states that flowered after their release from the burden of the overlordship of Melaka. The Achehnese, especially, opposed the Portuguese. Had the Achehnese and Malays cooperated, they could have, together, defeated the Portuguese at almost any time. But each wanted to rule the straits alone.

Immediately after their victory at Melaka, the Portuguese proceeded to the Molucca Islands—the fabulous Spice Islands—and they sent an envoy to the Thai court at Ayutthaya. Now they controlled strategic places along the entire trade route by which spices reached Europe, and they were in a position to bargain for the China trade, through Thailand. Direct trade relations with China were established in 1516, and China granted a trading center, Macao, to the Portuguese in 1557. Portugal had a monopoly. But it was only a monopoly of the European trade. Indian and Chinese ships passed through the Straits of Melaka unopposed, and even the Malays were able to smuggle goods past the Portuguese blockade of the straits. The Malays were mostly interested in the trade with India and, secondarily, with China. They always had been.

Their monopoly had been over only one segment of the East-West trade route. They had allowed others—Indians, Arabs, and Venetians—their own monopolies over portions of the route that lay to the west. The Portuguese innovation was that of aspiring to a monopoly over the entire route.

Their hold on the trade route was very weak. This was particularly the case during the northeast monsoon, when almost all of the available ships were loaded with spices and booty for shipment to Portugal. As many as twenty ships were required for this task, and the fortresses at Melaka and the Moluccas were left without adequate forces for their own protection. They usually timed the shipments late in the monsoon so that there would be just enough wind to reach Cochin or Goa on the western coast of India. The return voyage to relieve Melaka was delayed only briefly by the doldrums. Many times the fortress at Melaka was saved in the nick of time by the relieving force. Garrison troops left to protect Melaka rarely exceeded fifteen hundred, of which only two hundred were Portuguese. Much larger forces attempted to capture Melaka in 1550–1551 (Malays with Javanese troops), 1567–1568 (Achehnese with Turkish troops), 1571 (Achehnese), and 1575 (Javanese), and although the town was occupied several times, the fortress never fell.

During the sixteenth century, the only European power to contest the Portuguese monopoly was Spain. Spain was handed an opportunity to control the Spice Islands by a member of the unfortunate expedition headed by de Sequeira in 1509. He, Ferdinand Magellan, convinced the Spanish crown that the Spice Islands could be reached by way of the Pacific, and he received a grant of five ships for that purpose in 1519. Less than two years later, after having crossed the Atlantic and the Pacific oceans, he was killed while intervening in a local war in Cebu. But his lieutenant continued the voyage to Tidore, one of the Spice Islands, loaded spices, and returned to Spain by way of the Indian Ocean and the Atlantic. For eight years, until the Treaty of Saragossa in 1529, Spain sided with Tidore against Ternate, which was backed by the Portuguese. In 1545 and 1565, the Spanish sent expeditions from Mexico to the Spice Islands with the purpose of overthrowing the Portuguese monopoly. The expedition of 1565 was successful in establishing the Spanish in the Philippines. Manila was founded in 1571 as a competitor of Macao. Manila quickly became the more important port. Goods were paid for in silver Mexican dollars. The Mexican dollar became a standard currency of traders in Southeast Asia. It was not the only notable contribution of Mexico to the cultures of Southeast Asia. The Spanish administered the Philippines through Mexico. Their ships brought many New World plants to Southeast Asia such as chili peppers, peanuts, tapioca, tobacco, pineapples, papayas, maize, potatoes, and sweet potatoes. Southeast Asians almost immediately accepted these plants as supplements to their traditional food plants. The Portuguese may have introduced New World plants too, but this is less certain because there were no regular administrative or trade relations between Brazil and Portuguese outposts in Southeast Asia. There was no necessity for such distant relations since Portugal owned a short route to the islands. That the Spanish could rule from a greater distance and through an intermediating colony may account as much as the Treaty of Saragossa for Spain's acceptance of the Portuguese monopoly.

Portugal set the pattern of European interest in Southeast Asia for two hundred and fifty years although its monopoly lasted only half that time. The sequence of friendly visit, battle, fortress, and factory (warehouses for storing goods that would be shipped) was repeated many times by Europeans. There was no attempt to conquer large pieces of land or to settle large numbers of European immigrants. Living in Southeast Asia was a short-term adventure to be endured for the purpose of gaining a fortune that would enhance the enjoyment of life when one returned home. The fortresses protected warehousing sites (factories) and harbours where ships that protected the sea route could be refitted. Inside the fortresses, life was as nearly an imitation of Europe as possible. Even the factories were not dependent on European-owned plantations but on the tribute and trade of Southeast Asian kings and nobles. Europeans were protected from Southeast Asians and Southeast Asians were protected from Europeans. Culture contact occurred, but it was not intensive.

The Portuguese did not develop the old urban centers of Southeast Asia. The old centers that fell under its control, like Melaka, suffered because of the Portuguese interest in erasing memories of the former glory of native kingdoms. Other Europeans were to follow the same practice of raising the status of former villages to towns and of reducing the status of former cities to villages. It was in the interests of Europeans to reduce the scale of native kingdoms, and to this end Europeans often involved themselves in wars between local states and nations. Portuguese mercenaries were famous for their skill and courage and were much in demand by native kings who were at war with each other. Portuguese mercenaries served in the armed forces of both the Burmese and the Thai, for example, and French sailors served the Burmese during the sixteenth century. At the end of the sixteenth century, at the urging of Spanish and Portuguese adventurers in his court, the king of Cambodia pleaded for help from both the Portuguese and the Spanish governments against the Thai. The Portuguese government did not respond, and although the Spanish did, they stopped their naval force short of an actual invasion of Cambodia. Such interventions and threats of intervention remained commonplace during the next four centuries.

Portuguese contributions to the native cultures of Southeast Asia were surprisingly few in light of their importance in the commerce and politics of the region during the sixteenth century.[5] Although the Portuguese language was one of the standard market languages in the area during the sixteenth century and was so entrenched that Dutch and English traders in the seventeenth century were forced to learn it, it left little impression on present-day languages and cultures of Southeast Asia. Malay language and culture were influenced the most. Approximately one hundred common words in Malay language are derived from Portuguese. These include many words that relate directly or indirectly to Christianity. For example, the Malay word *minggu* is derived from the Portuguese *Domingo,* which means "God." In Malay, *minggu* is one of two words used after the word *hari,* "day," to denote "Sunday" (that is "God's Day"), and it is the common word meaning "week." The word meaning "cannon," *meriam,* is probably derived from the Portuguese explication "Por Santa Maria!" which was often shouted just as the fuse of the cannon was ignited. More often the words are direct borrowings such as *gereja,* "church," for *igreja* or *natal,* "Christmas," from *natal.* Other borrowings include words that mean "flag," "bullet," "making rounds when guarding," "soldier," "a fine," "permission," "treacherous," "change money," "surcharge," "partner," "false," "overseer," "stammering," "veranda," "bench," "window," "cart," "chain," "wheel," "sphere," "dice," "cigar," "towel," "soap," "pocket," "shoes," "lace," "ribbon," "pin," "shirt," "velvet," "pillow," "canteen," "fork," "broth," "butter," "cheese," "cabbage," "cupboard," "table," "ink," "writing pen," "violin," "lady," "young lady," "a stroll," "school," "though," and "time." Malays knew most of these meanings and things before they met the Portuguese. That words for these meanings and things were borrowed is mere evidence of behaviors and artifacts that Malays associated with the Portuguese way of life.

Perhaps the most noticeable impressions made by Portuguese culture on Malay culture are in the fields of women's dress fashions, popular dancing, and music. The same is true in Burma and Thailand, although the impress of Portuguese culture is less noticeable. The reason why these, rather than other, aspects of local cultures were so influenced is that the Portuguese did not bring their own women with them to Southeast Asia. They married local women, dressed them up in fashionable dresses from Lisbon, and danced with them to the familiar music of guitars and violins.

Portuguese enterprise in Southeast Asia was officially controlled entirely by the government, but the government's hunger for quick profits and its poor treatment of servants encouraged the development of private enterprise.[6] Portugal was a small country with a very small population and, therefore, lacked manpower for controlling the vast new commercial domains that it claimed in the sixteenth century. But the government could have maintained greater control over those domains for a longer period if more of the profits had been reinvested in better salaries, better living conditions, more and better ships, and better weaponry and forts. According to official Portuguese estimates in the sixteenth century, six of every seven men who shipped out to Southeast Asia died within the first year. Most of the deaths resulted from malnutrition and disease, but others resulted from battles in which Achehnese or Malays had more and better ships. Salaries were very low in the beginning, and there were no raises. Supplements were available only through acts of piracy, which differed from acts of war only in that the profits from captured cargoes were distributed among the crew members rather than being turned over to the Crown, through embezzlement of portions of cargoes of trade goods being shipped to or from Goa, and through use of government equipment and manpower for private enterprise, which usually affected government enterprise adversely. As noted previously, many Portuguese eventually chose to serve in the forces of Southeast Asian kingdoms. They found better conditions in the service of these other states. Last and perhaps most important, the Crown failed to build fortresses on the island of Java, which was strategically placed along the sea route between Portuguese strongholds in the Spice Islands and Melaka. The Dutch took advantage of this failure. The last 60 years of Portuguese control of Melaka, from 1580 to 1640, were especially bleak. The Indonesian kingdom of Acheh and the Malay kingdom of Johore had become great powers that controlled more trade than the Portuguese, and at the same time, Portugal itself was ruled by the Spanish Crown. It was in 1640, the year that Portugal regained independence from Spain, that Melaka fell to a combined force of Malays from the kingdom of Johore and of Europeans in the employ of the Dutch East India Trading Company. The fortress withstood a siege of three months, during the doldrums from June through August, and beat off many fierce attacks. But this time a relief force from Goa did not arrive, and the eighty or so Portuguese defenders, along with their Asian soldiers, gave up. The Portuguese were well treated, released, and allowed to continue living in Melaka or to leave as they wished. Many remained and were joined by later immigrants. It was certainly the end of what has been called "the Portuguese century" in Southeast Asian history, but it was not the beginning of a "Dutch century."

Dutch entry into Southeast Asian trade was probably inevitable in any case because the Netherlands had been a major market for spices for several centuries. In the thirteenth, fourteenth, and fifteenth centuries, Venetian merchants sold spices directly to the Dutch, or to the English or Portuguese who supplied the Dutch.

The Dutch, in turn, sold spices to Scandinavians. During the sixteenth century, Portugal sold most of its spices directly to the Netherlands, which resold the spices to all the other Europeans. First Antwerp and then Amsterdam became great spice markets. The Netherlands fell under domination by the Portuguese and Spanish. Quite naturally, Dutchmen yearned to buy spices at the source rather than from the Portuguese. This became an especially urgent matter after Portugal fell under the rule of the Spanish Crown and the Spanish restricted Dutch access to Portuguese spices. Spanish and Portuguese Jews who had been expelled and who had taken up residence in the Netherlands were well acquainted with the sea route to Southeast Asia and were familiar with the commercial arrangements employed at the eastern terminus of the spice trade. They imparted their knowledge to the Dutch. Also, a few Dutchmen had sailed as crew members on Portuguese ships, and others had spent time in Portuguese jails as distant as Goa. The Dutch knew the way to Southeast Asia. But they needed allies. Their oppressors were the Spanish and, coincidentally, the Portuguese.

The English were drawn into Southeast Asia through their hostile relations with the Spanish, too. Drake's circumnavigation of the earth in 1579 by way of the Philippines and the Spice Islands was in fact an extended patrol against Spanish shipping. In 1585, the English went to war with Spain and formed an alliance with the Dutch. Three years later, the famous Spanish Armada was destroyed and English and Dutch piracy of Spanish-Portuguese shipping began in earnest. The Portuguese *carracks* were favorite targets because they were so richly laden with spices. Their rich cargoes spurred further interest in Southeast Asia. Groups of merchants began to consider the possibilities of outfitting their own expeditions to Southeast Asia. The first expedition, outfitted by a group of London merchants, consisted of three ships under the command of James Lancaster. It set out in 1591. Only one ship reached Southeast Asia. Lancaster used Penang Island as base for this ship for several months while he pirated other shipping in Melaka Straits. After losing 26 of the ship's crew in fruitless attempts to capture valuable cargo, he returned to England. About this time, a Dutch adventurer, van Linschoten, published a manual of sailing directions to the Eastern seas. The cat was out of the bag. Many Dutch and English merchants outfitted voyages to Southeast Asia. The Dutch expeditions were most numerous. Unlike the British, they were immediately successful. De Houtman's voyage in 1595, the first, went directly to the one unguarded strategic point in the Portuguese spice route—Java. From their position in Java, they spread throughout the Indonesian islands, making treaties of trade with as many local rulers as possible. In these treaties, the Dutch often recognized an obligation to tolerate Islam thereby further undercutting the Portuguese, whose policy was strongly against Islam.

Within a few years, the various Dutch companies were amalgamated, and a headquarters was established in Batavia. Dutch interests were in the islands rather than in mainland Southeast Asia. They were not interested in using Melaka as a port when they helped the Johore Malays take it from the Portuguese. The Dutch merely wanted to end attempts to blockade the Straits of Melaka. Their presence in Melaka after 1640 was of such low profile that the Malays thought of them as allies rather than as successors of the Portuguese. Indeed, they were not the successors of the Portuguese.

England was not a great sea power in the seventeenth century. As allies against Spain and Portugal, ships of English companies were permitted by the Dutch to engage in the spice trade although direct access to the Spice Islands was denied them. At first this did not seem to be an important restriction because the English had not been so interested in buying spices as in selling woolen cloth. For centuries the ships of other European nations had carried the export cloth from English shores. Now, English merchants sought new markets, and they built their own ships. But they discovered that woolen cloth was not acceptable to Asians who for centuries had purchased the cotton cloth of India. English merchants generally preferred trading in Indian cottons to trading in spices. Although they continued to trade and even had a spice factory in Java until the end of the eighteenth century, they began to favor Sumatra over Java in the face of stiff competition with the Dutch. The English found not-very-willing allies in the Achehnese of northern Sumatra who sensed that the English would be a useful foil against the Dutch. It was a very good partnership from the English perspective because the Achehnese had easily the most powerful fleet in Southeast Asian waters.

Their association with the Achehnese influenced the English traders to take an interest in the affairs of the Malays. Rulers of Acheh saw themselves as successors to the Melaka sultanate. They were obsessed with the goal of reconstituting the old Malay empire, and they saw Johore as their greatest competitor. Much of their trade was in tin, a resource with which the English were very well acquainted because England had been a primary source of the metal for almost three thousand years. English traders sought treaties that assured supplies of tin both in Sumatra and Malaya. Naturally, they wanted a monopoly over supplies from both areas, and so did their allies, the Achehnese. Strangely enough, the Dutch invited the Achehnese to join them and the Johore Malays in what turned out to be the successful attack on Portuguese Melaka, but the Achehnese refused because of their intention of taking Melaka by themselves. English traders were discouraged from further involvement in the Malay Peninsula, but they maintained their treaties with Sumatran kingdoms. At the same time, they were losing in their attempt to establish viable trade relations with Thailand. They had been invited to enter into trade relations with the royal court at Ayutthaya in 1612. But, as usual, the Dutch had arrived earlier—in 1608. Ten years after they had been invited to trade with the Thais, the English traders had failed completely and were forced, because of financial difficulties, to close their factory and withdraw their commercial interests. Meanwhile, the Dutch had developed a profitable monopoly of the trade between Thailand and Japan. While failing or barely surviving as traders in Southeast Asia, the English were developing excellent trade relations in Indian ports during the seventeenth century. Their strong commercial and military base in India was one of five major factors that allowed them to reenter the commerce and politics of Southeast Asia by the beginning of the nineteenth century.

The other four factors—the Battle of Dogger Bank, Napoleon's occupation of Holland, Kedah's concession of Penang to England, and the Burmese invasion of British India—involved armed conflicts that reduced the military and commercial power of the Dutch and provided excuses for British intervention. Before and during the American Revolution, Dutch ships smuggled tea and other goods into the colonies. Americans used this fact to pressure the Netherlands government into recognizing American independence in the text of a commercial treaty which fell into British hands. A declaration of war against Holland was made in 1780, and in the following year at the battle of Dogger Bank, the English destroyed most of the Dutch navy. During the next three years, Dutch trading vessels were easy prey and could be taken in Southeast Asian or European waters. The British captured many Dutch trading stations which were returned after the war, but the temporary victories gave the British more rights in the commerce of the area. The Dutch company had not recovered from the war of 1780–1784 when Napoleon annexed Holland and all of its Indonesian trading stations in 1810. No French forces were available in Indonesia, so the English filled in, occupying the major posts in Java, Sumatra, and Malaya from 1811 to 1816. They turned the posts back to the Dutch without a fight, but their occupancy earned them an important chip in bargaining for Dutch withdrawal from the affairs of the sultanates of the Malay Peninsula (the Treaty of 1824) and gave Raffles the Opportunity to found British Singapore (1819). In the meantime (1789), the Malay sultan of Kedah had asked the English to protect him from the Thais and the Burmese. They accepted the offer of Penang Island in exchange for their trouble. The Malays came to regret having made the gift and the following year attempted to retrieve it. The protective reaction of the English resulted in their gaining a large strip of land (Province Wellesley) on the mainland across from their island. They kept it as a precaution against further attempts by the Malays to steal their island. And finally (1824), the imperialist-minded Burmese attempted to conquer British Bengal by way of Manipur and Assam. This time the reaction of the British resulted in their almost immediate conquest of Rangoon and in the great humiliation of Burmese two years later in the Treaty of Yandabo.

This conflict between European powers for monopoly of trade, which is so familiar to us, probably did not seem very important to Southeast Asians in the seventeenth and eighteenth centuries. The most noticeable Europeans were those who were more individualistic adventurers than agents of European governments or merchants. Ribeiro de Souza and Philip de Brito (Portuguese), self-styled rulers of a small Mon state near Rangoon; Constantine Phaulkon (Greek), superintendent of foreign trade at the Thai court; Richard Burnaby and Samuel White (English), Thai government agents and trade representatives; and Blas Ruiz (Spanish), sometimes advisor at the Khmer court, were simply exceptional individuals who involved themselves in the affairs of Southeast Asian countries. Their original national identities were not terribly exotic. Not only were there other European adventurers in Southeast Asia—especially Frenchmen and Danes—there were also Chinese, Japanese, Okinawan, Indian, Persian, Turk, and Arabian adventurers. Moreover, from local perspectives of the time, it was not any of these foreigners who threatened the stability of the region during the three centuries following the Portuguese capture of Melaka (1511).

In the first two centuries of contact between Europeans and Southeast Asians, Europeans seemed neither powerful nor numerous. And they did not appear to be wealthy. In rice-tribute states such as Thailand, there was not even much interest in trading with Europeans. Very probably, the royal Thai invitations to the Dutch and English, in the early seventeenth century, to send trade missions to the court were motivated more by political than economic considerations. From the Thai perspective, the Europeans were being invited to bring gifts as token payments of homage to Thai royalty. Long distance trade was entirely in the hands of agents of the Thai government and agents of other governments that had long traded with Thailand. For a time Europeans were no more successful than other foreigners in gaining control of trade officials although the Dutch succeeded for a time in controlling the Thai-Japan trade and for a very brief period the French gained control of virtually all of the Thai trade. French success, however brief, may have frightened the Thai. In any case, after the French scheme collapsed in 1688, the Thai government withdrew from further regular communication with European governments until the end of the

countries. It was not until the end of the eighteenth century and
the beginning of the nineteenth century that Europeans became
insistent imperialists in mainland Southeast Asia.

NATIVE IMPERIALISM

The imperialists during the sixteenth, seventeenth, and eighteenth
centuries were the Thais and Burmese who, a few centuries before,
had arrived from the north, and the Sumatrans and the Bugis (of
Sulawesi) who were arriving from the south. Basically, fluctuations
of political power were between the poles of Thai and Burmese
dominance. The expansion of the Thai domain was just retreating
from full flood when the Portuguese captured Melaka. As a result,
Thais regained hegemony over most of the sultanates of the Malay
Peninsula. But 20 years later, a new Burmese dynasty, the Toungoo, rose from the Burmese, Shan, and Mon remnants of the old
Pagan Empire. In the 1560s the Burmese encroached heavily on
Thai territory in Siam and Laos, twice sacking the capital at Ayutthaya. The collapse of Ayutthaya was so complete that it allowed
the Khmers to return to their old Cambodian capital at Angkor for
several decades.

A reverse of Thai fortunes began at the end of the sixteenth
century when Thais regained control of the Khmer regime in Cambodia and regained territory in the bordering areas of Burma. As
Burmese lost control over peripheral territory, the Mons in the
south broke away, reforming their old kingdom of Pegu for several
decades at the end of the sixteenth century and the beginning of
the seventeenth century. The Toungoo dynasty reasserted its control over the Mons and moved the Burmese capital to Pegu in 1628.
A brief period followed in which there was an attempted union of
Burmese and Mon cultures. But in 1635, the Burmese capital was
removed to Ava in the north. Although Burmese kings invited
European trade on several occasions during the seventeenth century, Burma closed itself from the outside world so that it could
concentrate on disturbances within its northern borders. These disturbances were closely related to the expulsion of Ming princes
from China by the Manchus. The Thais made good use of the dis-
tractions by overrunning Chiengmai and Pegu. In the 1680s the
French East India Company rose to briefly dominate the foreign
political and commercial relations of Thailand through special
favors from the Greek superintendent of foreign trade, Phaulkon.
French troops even manned Thai garrisons briefly. But after the
Thai king, Narai, died in 1688, his friend Phaulkon was executed
and French traders and soldiers were expelled. For more than a century afterwards, Europeans were not welcome in Thailand. The
apex of Thai power had been reached in the 1680s, and it declined

gradually during the next eighty years. Burma was no threat because its power was declining, too.

At the end of the seventeenth century, the Bugis of Sulawesi in the Indonesian islands began to migrate into the coastal areas of the Straits of Melaka.[7] (Their migration into the straits area has continued to the present day.) They were sailors, traders, and sometimes pirates. Because the Dutch never had had very strong control of the Melaka Straits and no control whatever of the Malay sultanates of the peninsula and because the power of the Thais was declining in the southern part of the peninsula, the Minangkabaus of Sumatra and the Bugis of Sulawesi had an easy entrance into the affairs of the sultanates of the Malay Peninsula. Minangkabaus had been migrating to the peninsula since the fifteenth century, and they founded a series of communities in the hinterlands of Melaka and nearby areas of Pahang. The migration increased in volume as time passed, and Minangkabaus moved into other areas such as Selangor and Perak. At the beginning of the eighteenth century, Siak, a Minangkabau state on the Sumatran side of the straits conquered the Johore Empire by capturing its capital at Riau. A few years later, in 1722, after defeating the Minangkabau forces at Riau and Lingga, a combined force of Bugis from Selangor and Sulawesi restored the Johore Empire to the Malays upon their agreeing to establish a special position, *raja muda* or "under-king," to be filled by a Bugis prince. A few years later, Minangkabaus were fighting to gain control of parts of Kedah, Perak, and Selangor. Again, their most important opponents were Bugis rather than native Malays or Europeans. The Bugis won most of the battles. They had developed a very efficient military style. Leaders claimed to be devout Muslims, asking their followers to join them in "the Mercy of Allah" during battle. Their ships and navigators were among the best ever in Southeast Asian waters. They wore chain mail and were excellent marksmen with their muskets, which they favored over crossbows or cannons. When they won major battles against Malay or Minangkabau sultans, they usually insisted that one of their princes be designated "under-king" by the sultan. The sultan retained his throne and dignity but gave up control of political and commercial affairs to the Bugis *raja muda*. Probably, Bugis and Minangkabaus introduced commercial agriculture—plantations—to the Malay Peninsula.

Minangkabaus fought with less efficient weapons than the Bugis. They were more numerous than the Bugis except perhaps in the Kelang district of Selangor. This and their exceptional interest in settling the land made them about equal in strength to the Bugis. Although devout Muslims, they still maintained Hindu-Buddhist attitudes concerning their kings and their inland capital at Sri Menanti in Negri Sembilan.

The Bugis and the Minangkabaus were usually careful to choose the time and place of battle with the Dutch East India Company. They developed skillful hit-and-run and shifting-settlement strategies that exhausted Dutch troops sent on punitive missions against them. The Dutch spent much energy trying to destroy their plantations of coconut, betel nut, and gambier pepper. On capturing a village, the Dutch usually found only old men, women, and children. And the Dutch forced them to bare their heads in respect for the presence of Dutchmen—a gesture of complete contempt in Minangkabau and Bugis cultures and an appropriate gesture in light of Dutch pretentiousness and ineffectiveness in trying to monopolize trade in the area. Of course, the Dutch had very effectively monopolized trade in Indonesia, and that may have been one of the major reasons for the migration of Bugis from Sulawesi. They were migrating beyond the area of strict control by the Dutch to reach more amiable customers and trading partners such as the other Europeans and the Gujaratis. Minangkabau immigration to the Malay Peninsula may have increased in the seventeenth and eighteenth centuries for the same reason. By the middle of the eighteenth century, all of the sultanates of the Malay Peninsula, except for Trengganu and Kelantan, were embroiled in the contest for dominance between Minangkabaus and Bugis.

At mid-century the imperialistic interests of the Burmese had been revived. The Burmese had nearly reached the nadir of their power in the 1740s when an army from Manipur besieged their capital at Ava and the Mon and Shan states were in open rebellion. The low point came in 1752, the year that the Mons captured Ava and controlled most of Burma. But Mon kings began to fight among themselves and lost what they had gained and more within four years. By 1759 they had lost everything, even the old Mon territories in the northern part of the Malay Peninsula, to the founder of Burma's Konbaung dynasty. The new leader was not of royal background but merely the son of a headman in a rural area north of Ava. Like most of the other kings of this dynasty, he thought himself to be a *bodhisattva*, "emerging Buddha."

In 1760, the Burmese again invaded Thailand. Seven years later, after one attempt failed, the Burmese succeeded in utterly destroying Ayutthaya, and the Thais were forced to build a new capital, Bangkok. In complete disarray, the Thais were ruled for a time by a half-Chinese provincial official, and a new dynasty, the Chakri, did not begin until 1782. Three years later, the Burmese renewed their efforts to conquer all of Thailand, attempting this impossible task five times between 1785 and 1802. The expense to the people of Burma—Burmese, Shans, and Mons—of these invasions was a dreadful toll in taxes and military service. Then, after the last invasion attempt in 1802, the king of Burma began to show his *bodhisattva* status through a very expensive program of temple construction. Morale was very low. Mons attempted a revolt. Shans chafed under the burden of Burmese military occupation. A new king had imperialistic designs for acquiring Bengal.

The Burmese attempt to acquire Bengal that began in 1819 and ended disastrously in 1824 was not as foolhardy as it now seems. Indians rarely fought against the Burmese and had not been especially successful when they did. Moreover, the Burmese had defeated the Chinese many times in battle and had lost only once to the Mongols. What the Burmese did not realize was that the British East India Company had trained and equipped the Bengali army in the latest military style and had placed the army under command of British officers. Moreover, the navy had grown rapidly, and with its supporting bases in India and Malaya, it had total command of the Bay of Bengal, allowing safe and rapid transport of troops to Rangoon.

At the end of the first quarter of the nineteenth century, the British interest in Southeast Asia had already developed beyond a mere interest in acquiring luxury goods from the native kingdoms. Cut off by the Dutch from direct access to the Spice Islands, frustrated in attempts to sell woolens to Southeast Asians, the British needed something to trade. Southeast Asians would trade for British silver. But supplies of it were limited. They tried to gain control over the trade in Indian cottons which were preferred by Southeast Asians. Although failing in that endeavor, they were thereby drawn deeply into the political affairs of India and into the problem of producing cloth that was competitive with Indian muslins. In the meantime, English traders discovered that iron and firearms were as acceptable as silver in trade with Southeast Asians. The British East India Company traded firearms to anyone. English forests that had supplied the necessary charcoal for making iron had dwindled, but another fuel and reducing element, coal, began to be substituted in its place, suddenly expanding the energy resources of England. At the same time, a new way of using this energy source through the conversion of heat to motion was tied to the development of machines that could make muslin cloth as fine as that made by hand in India. English cloth was now cheaper. Suddenly, in 1835, England was producing about half of the world's cotton cloth. Manufacturing of other kinds of products developed after the first innovations in the manufacture of iron and cotton textiles. England needed markets for its goods. Its newly developing colonial policy was directed toward this need. England was pushed into trade in mass quantities of common goods and away from trade in limited quantities of luxury goods. A new capitalism began to replace the old. Its onset was so gradual and the genius of its origin so widely dispersed that its proper history cannot be written in this short space, but it is true that Southeast Asians as well as Europeans helped to create the new capitalism and were deeply affected by it.

Nowhere was the force of this cultural transition more evident than in developments in Britain's official relationships with Burma and with the Malay sultanates. In both instances, the servants of British government found it impossible to follow the old company policy of non-involvement in native politics. New needs dictated new organizational means. The East India Company lost its franchise for trade with India in 1813 and with China in 1834. When the company's monopoly ended, the number of British merchants in Southeast Asia increased rapidly. Their influence on governmental policy was even greater than that of the company. The company had been an instrument of government policy, to be sure, but the less disciplined commercial interests of private enterprise were more powerful and more directly related to the development of colonialism.

In 1852, for example, the British occupied lower Burma on the pretext of punishing oppressive treatment of British merchants in Rangoon. Within three years, the British controlled the whole coastline of Burma. A great man, Mindon, became king shortly afterward. He was more reform-minded and more Western-oriented than his contemporary, Mongkut of Thailand, who was to become more famous. His reforms and maneuvers merely delayed the fall of Burma to the rule of British India. A few years after his death in 1885, a successor refused to marry four queens, the cosmological tables tipped, and Burma was conquered by British-led troops on the pretext of punishing an unlawful fine demanded of a British timber firm. Similarly, commercial interests finally provoked British government interference in Malaya in the 1870s. British advisors became the new "under-kings" of Perak, Selangor, Pahang, and Negri Sembilan.

I have not written much about the French involvement in Southeast Asia up to the time of the Industrial Revolution. There is little to add to the brief mention of French intrigue in Thailand. French missionaries were the only Europeans that were much in contact with the Vietnamese. They began their efforts in the 1620s, cooperating with Spanish missionary effort but also intent on demonstrating the importance of the French church to Catholicism. When they arrived, they found that the Vietnamese were divided into two kingdoms. The southerners were ruled by the Nguyen dynasty and the northerners by the Trinh. After the final defeat of the Chams at the end of the fifteenth century, the Vietnamese of the south outdistanced communication with Hanoi and gradually became a separate kingdom. Christianity was opposed by the mandarinate in both the north and south because it was seen as opposed to Confucianism, which was the basic value system of the mandarinate and the monarchy. Throughout the seventeenth and eighteenth centuries, the two Vietnams vacillated between persecuting Christians and trying not to antagonize the French government. Doggedly, French missionaries proselytized whatever the mood of Vietnamese officials. They may have gained as many as three hundred thousand converts by the beginning of the eighteenth century.

French priests meddled in politics in much the same manner as English traders. Probably, their efforts to put more amiable officials into positions of power were not very successful. In fact, officials became less sympathetic as the decades passed. Shifts of political power were frequent and violent but resulted in no advantage for the French. In 1777, for example, three brothers led a successful revolt against the Nguyen emperor, conquered the Trinh army of the north, defeated an invading Chinese force, and then divided the country into three parts, with capitals in Hanoi, Hue, and Saigon. Then a Nguyen prince recaptured Saigon and began a campaign to conquer all of Vietnam. Twenty-five years later, in 1802, he succeeded and made his capital at Hue. The next half century was the golden age of Vietnamese history.[8] It was a period of terrible persecution of Christians, however. Emperor Minh Mang issued the most fateful edict against Christians in 1833 when he declared that the penalty for being Christian was death. The French government was drawn more and more to its duty of protecting French priests. This was particularly true after the 1840s as England emerged as the chief benefactor of China's defeat in the Opium Wars (wherein China was forced to accept the British import of opium into China from India). Having lost out to England in the developed areas of China, France hoped to develop new trade in southwestern China, and to that end, a base in the Red River valley was valuable.

In 1859 combined Spanish and French forces invaded Da Nang to punish the deaths of Spanish and French priests. They conquered a large area that included Saigon. The Spanish were satisfied with revenge; the French wanted land. A treaty in 1862 confirmed this conquest, and five years later French forces conquered the rest of Cochin China, as they called the south, on the pretext of pacifying anti-French rebels. In the same year, Thailand ceded its protectorate over Cambodia and Laos to France. A small group of French adventurers captured Hanoi in 1873, embarrassing the French government, which disavowed the conquest. The Vietnamese emperor was embarrassed, too, and sent to China for help. Reluctantly, a small Chinese force moved into the north a decade later. Justly provoked, a French force took Hanoi again, this time for keeps. In 1883 the royal court at Hue recognized the French protectorate over Tonkin and Annam.

France, Britain, and Thailand controlled Southeast Asia at the end of the nineteenth century.

EUROPEAN COLONIALISM

The Industrial Revolution was dependent on mass markets and on mass supplies of raw materials. Both were most easily available through control over large populations. Colonialism was thus an important ingredient of the Industrial Revolution. Technically, however, many areas of Southeast Asia were never colonies. Thailand, of course, was never ruled by a European colonial regime. Only a small portion of Malaya—the so-called straits settlements of Singapore, Melaka, and Penang—was ever formally a part of the British Colonial Empire. The French, technically, held only one province in all of Indochina. Legally, most of the land in Indochina and Malaya was merely under the protection of the French and the British. But Burma was in every way a part of the British Colonial Empire. Worse, it was merely a province of British India, a fact that made its experience during the colonial period different from that of other states in Southeast Asia.

The people of Burma did not readily accept the fact of British occupation in 1885, and some of them were the object of what was called "pacification" in those times. Five years later, the British controlled all of Burma. They abolished the monarchy in 1886 and a few years later refused to appoint a head bishop or primate of Theravada Buddhism. They ignored traditional political structure, ruling from the top through a largely appointive privy council and from the bottom through salaried headmen at the village level. The civil service was a provincial variant of that in India, and its positions were at first entirely filled by immigrant Indians. Indians served as soldiers and as policemen. Some pro-British ethnic groups, particularly the Christian Karens, were singled out as early as the period of pacification to furnish British-led troops of soldiers and police. And non-Burmese ethnic communities were ruled separately from the Burmese—a suggestion of separate autonomy from the Burmese that is the background of many contemporary political problems. In time, and very slowly of course, the British attempted to introduce a parliamentary system of government by slowly increasing the proportion of elected representatives to appointed members of the ruling council. By 1937 an elected parliament was achieved, but its powers were limited. Always, the ultimate power was in British hands.

British control over the Malay sultanates was very different in form. Four of the sultanates had signed treaties of advice with Britain in the 1870s and had been federated into a single administrative unit in 1895. Four other sultanates—Kedah, Perlis, Kelantan, and Trengganu—were freed from Thai suzerainty in 1909 and signed treaties of advice the same year. Johore was the last to sign such a treaty, in 1914. The last five refused to join the federation and were known as the Unfederated Malay States. The treaties of advice required that the sultan of each state follow the advice of a British advisor in all matters except religion and custom. From the British point of view, which usually but not always prevailed, "religion and custom" was a very small universe. From the Malay point of view, it was a universe that included practically everything. In any case, the sultans and their royal courts were preserved. The sultans were nothing without their chiefs, however, and the chiefs who had not been killed in the British-sponsored tin wars of the 1870s were bought with salaries and pensions. At first, members of the staff of the British advisor (Resident) filled the day-to-day administrative vacuum left by the removal of the Malay chiefs. Later, regular administrative clerk services headed by the British Residents developed in all of the states, and after 1895, a federal service developed in the Federated Malay States (Selangor, Perak, Negri Sembilan, and Pahang). Malay leaders at the subdistrict level, whose positions in many areas were inherited, continued in their traditional roles. But they were given "bicycle money" to perform certain duties for the British-controlled administrative services. At the village level, traditional leadership remained intact. In Malaya, the British controlled the sultanates through their hold on the middle level of political structure.

The technical hold that the French had in Indochina was no less tenuous than that of the British in Malaya. Only Cochin China, the southern delta area of the Mekong River, was technically a colony. Tongkin, Annam, Cambodia, and Laos were protectorates. However, they were members along with Cochin China in the French-sponsored Indochinese Union that was administered by a governor-general who was responsible to the Ministry of Colonies in Paris. The French government tinkered and meddled in the affairs of the union, as evidenced by the frequent change of governors-general (23 between 1892 and 1930), but lower-ranking Frenchmen, who spent much of their lifetimes in the administrative service of the union, made the important decisions about colonial policy. Cochin China was ruled at the national level by a French governor and two assemblies, and at the provincial level by French province chiefs and provincial assemblies. Tongkin, in the area of the Red River valley of northern Vietnam, was ruled by cooperative Vietnamese mandarins who assiduously followed the advice of a French Resident. Annam, the central region of Vietnam stretching from Tongkin in the north to Cochin China in the south, retained its emperor and his court at Hue. But the powers of the emperor and his mandarinate were so circumscribed that he was no more than a national symbol. Actual power was in the hands of the French administrative service. French power reached from top to bottom in all three Vietnamese regions but was especially strong at the local level in Cochin China, where even the local policemen and judges were French.

Cambodia and Laos, as buffer states between Vietnam and Thailand, were subject to much less French control. Both had chosen French rather than Thai suzerainty. Both feared the Vietnamese more than they feared the French. The enmity between French and Vietnamese made for a certain community of interests between the French and their protectorates in Laos and Cambodia. The political structures of Laos and Cambodia were modified very slightly toward Western models. Throughout Indochina, the French maintained separate administration for the hill peoples.

Thailand, too, westernized the structure of its governmental institutions slightly in accord with the advice of European technical advisers. Certainly, the Thais were not directly forced to westernize the structure of their government, but the changes did weaken European arguments that Thai justice was not adequate for judging the crimes of European citizens in Thailand, thereby obviating claims to extraterritoriality and bringing about changes that probably enhanced Thailand's ability to respond effectively to other economic and political ploys of European nations. The Thai government did not accept advisers from any one European country; rather, it accepted a few technical advisers from several —Germany, Denmark, France, England, Belgium, and the United States. American missionaries were quite influential, too, in an informal way. Their wives sometimes served as teachers of English and science in Thai schools. Although Thailand lost suzerainty over extensive territories—Laos and Cambodia to the French and the northern Malay states of Perlis, Kedah, Kelantan, and Trengganu to the British—it remained in firm control of its old central territories and insisted on more firm control through its efforts to assimilate Shan and Lao tribesmen and even Malays and Chinese into the Thai national identity. Although Westerners never achieved firm control over Thai resources and customers, the Thai government adopted many of the western means of such control for its own purposes. To some extent, the effect was the same.

English became the official language in Burma and Malaya; French, in Vietnam, Cambodia, and Laos; and Thai (Central Thai), in all of Thailand. In each instance, other language loyalties were weakened by reducing their use in official governmental business or by restricting their use in higher education. Peasants and lower class urban dwellers were not much affected, but the urban elites were so deeply affected that in some instances they initially lost interest and facility in their native languages. Later, they reacted against the new languages as symbols of imperialism. This was particularly the case in Burma and Malaya, where English was associated with the dominance of foreign Asian elites, Indians and Chinese, as well as with British colonial officials. Indians had a head start in the use of English through their experiences with the British in India and through their positions in the colonial administrative services. Both Indians and Chinese often attended Christian missionary schools, too, where English was the medium of instruction from the first year of schooling. Malays, particularly, feared that their children would become Christians if they attended missionary schools; as good Muslims, they would not allow their children to attend even though the advantages of an English education were clear. Malay fears were not unfounded. They were aware of Thai efforts to win converts to Theravada Buddhism and Thai language among the Malays of southern Thailand. The British did offer English education to Malays of noble birth, establishing the Malay College for purposes of training Malays to fill high positions in the civil service. Chinese immigrants to Thailand were subject to the same pressures to assimilate, but they were given an economically advantageous position in Thai society at the same time.

Native educational systems in Malaya, Burma, and Thailand had been religious in emphasis and primary in level. Village schools taught religious orthodoxy and basic literacy. There was virtually no secondary or advanced level except by tutorial from religious officials and within the context of the royal court. Westernization actually added to the educational establishment in these areas. In Vietnam, however, the native system was very highly developed and well integrated with government administrative services. There were schools at the village, district, provincial, and national levels. The French reformed village schools to teach the Roman orthography and French language and disbanded dozens of schools at other levels, substituting 14 secondary French language schools. A national college, more or less equivalent to the disbanded Vietnamese university at Hue, was opened briefly by the French in Hanoi, but it soon closed. The French destroyed an elaborate native system and offered no adequate substitute. However, French language was taught at the village level, and it was more widely used by the Vietnamese than was English among the Burmese or the Malays.

National economies changed even more rapidly than educational systems during the last half of the nineteenth century. Developments in the technology of transporting bulk goods were revolutionary in effect. A French engineer directed the cutting of a canal across the Isthmus of Suez. This new canal linked the Mediterranean and the Red Sea more directly and was much wider and deeper than the old canal between the Red Sea and the Nile River which had not been used since Arabs controlled the East-West trade. Most important, Europeans controlled access to the canal through a treaty with Egypt. The long and hazardous trip around the Cape of Good Hope was eliminated. Steam power increased the speed, capacity, and dependability of ships, lowering the cost of transporting goods in bulk. Railroads in Europe and in Asia opened large regions as sources of raw material and as markets. And European colonial regimes brought peace to Southeast Asia so that internal and international trade was much less hazardous than it had been for centuries.

The European contribution to economic development in Southeast Asia is not disputable. However, much of the actual development was accomplished by natives or by immigrant Asians. Peasants from central Burma opened the rich lands of lower Burma in response to a high demand for rice in India and Southeast Asia. Indian Chettyars were an important source of capital for these Burmese peasants, and the Chettyars' acquisitive ways continually pushed the peasants into developing new areas for cultivation. The Burmese pioneered, and Indians gained control and continued farming, the rice lands. Taxes consumed major portions of the profit of the Indians and financed public projects and improvements credited to the colonial regime. Much of the profit found its way to England or to India and was not reinvested in Burma. The lot of the Burmese peasants was not much improved, and the possibility of "economic takeoff" was stifled by the British and Indian absorption of surplus. Still, it was one of the most spectacular instances of agricultural development in the nineteenth century—cultivated rice lands in southern Burma increased from three million to ten million acres within half a century (1880–1930). About seventy percent of the rice was exported. Most of it went to India; more than half of the land that produced it was controlled or owned by Indians; and the colonial officials who administered land laws pertaining to rice production and who collected taxes on its profits were Indians. The British invested in mineral production (petroleum, tin, and other metals) and in banking. Economically, Indians, rather than Britishers, were the colonial masters of Burma.

Rice production was never very important in Malaya. Malay peasants rarely produced more than enough for their own subsistence, and they were never able or willing to produce enough for the urban centers. Early Malay kingdoms in the peninsula had imported rice from Java and Thailand before the arrival of Europeans. The volume of rice imported from Java became smaller as Europeans developed monopolies over trade in different areas and as the population pressure on the rice lands of Java increased. Thailand became the main rice supplier of Malaya, and Burma provided additional supplies as necessary. British colonial officers were not especially interested in developing rice production in Malaya; other crops and other economic enterprises seemed more important to them.

The British were especially interested in developing the tin-mining industry of Malaya. Malays, of course, had pioneered in this field. Tin was the major export of fifteenth-century Melaka. But even then, non-Malays, aborigines, probably collected most of the tin ore. Later, as the newly opened European market increased demand for tin, Malay chiefs imported Chinese laborers to open new areas for tin mining. The Chinese worked under a "Captain

China," selected from among their own ranks, who was directly responsible to the Malay chief (from the Malay point of view) or who sold the tin to the Malay chief of the area (from the Chinese point of view). Chinese involvement in tin mining increased dramatically from 1850 to 1870 when almost all of the tin produced was mined by Chinese. The tin wars of the 1870s wrested control of the export of tin from the hands of the Malay chiefs and placed it in the hands of Chinese entrepreneurs. British merchants encouraged this development and began to acquire a financial interest of their own in tin mining. They introduced mechanical methods of extracting tin ores from the soil and improved methods of smelting in the hope of increasing production. The Chinese "open-cast" mining techniques were very inefficient. Britishers had had much more experience (England still produced more tin than Malaya in 1870) than the Chinese, but the Chinese were quick to copy British methods. They continued to dominate tin production through the first quarter of the twentieth century. Then, food canning and automobile manufacture in Europe and the United States spurred British capitalists to invest increasing amounts in tin-mining properties in Malaya. Just before World War II, the Chinese share of tin production had fallen to about one-third of the total and British-owned companies accounted for most of the remaining two-thirds.

British capitalists began and developed the rubber industry of Malaya. Other commercial crops such as pepper, cloves, and coffee had been tried earlier and had not been especially successful. Rubber-tree seedlings from Ceylon, originally smuggled from Brazil, were introduced into commercial plantings at the end of the nineteenth century. The development of automobile manufacture in Europe and the United States began soon afterwards, greatly expanding the demand for rubber. British capitalists imported large numbers of Chinese and Indian laborers to work on their rubber plantations, and tens of thousands of Indonesian Malays migrated to Malaya, too, to work on commercial plantations. Chinese entrepreneurs followed the British example, developing and working their own smaller plantations and employing cheap Tamil and Chinese tappers. Indigenous Malays and Indonesian Malays, taking advantage of land codes that reserved small holdings of lands for the exclusive use of Malays, developed thousands of independently owned rubber-tree orchards, varying in size from 1 to 20 acres, which were tapped by the owners, members of their families, and their neighbors. The Chinese and the Malays quickly caught up to the British. Small Chinese plantations and Malay small holdings accounted for more than half of the acreage in rubber trees before the beginning of World War II.

In Malaya, Indian Chettyars did not gain control of extensive lands as they did in southern Burma. Southern Burma had been a sort of no-man's-land, abandoned to the control of British India by the Burmese court in its retreat to Mandalay in the north. Moreover, much of it was swamp land that had never before been brought under cultivation. Individual Burmese pioneered it and thereby had rights to it, but these were only "natural rights" that were not reinforced by Burmese custom. Indeed, the pioneers were mere individuals and were neither bound nor protected by traditional claims to the land. Their claims and the claims of Chettyars to whom they mortgaged their land were always within the context of British law. The situation was different in Malaya, where in principle, if not in fact, the sultans of the various states controlled the use of all land. Acting in the spirit of the Malay principle that all land belonged to the sultans except as they themselves wished to dispose of it, British administrators reserved large tracts of agricultural land for the exclusive use of Malays. Such land could be neither sold to non-Malays nor used as collateral for loans from non-Malays and was thus available to Malays only. Also, except for a brief period in the limited area of the straits settlements (Penang, Melaka, and Singapore), Malaya was never ruled by the administrative services of British India, which brought many Indians to Burma. Overseas Indians were never a serious problem in Malaya.

Overseas Chinese in Malaya, in a very general sense, were the functional equivalent of overseas Indians in Burma. The Chinese became great entrepreneurs and moneylenders in Malaya. The success of Chinese immigrants was less the product of their experience in business than of their determination to rise above their low status in southern China from whence most of them came. There, they had been mostly the poorest peasants or landless urban folk. British administrators encouraged their entrance into entrepreneurial positions by suppressing the business activities of the Malay chiefs and sultans, by encouraging Malays to remain or to become rural farmers, and by discouraging immigrant Chinese from becoming independent farmers. Some features of Chinese social organization, the patrilineal extended family and mutual aid societies, were important in establishing an advantage for the Chinese in competition with Malay businessmen.

Like the Indians in Burma, the Chinese of Malaya were a very transient population. They sent much of their earnings home to relatives in China, and many returned to China after having become wealthy in Malaya. But they made a large contribution not only in labor and skill, but also in capital. Tax revenues from Chinese commercial enterprises, especially tin mining, supplied most of the capital that the British used for developing transportation facilities and other public works. And after 1920, the proportion of female to male Chinese immigrants increased. Family life became more common and settlement became more permanent. The Chinese had come to stay after all. Their strength in wealth and numbers made them serious rivals to the Malays, who became increasingly fearful of the potential political strength of the Chinese.

The Thai government did not import tens of thousands of foreign Asian laborers as the British did in Burma and Malaya. Still, there was much immigration of Chinese. They came to comprise about twenty percent of the population, and they gained control of most of the entrepreneurial positions in Thai society. They were moneylenders, and they owned market gardens, rice mills, rubber plantations, and tin mines. The Thai government used them as tax collectors and employed them in government-controlled banks. They were allowed, even encouraged, to develop commercial enterprise. But the government nationalized some of their enterprises and forced many of them to assimilate to Thai ethnic identity.

Europeans, especially the British, invested in the Thai economy, but economic growth was not rapid. Even the development of commercial agriculture reached a plateau by the beginning of the twentieth century. Such slow development had its compensations. The value of imports was not allowed to exceed the value of exports, credit was not too easily available to cultivators so that they were not deprived of their land, and traditional social structure was not disrupted. New economic and political forms of the West were displayed in Bangkok. A stone palace replaced the carved wooden one, a military junta replaced the king (in 1932), office buildings and banks replaced some shophouses; but peasants remained on their traditional lands, producing enough for their own needs and a little surplus for the Buddhist monks and the tax collector and remaining loyal to the king, not caring that others ruled in his name.

French economic development of Indochina was concentrated in the south, in Cochin China. French capital transformed lands of the Mekong delta into a vast area of irrigated rice fields and rubber plantations. It was like southern Burma in being a newly opened area in which Western law, rather than native traditions, guided the development of economic institutions. But it was different in that Europeans, rather than foreign Asians, controlled the land. Foreign Asians were not imported as agricultural laborers. Rather, Vietnamese were imported from the north. In time, as some of them managed to leave agricultural labor, they moved into towns and cities, where they worked as unskilled laborers. Their importation from the north created a landless proletariat in both rural and urban areas. Chinese construction laborers were imported to build railroads, however, and most of them eventually came to live in Cochin China where economic opportunities were more certain because of the relatively sparse population and the investment of French capital. They concentrated in towns and cities, becoming businessmen, moneylenders, and skilled laborers.

The major ills of the European presence—deterioration of traditional political order, economic dependence on a few specialized and fluctuating segments of the world market, intrusion of masses of transient foreign Asians, and the admission (by default) of the superiority of foreigners and foreign ways to regulate and fashion life—were made painfully clear to Southeast Asians by the economic and military failures of Europeans in the 1930s and early 1940s. The failures showed that Europeans were no longer omnipotent and that they could not be trusted to provide the economic and political security that many Southeast Asians had been willing to purchase by forfeiting their independence. Nationalistic sentiments among Southeast Asians had not died after Europeans took control. They had merely faded under pressure of economic well-being and political suppression. Economic depression and Japanese military conquest released the pressure of rising irritation with the European presence.

REFERENCES

[1] Maurice Collis, *The Land of the Great Image* (New York: Alfred A. Knopf, 1958).

[2] Collis, *The Land of the Great Image,* pp. 18–19.

[3] B. Harrison, *South-east Asia: A Short History* (London: Macmillan & Company, 1963), p. 64; Paul Wheatley, *The Golden Khersonese* (Kuala Lumpur: University of Malaya Press, 1961), p. 313, fn. 1.

[4] C. C. Brown, trans., *Sejarah Melayu "Malay Annals"* (Hong Kong: Oxford University Press, 1970).

[5] See, for example, A. P. da Franca, *Portuguese Influence in Indonesia* (Djakarta: P. T. Gunung Agung, 1970).

[6] A good general history of Southeast Asia is D. G. E. Hall, *A History of Southeast Asia* (London: Macmillan & Company, 1964).

[7] The standard history of Malaya before independence is R. O. Winstedt, *A History of Malaya* (Singapore: Marican and Sons, 1962).

[8] See pages 104–107 of H. J. Benda and J. A. Larkin, eds., *The World of Southeast Asia: Selected Historical Readings* (New York: Harper & Row, Publishers, 1967).

FOUR

THE REBIRTH OF NATIONALISM

Many Western writers persist in viewing "real nationalism" as a nascent or recent phenomenon that has developed through gradual appreciation of Western political precepts by Southeast Asians.[1] Such a view ignores the existence of native states and imperialism in the area before the European arrival. As we have seen, Europeans did not gain economic and political control of Southeast Asia until the last quarter of the nineteenth century. Even then many Southeast Asians did not acquiesce to European dominance. The extent of their resistance, although difficult to measure, was nonetheless substantial. Europeans won control on the strength or the threat of their military superiority, but open rebellion and guerilla warfare continued for years after the treaties were signed in Indochina, Burma, and Malaya. The historical record is not clear because of the tendency of officers to report anti-European incidents as acts of piracy and banditry. Incidents of noncooperation, many of which were recorded in correspondence files of district officers, were viewed as the results of misunderstanding, ignorance, or laziness on the part of Southeast Asians. Leaders of anti-European incidents were seen as self-serving troublemakers at least and at most as religious fanatics, common criminals, or mere lackeys of other European nations. It was not in the European interest to recognize the existence of genuine nationalistic sentiment among Southeast Asians.

Resistance to European control through violent acts or non-cooperation gradually decreased, not because Southeast Asian leaders lost interest, but because they were outmaneuvered by the ingenuity of European colonial officials and the superiority of European armed forces. In many ways, the first European officers were the best suited to deal a deathblow to traditional nationalism. They were young and knowledgeable and daring. Some had just reached their majority. They learned the local languages and customs quickly, respected the acuity of their adversaries, and dared to earn respect. Few of them had been formally trained as diplomats or administrators. Indeed, their duties were not at first clear, and they had to define their own positions. They were drawn from various occupations and classes—trader, lawyer, physician, seaman, and soldier. They were more than just imaginative colonial officers who became advisers of the kings, aristocrats, and headmen whose pensions they arranged and whose challengers they subverted or compromised. They also wrote the first extensive accounts of the customs and traditions of various ethnic groups in Southeast Asia. Generally, they were sympathetic to the interests of the people whom they advised and ruled. But the effect of many of their liberal programs was the subversion of nationalistic movements. This was particularly the case in the Malay states and in Indochina where colonial officials manipulated rather than destroyed traditional symbols of nationalism. In Burma, of course, the traditional symbols were destroyed (royalty) or terribly weakened (Buddhist officialdom).

The traditional varieties of nationalism in Southeast Asia were as "real" as the European variety. But they differed in that nations were defined according to hierarchies of foci rather than by boundaries that enclosed territories. Ordinarily, such nations consisted of at least three levels of foci. Villages focused on towns that were the seats of principalities. Principalities focused on cities that were the capitals of nations. Capitals often contained large numbers of resident and transient foreigners housed in the more profane districts, and they were the ceremonial sites of pacts and alliances with lowland minorities and mountain tribesmen. However, each capital, each nation, belonged to the people of a particular ethnic identity—"major people." Others were often welcome, but as guests not co-owners.

Capital cities and, to a lesser extent, principal towns were cosmologically defined as centers of universe with magically central leaders and paraphernalia.[2] Warfare between nations was an attempt to discredit the image of the other capital as a magical center of universe while aggrandizing the image of one's own center, and secondarily, it was an attempt to capture the material resources and markets controlled by the other center. Europeans excelled in the pursuit of these locally defined purposes of warfare but did so in rather novel ways. The only situation in which they relied more on force than on ingenuity was in Burma where the British dismissed royalty, restricted the authority of Buddhist monks and bishops, and placed villages directly under the authority of colonial officials. In Indochina and Malaya, the Europeans avoided any challenge of royal privilege. They sponsored candidates for royal office who were pro-European, and they kept favored members of royalty on substantial pensions. They avoided any appearance of taking over the old capitals, which were left as traditional residences for royalty, and they built their own cities, which became centers of trade in bulk materials and manufactured goods and centers of colonial administrative services.

The old centers of nationalism were discredited by compromising the position and image of members of royalty and by creating new commercial and administrative centers that quickly outdistanced the old centers in size and everyday importance. Not only were members of royalty selected for office according to their willingness to cooperate and paid large sums of money to secure their friendship, they were treated to rather complete Western educations and given responsibilities in colonial government. To the extent that they became intellectually westernized and a part of colonial regimes, they became less effective as foci for traditional nationalism. The Western seduction of traditional elites proceeded downward from royalty through the ranks of aristocratic families. Royal and aristocratic families usually managed to gain large financial interests in mineral and agricultural resources, and many of them even came to own valuable tracts of land in the new urban centers. The royalty and aristocracy had been the primary entrepreneurs and capitalists of earlier days, so their interest in capitalism was not new, but the effect now was to help in the establishment of European centers that outshone traditional centers.

Southeast Asians were stymied in their expression of nationalistic sentiment by a tremendous loss of confidence in traditional symbols of cosmological power—their capital cities and their kings. Moreover, control over economic ventures of foreign Asians was lost and never fully grasped again by the Europeans. To lose to a people who seemed as magically endowed as the Europeans was perhaps less bitter than to be put on more equal footing with other peoples—mountain tribesmen and lowland minorities and foreign Asians. A large part of nationalistic effort was devoted to protecting special rights and the higher status of the major peoples of Southeast Asia who had surrendered power to the Europeans. These efforts came quite naturally from royalty in their everyday associations with European officials. They were successful to a degree in gaining guarantees of land, of education, and of positions in the administrative services for their followers, but they failed otherwise to guarantee economic success vis-à-vis foreign Asians. Foreign Asians were more inclined to engage the European-controlled economic system because their entrepreneurial enterprises were less affected than their other activities by colonial regulation.

Native royalty and aristocracy were at first complacent about the economic success of foreign Asians. They had profited directly from such success in the past when they controlled the system of trade in luxury goods. But the new capitalism of bulk goods was controlled by Europeans. Foreign Asians were able to increase their participation in this new system before indigenous entrepreneurs adjusted to the fact of European control. Gradually, foreign Asians had gained control over all but the upper levels of entrepreneurship, which were controlled by Europeans. Finally it became apparent that in the new political order introduced by the Europeans economic power could be easily translated into political power. This realization was slow in dawning because foreign Asians were so concerned initially with political events in their own homelands that they did not participate much in local politics. Southeast Asian leaders were willing to concede some economic advantage to foreign Asians in order to better concentrate on gaining administrative power. Traditionally, such power had been closely allied to ultimate (cosmological) power, and economic success had been viewed as merely an attribute rather than a source of power. In the new social order, economic success was a major source of power. Foreign Asians became more visible than Europeans as competitors for power. A major portion of the content of nationalism was anti-foreign Asian. And, because foreigners enjoyed greater success in the capitalism controlled by Europe, a portion of the content of Southeast Asian nationalism became anticapitalist.

Under European colonial regimes, hill tribes and lowland minorities regained much autonomy that they had lost to Southeast Asian kingdoms. They did not so much side with the Europeans as welcome independence from the previous regimes. Nationalistic sentiments of tribes and minorities were rekindled, but of course, their nationalisms were distinct from those of lowland majorities.

REVITALIZING TRADITION IN BURMA

Many of the movements that signalled rebirth of nationalism had as their apparent goal the reform or development of traditional culture.[3] Religion and language were common foci of such movements. Religious movements attempted to recover central position in a cosmological order that had been disturbed by the Europeans. Language movements attempted to enhance images of cultural excellence that had been outshone by the magical successes of Europeans and foreign Asians. Because religion and language are the most important dimensions of communal identity in Southeast Asia, they were natural foci of nationalistic sentiment.

Although not traditional forms for organizing political activity, voluntary associations were important vehicles for the expression of nationalistic sentiment. They were modeled after associations in Europe and China. Probably, they drew inspiration more directly from Chinese than from European models. Much of China's resistance to European imperialism since before the middle of the nineteenth century had been through voluntary associations. Political associations found it easy to coordinate their activities and resources with those of traditionalist movements. Traditionalists tolerated modern political associations. Their goals were basically the same—regaining control of their society from Europeans and foreign Asians. Their methods—whether to borrow the mundane tactics of Europeans and foreign Asians or to emphasize traditional symbolic strategies—differed.

The history of nationalistic movements in Burma best illustrates the degree to which modernist and traditionalist elements combined in their efforts to regain independence. This circumstance is best understood as resulting from a combination of the savagery of British/Indian efforts to destroy Burmese national identity and the Burmese belief that their defeat was a temporary cosmological quirk. An end to Burma's monarchy had been declared by the British in 1886, shortly after their conquest of Mandalay. The royal court was itself a major aspect of national identity for Burmans, and it was the main source of support for traditional law and literature and of Buddhist piety, which were the other pillars of Burmese nationalism. Five years of intense rebellion, led by Buddhist monks *(pongyi)*, followed the British declaration. Non-Burmese minorities attempted to regain their own autonomy at the same time. With an army of more than thirty thousand Indians, the British routed Burmese rebels and gained control of the Shan states (1888), the Kachin (1892), and the Chin (1895). Christianized Karens joined with Indian and British forces in the fight against Buddhist Burmese forces, reinforcing their antipathy towards the Burmese. Then, as a final blow to Burmese national identity, the British refused to allow appointment of a new Buddhist primate *(thathanabaing)* in 1895. The kingpin of the structure of Burmese Buddhism had been removed. The last symbol of national identity had been abolished.

Buddhism, although no longer integrated hierarchically into a single national organization, continued as a major experience of Burmese ethnic identity. Every Burmese male was initiated as a monk when he became adolescent. Although only a very few remained monks for more than the period of initiation, being a Buddhist monk was a common experience of all. Monks who remained for longer periods and senior monks, bishops, or abbots, who managed the monasteries, were universally revered.

One of the first voluntary associations that had nationalistic goals was the Young Men's Buddhist Association, founded in 1906. Its members were aware of the brilliant Japanese victories over Europeans (Russians) in 1904 and 1905, and they quickly learned of the founding of the Congress Party in India whose leaders intended to gain independence from the British. Sun Yat Sen provided them with further inspiration in 1911. From the beginning, they employed laymen rather than monks as teachers of Buddhism, and their political intentions were sufficiently clear so that the colonial administration forbade its clerks from joining the organization. However, a decade passed before the YMBA grasped an issue to contest with the British.

In 1916, the YMBA protested to the colonial administration that Europeans and non-Buddhist Asians failed to remove their footwear when visiting Buddhist temples. Despite its inconsequential appearance, the issue was basic. Were Britishers exempt from the proprieties of Burmese tradition? Could Britishers rule without regard for Burmese culture? The point was all the more painful for British administrators because of the announced British policy, known to leaders of the YMBA, of protecting indigenous culture in Malaya. Protests were organized throughout Burma, and in 1918, the colonial administration capitulated, ruling that visitors to monasteries and temples must conform to standards of dress decided upon by the local abbot.

Winning the issue over footwear in temples gave the YMBA a great deal of confidence. Also, a few thousand Burmese had served the British Empire in Europe and Iraq as policemen and laborers during World War I. Experience with the political institutions of these other societies must have reinforced their hopes of regaining independence. The ideal of national self-determination that was expressed by some of the victors of World War I was stimulating, too, especially in light of the British declaration of interest in developing greater self-government for India.

At first, the leaders of the YMBA feared that Burma would be swallowed into an independent India, and they requested that they be separated from the colonial administration of India. Then they feared that Burma would be denied steps towards self-rule if separated from India, and they changed their requests. In spite of the confusion over the issue of relationship with India, YMBA leaders began successfully to persuade the British to establish a constitutional dyarchy in which Burman ministers, responsible to a Burman majority legislative council, governed all internal affairs except for finances, police, labor, and minorities. Before they gained the concession of a constitutional dyarchy from the British, they had to seek support from among Indians and Christians. To this end, they changed the name of their organization to the General Council of Burmese Associations in 1920. As the GCBA, they led the boycott against government schools for teaching Western values, guided the development of peasant political associations (ethnic societies), encouraged the increased political participation of Buddhist monks by helping to found the General Council of Monkhood Associations, and finally, gained the concession of constitutional dyarchy from the British. All of this was accomplished by 1923 but at the cost of fragmentation as various factions took advantage of different political opportunities that had been won. Struggles for power within the nationalist movement consumed the next seven years.

Burmese peasants had recognized the nationalistic intent of the GCBA and on several occasions had treated GCBA leaders as if they were members of traditional Burmese royalty. A minor officer of the GCBA who was responsible for surveys of agrarian conditions in 1927–28 understood the interest of peasants in restoring royalty. A former monk and folk healer, he was very familiar with the doctrine of the *bodhisattva* or "Emergent Buddha" as king. In 1930, when the price of rice had been halved within a year by the world economic depression, Saya San began his peasant revolution in lower Burma. He moved north to an ancient place rich in sacred power with which a charismatic leader might anoint himself. He built a capital there in the jungle and acquired royal paraphernalia. His followers, like many Burmese males at that time, were tattooed in the traditional manner from navel to knee with figures of tigers, monkeys, pigs, and birds, which provided protection from natural as well as supernatural dangers. They also wore traditional amulets made of metal and bamboo and of cloth or paper upon which were inscribed magical runes that were supposed to protect their lives until the new Buddha had emerged. They attacked police posts, Indians, Chinese, and village headmen who opposed them. Twelve thousand colonial troops broke the back of the revolution within two years, but the British were frightened by the possibility of wider rebellion. They responded by allowing a greater amount of self-government.

The GCBA was associated with Saya San, the storied rebel, and harvested his popularity in the general elections of 1932. In the years that followed, leaders of GCBA as members of the legislative and administrative establishment failed to improve general economic conditions and were challenged by university students who had learned something of European Marxism. The Marxist students called each other *Thakin* (Lord) to illustrate the right of Burmans to rule themselves. They organized labor unions and university students. But their timing was wrong. Their efforts to obtain greater self-rule were undercut when the British implemented the new constitution in 1937, honoring promises made two years before to the GCBA leadership. Under the new constitution, Burma was ruled by nine ministers who were responsible to an elected house of representatives and senate. The British-appointed governor retained control only over defense, foreign relations, monetary policy, and certain minorities.

No party had gained a clear majority in the 1936 elections. Dr. Ba Maw, a socialist lawyer and Anglophobe who had defended Saya San, developed a coalition and headed the first government. It lasted until 1939 when it was toppled by legislative problems that

were an outgrowth of anti-Indian riots led by Buddhist monks.
World War II began the same year.

Ba Maw and leaders of the Thakin movement formed a group which demanded complete independence from England as the price for Burma's cooperation in the war effort. Some members of the group, including Dr. Ba Maw, were imprisoned for treason. Others fled to Japan. Thirty of the Thakin, including Aung San and Ne Win, returned to Burma with the Japanese invasion of 1942. They headed a small force of about a thousand that had been assembled in Thailand. It grew to more than thirty thousand as the British and Chinese Nationalist forces were defeated. Although their force was small compared to that of their allies, the Thakin-led Burmese army made a definite contribution to the defeat of their former overlords. The Japanese nominated Dr. Ba Maw to be head of state, and Ba Maw selected a cabinet from among his personal friends and the Thakin. Ba Maw and his colleagues made frank public statements about the inadequacy of Western democratic institutions for ruling Burma. Ba Maw increasingly adopted the style of a king and assumed the title of *Mingyi*. He sought and gained control over the Shan states. Ba Maw was more Burmese than westernized socialist, after all. He gained full independence for Burma from the Japanese except that Burma had to honor the needs of their army.

The Japanese were no less arrogant in their treatment of temples, tradition, and people than the British. The economic situation was much worse than under British colonial rule. Food was scarce and people were pressed into service as laborers for military projects, the most famous of which was the railroad into Thailand. When the British successfully counterattacked the Japanese thrust into India in 1944, it was clear to the leaders of the Thakin that the Japanese were going to lose the war and that arrangements ought to be made to become allies with the British army. As the Japanese defeat turned gradually into a rout, the Thakin group offered to help speed victory by attacking the Japanese army from behind. The offer was finally accepted when it appeared that the British advance could not be concluded before the onset of the southwestern monsoons unless aided by the Burmese. With the help of the Thakins' Antifascist Peoples Freedom League, the Japanese army began to fall back into Thailand in May of 1945.

The war was won. The Burmese were on the right (winning) side after all. And the British really could not deny the Burmese what they had already gained—their independence. Officials of the colonial administration (including the governor) were against Burmese independence, and they interfered with the transfer of power in many ways, even suggesting at one point that the leader of the Thakins, Aung San, be imprisoned. But the British home government of Clement Attlee took effective measures to ensure a smooth transition. Thakin Aung San and his closest associate,

Thakin Mya, and five others were assassinated just before the realization of independence. Thakin Nu, a schoolboy friend and longtime associate of Aung San, replaced Aung San, becoming the first premier of the Union of Burma in 1948.

The new old nation was in complete disarray. Much of the cultivated area had reverted to jungle. Railroads, highways, and port facilities had been destroyed in the war. Public services no longer existed. Cities and towns were crowded with refugees. Indians, who had managed the major businesses and the distribution of goods and services in the past, fled back to India rather than face the prospects of retribution under Burmese rule. The minority ethnic groups began to long for their own independence, and even the communists split into two factions, each of which planned to gain control of the whole country.

U Nu, the Marxist Thakin, began to take the necessary pragmatic steps to pull the country back together. The Burmese army was sent out to fight rebels and to begin reconstruction of the transportation system. Efforts were made to redevelop agricultural lands. The economy was nationalized. Promises were made to Kachin, Chin, Shan, Arakanese, Mon, and Karen nationalists. However, U Nu's major contribution was a very traditionally Burmese one. Through personal advocation and leadership, he reinvigorated the Theravada Buddhist religion in Burma. He placed Burma in the cosmological vortex of the Buddhist world by convening the Sixth World Buddhist Council (1954–56). If only he had not been an elected leader, tainted by baptism in the stuff of Western political systems, he might have become a king and an Emergent Buddha.

Another of the prewar Thakins, Ne Win, seemed to lose patience with U Nu's overriding interest in Buddhism and his inattention to socialism. U Nu surrendered power voluntarily to Ne Win and the army for a period of 18 months in 1958–60 and returned to power after elections in 1960. In 1962, he announced his intention to retire, and the subsequent struggle among others to succeed him led to the army's final intervention. Ne Win's "Burmese socialism" succeeded U Nu's "Buddhist socialism," and Burma began to close its borders to outsiders, turning to the task of internal reconstruction and introspection so necessary to recapture its proper place in the cosmos.

The military rationalization for the take-over of civilian government was that there was widespread dissatisfaction with politicians who had not learned during the interim military regime to discipline themselves to form functioning coalitions from the various political parties. The occasion for the take-over was the strong indication that the civilian government was about to acquiesce to Shan demands for the formation of an independent Shan state. Further existence of the country was additionally threatened by the Kachin Independence Army, the National Progressive Party of the Chin, the New Mon State Party, the Karen National United Party, the

Karenni National Progressive Party, the Arakan Communist Party (Red Flag branch), the National Red Flag Communist Party, and the White Flag Communist Party, all of which had military units of some sort.

Unfortunately the first field operations by the military government were against students at Rangoon University. Students were killed and wounded and driven from the university, which was converted completely to the teaching of Burmese socialism. Later the military regime began operations against Shan rebels. Military operations were not very successful, and an amnesty period from April 1963 to January 1964 was granted with the hope that persuasion would succeed where force had failed. By July of 1964, the military government was in communication with all rebel leaders, but all negotiations broke down by the end of 1965 with the exception of the agreement reached with the Karens in March of 1964. But negotiation was a successful tactic because the Karen had posed the greatest threat. They were better organized and more experienced in warfare than the other rebel groups.

Other rebel groups have continued their insurgency against the Burmese government, but the pressure has eased. The release of many political prisoners by the government in 1968 was an indication of substantial restoration of civil order. Another indication was the assassination of the head of the White Flag Communists by one of his own followers in September of 1968. Operations against rebels have not been brought to a ruthless conclusion because of fear of disaffecting China and Thailand and because continuation of the military operations strengthens the political position of the army. Also, the senior officers who have learned to be effective against the rebels are removed to become administrators, and inexperienced junior officers are left to command field operations. When they become experienced, they, too, will be promoted to administrative posts.

Civil war continues to interfere with government economic planning. The stagnating economy of Burma poses almost as much threat to the continued existence of the Union of Burma as threats of secession by ethnic minorities. Production of all sorts is still below pre-World War II levels. In the meantime, Burma's population is expanding rapidly, at the rate of about three percent each year. It seems improbable that Burma will ever again be a major exporter of rice.

Probably, most Burmese are aware that the military has not been much more successful in developing the economy than were the earlier civilian governments. They most likely accept military rule because it is more familiar to them than monarchy or parliamentary democracy. The British destroyed the traditional monarchy almost a century ago. They severely limited Burmese experience with parliamentary democracy, and worse, they made a mockery of the parliamentary system by keeping real power from it. The Burmese were prepared to scorn parliamentary democracy on the basis of previous experience. Military police and civil servants had been more powerful than the parliament during British rule, and they were the institutions of government experienced most by ordinary people. Also, the independence movement was as much military as socialist, and it was aided by a Japanese military regime. It is amazing that parliamentary democracy lasted as long as it did in Burma, and it seems improbable that the Burmese will turn again to democracy in the near future.

THE PERSISTENCE OF VIETNAMESE NATIONALISM

French repression of Vietnamese nationalism was almost as harsh as British repression of Burmese nationalism.[4] The French had less opportunity than the British because they had not conquered the whole of Vietnam. They had to use Vietnamese royalty in order to gain access to the whole country. The French consolidated their rule of Vietnam in 1883, but nationalist resistance continued. Until the 1920s, nationalist movements were led by mandarins of high rank and dissident princes and were oriented toward a full restoration of the traditional Vietnamese Empire. Leaders of these movements viewed the French as simply usurpers of political power. Although they resisted French efforts to convert Vietnamese to Christianity, their attitudes about French culture were not entirely negative. Like leaders of all the other major nationalist movements that followed, they encouraged the use of the Roman alphabet because it made literacy easier for ordinary people thus facilitating communication.

Another kind of nationalist movement developed in the 1920s when it became clear that the focus of French political as well as economic power in Vietnam was the Bank of Indochina. By the 1920s, French commercial enterprise was very firmly established in the middle and upper echelons of the economic system. Foreign Asian entrepreneurs, consisting almost entirely of Chinese, were confined to the lowest echelons except in the rice trade, where they reached only the middle echelons. The Chinese were ancient enemies and thoroughly disliked, but they were obviously not the cause of the economic disenfranchisement of lower-class Vietnamese. French institutions were blamed. Moreover, members of royalty and high mandarins were profiting from the colonial regime through rents they received as landlords and through interest on loans that they made to Vietnamese entrepreneurs. They were suspect. And they had become less and less interested in nationalism as they enjoyed, more and more, their prerogatives as wealthy Frenchmen. They vacated their leadership of nationalist movements. Other, less traditional, leaders took their places.

The new nationalist leaders were drawn from diverse sources, but all were interested in some revision of the traditional order and all pursued their goals through the organizational device of voluntary associations. Leaders of the most important nationalist association in the 1920s, the Vietnamese Nationalist Party (VNQDD), were educated in French language schools in Vietnam and France, and they modeled their organization and political ideals on the Koumintang party of Sun Yat Sen. They did not want a return to the traditional Vietnamese Empire, but rather they wanted to establish a republic that would be entirely free of French political and economic domination. Leaders of another nationalist association, the Association of Revolutionary Youth, were educated in French language schools in Vietnam and in revolutionary schools in southern China, and they drew their inspiration from Lenin's communist movement. Their goals were the ending of French domination and the founding of a soviet state. Three religious associations that were founded in the 1920s—Cao Dai, Hoa Hao, and Binh Xuyen—had strong nationalistic orientations and represented different kinds of Buddhist reactions to Catholicism and colonialism.

Cao Dai has doctrines drawn from Christianity as well as from Hindu-Buddhism. One of its saints is Victor Hugo. Its hierarchy of religious officials is modeled on that of the Catholic church. The Hoa Hao is a more orthodox Buddhist sect. Its separatism is based on the Emergent Buddha status of its founder, Huynh Phu So, who started the sect in the village of Hoa Hao. Binh Xuyen is a revolutionary sect patterned on the Heaven and Earth Leagues or Triad Societies of China, which opposed the Manchus and worked for a return of the Ming dynasty. Like the Triad Societies of overseas Chinese, the Binh Xuyen is a total institution that provides economic as well as social insurance, and it is deeply involved in the organization of all sorts of behavior—even "antisocial" behavior such as extortion or prostitution.

The leaders of these religious sects were monks and priests. They excelled in recruiting and training military forces. All were xenophobic. They were educated in local schools. Their goals were the expulsion of all foreigners and the development of local rule by religious people that would not be within the traditional framework of the Vietnamese Empire.

No one of these various nationalist groups consistently led the others in popularity or power. In the 1920s, the Vietnamese Nationalist Party was most important. The VNQDD organized strikes among peasants and workers and, in 1930, attempted to promote a general uprising against the French. It was so fiercely repressed by the colonial government, however, that it virtually ceased to exist by 1931 and did not reemerge until World War II. The demise of the Vietnamese Nationalist Party left a sort of leadership vacuum that was quickly filled by the Communist Party of

Indochina (CPI), which had developed from the Revolutionary Youth Association. Like the VNQDD, its primary activity was organizing peasants and workers. It also formed soviets in two provinces of north-central Vietnam. Nguyen Tat Thahn (alias Nguyen Ai Quoc alias Ho Chi Minh) founded and led both the youth association and the political party. Much of the success of the CPI during the 1930s must be attributed to his talents as an organizer and to the extent of his previous involvement in the French Socialist Party (a regular member), the French Communist Party (a founding member), the Third International (a delegate for France), and the Chinese Koumintang (interpreter for a Russian adviser).

The CPI was the first of the nationalistic movements to have international support, but more important was the fact that for the first time a large number of Frenchmen—socialists and communists—were sympathetic to the cause of Vietnamese independence. Socialists and communists in the French government restrained colonial officials from harassing the CPI as consistently or as harshly as they had the Vietnamese Nationalist Party. Moreover, the military forces of the three new Vietnamese religious sects—Coa Dai, Hoa Hao, and Binh Xuyen—began to engage French colonial troops in the 1930s, thereby diverting French action against the CPI and extending the period during which the CPI dominated other nationalist organizations.

By the late 1930s, however, the leaders of the CPI had been driven to refuges in the borderlands of South China from which their forces made occasional excursions into Vietnam to fight French colonial forces. At the same time, the forces of the Cao Dai held the Mekong delta, Hoa Hao forces were ranged along the Cambodian border, and the Binh Xuyen controlled an area near Cholon-Saigon. Thus, the war of Vietnamese independence was well under way by the 1930s. Indeed it had been going on since the beginning of French domination except for a brief period between 1916 and 1920 when the Vietnamese half believed in the sincerity of European pronouncements of the principle of self-determination. After that brief pause in the struggle for independence, the organizational style of nationalists changed from the traditional networks of local leaders and high mandarins that were focused on a single royal leader to the development of voluntary associations that had mass membership and special committees—organizational forms that were more effective for overthrowing the governmental institutions of European society. It was this aspect of Marxist theory—organizing the overthrow of European institutions—that fascinated Vietnamese nationalists.

In 1941, the Japanese took possession of French Indochina for the Vichy government in France. French colonial forces were directed by the Japanese military. From the viewpoint of Vietnamese nationalists, the change was hardly noticeable. The soldiers whom they fought were still Frenchmen. In a brief period in 1941, these French troops, acting as part of the Japanese command, very nearly extinguished the forces of the Coa Dai and Hoa Hao. Of all the nationalist forces, only those with sanctuaries in South China were not seriously crippled. Various sorts of nationalists united to fight under the leadership of Ho Chi Minh because his were the only intact forces that had experience in fighting the French. He had formed the various nationalist associations into a single organization, a popular front named Viet Nam Doc-Lap Dong Minh Hoi (League for the Independence of Vietnam) or "Viet Minh" in 1939, just before the Japanese intrusion. French colonial troops did not fight the Japanese during the invasion of 1941. Instead, they fought Vietnamese nationalists with devastating effectiveness. The United States gave arms and supplies and training (especially in the use of mortars and rockets) to the Viet Minh as allies in the war against Japan. The Viet Minh, of course, also used their American training and arms against French troops of the Vichy government who were nominally a part of the Japanese command in Indochina. French and Japanese authorities collaborated in an effort to eradicate Vietnamese nationalists. Such cooperation continued until March of 1945, when the Japanese finally disarmed the French troops.

By August of 1945, the Viet Minh had defeated the Japanese army of Indochina. Boa Dai, the puppet king of the French and the Japanese, abdicated in favor of the Viet Minh government. On 2 September, the Viet Minh issued a Declaration of Vietnamese Independence quoting parts of the American Declaration of Independence and the Declaration of the French Revolution. But the Japanese had been defeated elsewhere by the Western allies who sent armed forces to take the surrender in Indochina.

European and American interests in Southeast Asia were opposed. Americans wished to end colonialism, Britishers and the Free French wished to prolong it. At the Potsdam Conference, Americans agreed that Britain would take the Japanese surrender in Southeast Asia on the condition that the Chinese would take the surrender north of the sixteenth parallel in Vietnam. In this way, the United States offered something to its Chinese allies while denying full recovery of colonial areas by Europeans.

Indian troops of the British Empire began to arrive in southern Vietnam by mid-September 1945. British commanders ignored the Viet Minh claim of being the legitimate government, rearmed the five thousand French troops who had been disarmed by the Japanese, and ordered the Viet Minh to surrender their weapons. On 23 September, the highest French officer staged a coup d'etat, evicting the Viet Minh government in Saigon from its headquarters. French colonial government had returned to southern Vietnam. The Viet Minh began their war of independence again, fighting Indian and Japanese troops commanded by British officers and French troops. By Christmas the French had increased the number of their own troops to about fifty thousand, and the British left, having fulfilled their obligation to their French friends.

Nationalist (Koumintang) Chinese troops did not interfere with the Viet Minh government of Vietnam north of the sixteenth parallel. They kept the French troops unarmed and in custody, and they disarmed the Japanese troops and placed them in detention. The Republic of Vietnam lived for four months while the Chinese negotiated with the government of France. Two additional months elapsed while the French negotiated with the Viet Minh for the right to move their troops into northern Vietnam. French troops entered peacefully, but local frictions with the Viet Minh troops burst into a war that lasted until 1954.

The Viet Minh wanted an independent Vietnam that included all three of the traditional *Ky* or "provinces" (Bac Ky-Tongkin, Trung Ky-Annam, Nam Ky-Cochin China). And they expected to reinstate their superiority vis-à-vis Khmers, Laos, Chams, and other "lesser" people whom they had dominated before the French conquest. The French wanted to retain possession of Cochin China because most of their capital was invested there. They were willing to concede "freedom," if not full independence to separate states, for the Vietnamese of Tongkin and Annam, the Khmers of Cambodia, the Laos of Laos, and the "Montagnards" (the various kinds of "hill people") of Indochina. All of these states were to be members of the French Union.

Viet Minh refusals to compromise the full independence of Vietnam led the French to cease negotiating with them and to establish another "legitimate" Vietnamese government that would be more amenable to French interests. The former puppet emperor, Bao Dai, was finally persuaded to set up a provisional government in May of 1948. Bao Dai was not easily persuaded. His price was the return of Cochin China to Vietnam. This alternate government, the Provisional Central Government of Vietnam, signed a treaty with France in June. The treaty gave independence to Vietnam as an associated state within the French Union. The stage was set (by the French) for a civil war.

A civil war did not begin. Very few Vietnamese could be found who supported the emperor and the new version of colonialism associated with his government. The war continued to be between France and the Viet Minh. It was the overwhelming support of Vietnamese of all cosmological perspectives—Buddhists, Catholics, Communists, Republicans, and Royalists—for the Viet Minh that made the defeat of the French inevitable.

Giap of the Viet Minh was an excellent general, but his tactics were not novel. Neither were French tacticians stupid. The Vietnamese were simply more intent on regaining their independence

than the French were intent on regaining their colony. That the 85
French were not finally defeated until the spring of 1954 is a tribute to the courage and skill of their soldiers. During the two years before the French defeat at Dienbienphu, the people of France had not supported the war in Indochina. In fact, almost eighty percent of the cost of the war in those years had been borne not by France but by the United States.

American economic aid for French armed forces in Indochina evolved from aid to Vietnamese nationalists. Immediately after World War II, the American State Department had urged Europeans to follow the American example in the Philippines of granting independence to former colonies. As a part of this policy of anticolonialism, the State Department helped newly emergent nations to arm themselves for self-defense. American efforts to help the Vietnamese were thwarted by the French, who insisted that all such aid should be channeled through the French military because of the "disorganization" of the Vietnamese army. Eventually, the American State Department concurred. Later, as the cold war and then the Korean War developed, the policy changed to one of strongly supporting anticommunist forces. Then France convinced the State Department that the Vietnamese war of independence was a communist war of aggression not unlike the North Korean war against South Korea. It was this conviction that led to increasing American opposition to the Republic of Vietnam.

The terms of peace that were signed at the Geneva Conference in 1954 were entirely favorable to the Republic of Vietnam. A plebiscite was to be held in 1956 to decide whether or not the southern half of Vietnam would join the Republic. Given the popularity of Ho Chi Minh, it was almost certain that Vietnam would be reunited in 1956.

The Boa Dai regime in the south was not popular. Its reliance on the sects for military forces seemed to indicate further weakness. The United States supported another political clique that seemed more likely to succeed against the communist regime in the north—the Catholic League headed by the wealthy and aristocratic Ngo family.

With American support, the Ngo family established the Diem regime, defeating Bao Dai in an election and the religious sects in battle. The Diem regime refused to submit its fate to a plebiscite. Nineteen fifty-six passed. The Republic of Vietnam decided to take by war what it would have won in the plebiscite. Diem's generals were quite successful against the armed forces of the republic and against the forces of the Popular Front government in the south. His family was overthrown because of its Catholic chauvinism. Buddhist monks led demonstrations in the streets and Buddhist generals plotted Diem's assassination. In the confusion that followed the fall of his regime, forces of the Republic of Vietnam and of the Popular Front government of the south made substantial gains. The United States had a choice—allow a communist victory or commit large numbers of American soldiers to battle against communist forces. Large numbers of American soldiers, more than half a million at a time, were eventually brought to Vietnam. American policy-makers failed as dramatically as the French. They mistakenly viewed the major conflict as being between communists and noncommunists rather than between different cliques of nationalist leaders, different religious groups, and different ethnic groups. The American-Indochinese war lasted a decade, until 1973, when American forces were withdrawn. Then, once more, the Vietnamese were left to solve their own problems of national destiny. Nothing had been solved. Solutions had been merely delayed.

Western democratic forms of government would not survive in any case. Western Marxist forms had been transformed and would be further transformed to fit Vietnamese culture. Vietnamese appetite for imperialism in Khmer and Thai worlds was not yet satisfied, but the traditional royal empire of Vietnam would not be revived.

NATIONAL SURVIVAL: CAMBODIA AND LAOS

Nationalist movements in Cambodia and Laos were not directly related to those in Vietnam.[5] The circumstances of colonialism were different. By conceding suzerainty to France, the Laos and Khmers almost certainly avoided Thai imperialism, which would have been much less sympathetic. Moreover, French rule was less direct in Laos and Cambodia than in Vietnam, and there was less nationalistic reaction. Finally, Laos and Khmers viewed the Vietnamese as foreign Asians and did not trust them. The pre-European imperialism of the Vietnamese was well known, and they were also closely associated with French imperialism. Vietnamese were brought into Laos and Cambodia by the French to serve as clerks and as laborers on rubber plantations. Many became entrepreneurs. Their position was similar to that of overseas Chinese and Indians.

Khmers appreciated the fact that the French had stopped Vietnamese expansion and had continued to respect important Khmer institutions such as Theravada Buddhism and the prerogatives of royalty. The French government sponsored the restoration of Angkor Wat and Angkor Thom and helped Khmers develop an institute for the study of Theravada Buddhism. There had been some armed resistance to the French assumption of civil administrative authority in 1884, but after that there was virtually no conflict between French authorities and Khmers until 1941 when Buddhist monks protested the arrest of one of their number by French authorities for speaking out in favor of independence. Khmers had also resisted introduction of the Roman alphabet, preferring their own syllabary, and they had objected to abolition of slavery.

The first effect of the Japanese occupation was to increase Khmer appreciation of French protection. Japan had little interest in Cambodia except as a corridor between Vietnam and Thailand. Military requirements for food were less burdensome, and French authorities were able to retain more authority and respect than in Vietnam. However, Japan assisted Thai imperialism by adjudicating the return of border areas that Thailand had lost to the French protectorate of Cambodia in 1904. From the Khmer perspective, Thailand was a greater threat than either Japan or France.

Thailand sponsored a Free Cambodia movement (Khmer Issarak) among Khmers in the reacquired territories with the view of expanding Thai influence even farther into French territory. Japan complicated this effort by staging a coup d'état in 1945 that toppled the façade of the Vichy colonial regime. A Khmer government headed by Prince Sihanouk was granted complete independence by the Japanese within a few months. But when French troops reoccupied Cambodia at the end of World War II, Cambodians did not resist. The Allies forced Thailand to return the border areas to Cambodia, and until 1955, when France granted complete independence to Cambodia, the Khmer Issarak competed with Prince Sihanouk's government for the support of the Cambodian people. French educated, Sihanouk appreciated the importance of popular support. He abdicated as king in order to gain a more popular following and he succeeded. Additionally, his skillful and successful negotiations with the French helped to win his government the overwhelming support of the Cambodian people. The Khmer Issarak did not become active again until Sihanouk began to soften his government's objections to North Vietnamese encroachments into areas bordering South Vietnam—a softening that Thailand viewed with alarm. Elements of the Khmer Issarak participated in the overthrow of Prince Sihanouk's government in the spring of 1970. Lon Nol, at best an unpopular leader, took control of the government. As in the overthrow of the Diem regime in Vietnam, the American Central Intelligence Agency was very much aware of the coup d'état but could not control the selection of a new head of state. Sihanouk reluctantly went into exile in China. North Vietnamese forces spread into Cambodian territory. The old spectre of Thai and Vietnamese imperialism, which had been laid to rest for a time by French protection, had returned to haunt the Khmers.

Laotians, too, had been caught between Thailand and Vietnam. But culturally and linguistically, they are very closely allied to the Thais and they are somewhat insulated from the Vietnamese by mountain tribes. Laotians were less well integrated politically than Cambodians when the French arrived. Their state, Lan Ch'ang, had just emerged in the fourteenth century and had briefly controlled extensive areas of the middle Mekong Valley, Chiengmai, and the entire Korat Plateau before it declined at the end of the sixteenth century and became four separate principalities—Vientiane, Luang Prabang, Champassak, and Xieng Khouang. In 1893, Laos had welcomed French protection from Thailand and Vietnam. Vientiane and Xieng Khouang had lost their suzerainty to the Vietnamese while the other two principalities were under the control of the Thais. Laos did not have the same potential for ordinary commercial agriculture as Vietnam or even Cambodia. The French did not develop extensive rice and rubber plantations in Laos. But they did stimulate the production of opium in the hills of Xieng Khouang surrounding the Plain of Jars. Before World War II, the opium crop was sold in southern China; afterwards it found its way to southern France. However, the opium trade was probably not as rewarding economically as commercial agriculture in the Mekong delta area of Cambodia and Cochin China.

French colonial administrators did not interfere with the daily lives of the people of Laos. Only members of royalty received a Western education. French officials respected Buddhist and royalist institutions. Laotians objected only when the French brought in Vietnamese as minor colonial officials and when the French discussed the possibility of transferring a small piece of Laotian territory to Vietnam. Mountain tribes rebelled several times. The Kha, subsistence farmers and gatherers who were sometimes engaged in the slave trade, contested the French abolition of slavery, and other tribes fought to gain or retain control of poppy-growing areas during the seasons of opium harvest.

During World War II, the Japanese ignored Laos. It produced nothing that they needed, and it seemed to have no strategic importance. Japan helped Thailand to regain border areas that had been ceded to the French protectorate of Laos in 1907. A Free Laos movement (Lao Issara) was developed in these border areas after their return to Thailand. Several Lao princes joined the Lao Issara with the view of building their own political movements to gain control of the four Lao principalities. They hoped to outdistance their rivals who were their brothers and cousins and uncles—other members of Lao royalty and of the same vice-regal patrilineage.

At the end of World War II, Nationalist Chinese troops who were supposed to take the surrender of Japanese forces used their occupation of Laos as a bargaining chip in negotiations with France. The return of Laos to French control was delayed, and French authorities feared that Laotians would develop a taste for independence. But even after the delay, returning French forces were welcomed by Laotians. Pressured by war in Vietnam and diplomatic demands from Cambodia, France gradually granted full independence to Laos. The final step to full independence came in 1954.

Royal cliques began almost immediately to contend for political power. A pro-Thai faction headed by Prince Boun Oum and Phoumi Nosavan of Champassak received a considerable amount of military aid from the United States. An anti-Thai faction (Pathet Lao) headed by Princes Souphanouvong and Petsarath were based in Xieng Khouang, and they sought aid from the Republic of Vietnam. The neutralist faction was based in Luang Prabang and Vientiane and was led by Prince Souvanna Phouma. Souvanna Phouma, who headed the first independent government, convinced the other cliques that it was best to collaborate with each other in ruling Laos.

The CIA, ever watchful to improve conditions for America's ally, planned and supported a coup d'état which placed the pro-Thai clique in power. Neutralist forces (commanded by Kong Le) joined the forces of Prince Souphanouvong in civil war against the pro-Thai clique. Other kinds of conflict, between Laotians and tribesmen such as the Kha and between Laotians and Vietnamese, were mixed into the general upheaval. Even the annual conflict over rights to harvest the poppy fields became an aspect of the civil war. Eventually, the neutralists were restored to power, but they accepted American military aid and lost the support of Souphanouvong's Pathet Lao. In 1973, as Americans were withdrawing from Indochina, conditions seemed good for revival of a governing coalition of all princely cliques in Laos.

NATIONAL REFORM: THAILAND

Thailand, of course, never lost its independence. But it did lose territory to the British and French colonial regimes that surrounded it. Also, the Thai government had to change its political and economic system to counteract the threats of English and French imperialism. These counter measures are usually described as "reforms" or "modernization" in the scholarly literature of the West.[6]

The initiator of modernizing reforms in Thai government, Rama IV, had been a Buddhist monk for more than twenty-five years before becoming king. His long tenure as a monk preserved him from attack by his older half brother, King Rama III, and gave him time to study religion, languages, and Western science. He studied Buddhism with Mon monks, Latin with Catholic missionaries, and English and science with American Protestants. Americans had a favored status because they had no colonial ambitions in lands adjoining Thailand and they had sold firearms to the Thai government in 1818 and 1820. From among all Western visitors, Americans seemed to be the least ambitious as imperialists, and for that reason, they were most acceptable as teachers of Western culture. The scholar-monk, Prince Mongkut, learned his lessons well. When he became King Rama IV in April of 1851, he was the only ruler in Southeast Asia who could understand Western rationalizations for imperialism and who could communicate that understanding directly to representatives of England and France. He relieved the West of its self-appointed responsibility to civilize other societies and to promote free trade. He westernized the legal, economic, political, and educational institutions of his country to the minimum extent that was necessary to avoid conflict with England or France. The United States and other Western nations who were asked to provide technical advisers served as a powerful and sympathetic audience for Thai efforts to reform traditional institutions in the face of imperialist pressures from England and France. Thailand lost only the most far-flung portions of its realm—two Shan states, two Cambodian principalities, and four Malay sultanates. Westernization, like Western advisers, remained in Bangkok. But their Western influence on the governing Thai elite eventually affected the lives of rural people.

Members of the nobility and bureaucratic elite had been thoroughly exposed to Western culture by the end of King Chulalongkorn's reign in 1910. They had learned to respect Western administrative procedures and to question traditional forms. If they needed examples of how to suspend or abrogate the rule of traditional monarchs, Western colonial regimes provided them. When the bureaucratic elite removed King Rama VII from power in 1932, he and other members of Thai royalty hardly objected.

The new constitution stripped the monarchy of all significant power and gave it to the bureaucratic elite. However, royalty retained its prestige and symbolic prerogatives. Pridi Phanamyong, a French-trained lawyer, took control of the new government. His proposals for economic and political change have been characterized as socialistic or communistic by Western writers, but such characterizations do not explain the changes in Thai society that became apparent after the revolution of 1932, nor do they explain Pridi's continuation as a minister of government after the so-called conservative, Pibun (Luang Pibun Songgram), took over the leadership in 1934.

By stripping the monarchy of its power and yet sustaining its prestige, all without resorting to popular democracy, the government gained the greatest possible advantage in its pursuit of Thai nationalism. Western advisers, no longer appointed by the king, were for the first time lower in rank and much less influential than the highest ranking Thai bureaucrats. Chinese businessmen, denied the patronage of Thai royalty, were for the first time subject to taxation and other legal controls. Other minorities, too, lost special protection accorded them by the monarchy. Furthermore, the new Thai government felt free to plan the reacquisition of territories lost by treaty to British and French colonies.

Marshal Pibun's government sent most of the Western advisers home. At the same time, the armed forces were increased and modern military equipment was acquired. The Japanese military establishment was much admired and imitated—even to the point of trying to establish a Thai version of the bushido ethic of Japanese samurai.

Minority groups were subjected to a Thai-conformity campaign. Chinese businesses were nationalized, and Chinese tax collectors lost their franchises as Thai officials were appointed to collect taxes. A high tax on foreign businessmen forced many Chinese to take Thai names. Private Chinese schools were closed. Only Thai language could be used as the medium of instruction in public schools. This measure affected Mons and Malays as well as Chinese. Proselytizers of Theravada Buddhism were encouraged to convert tribesmen in the north and Malays in the south of Thailand. Thai nationalists insisted that everyone behave in accord with the customs and standards of the central (Sukhothai) variety of Thai culture.

Traditional government, almost entirely in the hands of the monarch, enjoyed the full confidence of the Thai people. Constancy was the monarchy's major virtue in maintaining internal tranquility and its major flaw in developing a flexible foreign policy that could prevent further encroachments by European colonial powers. The revolutionary government recognized the chief virtue of the monarchy and retained it while substituting more flexible, westernized political institutions to deal with foreigners. A single nationalist political party controlled the new government, which consisted of a legislative assembly and a ruling council. Half of the members of the legislative assembly were selected by and from local leaders who owed allegiance to the party. The remainder were appointed directly by the national leaders of the party. Members of the legislative assembly elected members of the ruling council. Thai peasants were not drawn into the disturbing influences of contending political parties, but the new system allowed flexibility in policies and leadership so necessary for success in dealings with foreigners.

As the interest of Europeans was diverted by events in Europe that preceded World War II, the militarist faction gained absolute control of the government in Bangkok. They developed a pan-Thai movement to attract the loyalty of the Shan of Burma, the Lao of Laos, the Tai of Vietnam and southern China, and the Thai of northern Malaya. They changed the official name of the country from Siam to Thailand, and they spoke openly of annexing the Shan states, the northern Malay sultanates, southern Burma, and portions of Laos and Cambodia. Thailand welcomed the support of the Japanese in regaining all of these territories during World War II.

When it seemed certain that the Japanese would lose the war, in 1944, the militarist faction of Marshal Pibun lost control of the nationalist party to a faction headed by Pridi whose friend, Prince Seni Promoj, was ambassador in exile in the United States. After the war, the United States interceded on Thailand's behalf, softening the demands of Britain and France that Thailand be punished for collaborating with Japan. All of the recently reacquired territories had to be returned, and for a time rice had to be supplied at a very low price to Britain and France. But Thailand was quickly accepted back into the community of independent nations.

Marshal Pibun returned to power in 1947 as communist-led insurgency developed among minority groups in border areas. Other military factions developed in the nationalist party, and by 1957, the Pibun faction had been replaced by another led by Marshal Sarit. The Sarit faction cancelled the constitution and assumed full dictatorial powers. Marshal Sarit and his successor, General Thanom Kittikachorn, were more willing than Pibun to form a military alliance with the United States. They drew the American interest by emphasizing the massive influx of Vietnamese peasants into northeastern Thailand and by claiming that disturbances there and among Malays in southern Thailand were communist-inspired. It is easy to imagine that the famous domino theory of communist expansion in Southeast Asia was first expressed in Thai words. American military forces, mostly air force units, came to Thailand in large numbers. From their bases in Thailand, they fought wars in Vietnam, Laos, and Cambodia. As American participation in the conflicts in Vietnam, Laos, and Cambodia came to a close in 1973, American forces began to withdraw from Thailand. Problems with Lao tribesmen and Vietnamese in the northeast and with Malays in the south had not been resolved.

EXPERIMENT IN MULTIETHNIC
NATIONALISM: MALAYSIA

The history of nationalist movements in Malaysia has many points in common with histories of such movements in other Southeast Asian countries, but totally, it is the most peculiar.[7] In some ways, colonialism transformed Malaysia more thoroughly than other Southeast Asian countries; in other ways, colonialism transformed it less. Two characteristics of the colonial experience in Malaysia have been most significant.

The territorial boundaries of Malaysia do not conform to those of its predecessor state, the empire of Melaka, which controlled not only Malaya but most of eastern Sumatra and none of northern Borneo. Like Lan Ch'ang, the predecessor state of Laos, the empire of Melaka was dismembered before its modern successor began to emerge. However, Lan Ch'ang was dismembered by other Southeast Asian states, and its major principalities were eventually reunited by a European colonial regime. Europeans helped dismantle the empire of Melaka and separated it into its constituent sultanates, some of which are part of Malaysia while others have been absorbed into Indonesia. Other territories in Borneo, which were formerly controlled by Britain but had never been a part of the empire of Melaka, have become a part of the modern successor of Melaka—the Federation of Malaysia.

Immigrants have played important roles in the history of Southeast Asia. Only Singapore, a part of Malaysia from 1963 to 1965, has been more affected by immigration than Malaysia. An estimated eighty percent of Malays in the west coast states of Western Malaysia (or Malaya) were either born in Indonesia or are descended from recent Indonesian immigrants. Even counting these naturalized Malays, the Malays constitute only a plurality of the total population in their own country. Overseas Chinese are almost as numerous as Malays, and overseas Indians, although comparatively few in number, comprise as large a percentage of the population as do all foreign Asians in most other Southeast Asian countries.

These two features of the Malaysian colonial experience —division of the territories of the previous state and a subsequent influx of many immigrants—have shaped Malaysian nationalism significantly.

Colonial rule settled gradually into Malay sultanates after the Portuguese, Dutch, and English dismantled the empire of Melaka. The dismantling process was itself quite gradual. It had begun at the start of the sixteenth century and was not completed until the end of the nineteenth. Then, British advisers arrived. At first, they were alone. Later, they developed large staff organizations, which gradually developed into administrative bureaucracies. Some overseas Indians, experienced in the colonial services of India and Burma, found places in the administrative services of the Malay states. Chinese tin miners who had labored for Malay sultans and chiefs became independent producers as the British market absorbed more and more of the tin that was produced. Chinese laborers were imported by Chinese and British tin-mining companies. Later, as the British developed the rubber industry, hundreds of thousands of Indonesian, Indian, and Chinese immigrants arrived to work on large rubber plantations or to develop their own small plantations.

Most of these immigrants did not plan to remain in Malaya. They hoped to return to their home country and were more interested in political events there. Chinese in Malaysia formed associations that were concerned with Sun Yat Sen's revolution in China. They became the major financial contributors to the revolution and, after 1911, continued as the major source of capital for the economic development of China by the Koumintang government. Fiercely concentrating on the welfare of their home government, overseas Chinese hardly noticed local political events except for their own harassment by British officers who mistakenly believed that the Koumintang associations were a threat to British colonial rule in Malaya. Indians followed the Indian independence movement and the Indian labor movement after World War I. They brought the ideology of Indian labor movements to Malaya and were thereby sometimes in conflict with British authorities. But they were chiefly concerned with India rather than Malaya. Most of the Indonesian immigrants were Sumatrans from the old territories of the empire of Melaka. Their customs and languages were very similar or even identical to those of Malays. They accepted the social order of Malays and the Malay sultans as their own. In turn, they were accepted. They became loyal subjects of Malay sultans. But they drew on their experiences with the comparatively virulent nationalistic movements of Indonesia to help found Malay nationalist movements. Indigenous Malays welcomed immigrants from Indonesia because they helped to offset the numerical superiority of foreign Asians.

Malay nationalism was, from the beginning of colonial rule, more anti-Chinese than anti-British. But Malays rebelled against British administration occasionally. The Tok Janggut rebellion of 1915 is the best known case of armed resistance. Tok Janggut ("Bearded Grandfather"), Haji Mat Hassan, led an army of several hundred Malay men who objected to new land taxes imposed by the British administration in Pasir Puteh district of Kelantan. Acting with the approval and encouragement of the territorial chief, they attacked and destroyed the district office and began a march to Kota Bharu, capital of the State of Kelantan. British military reaction was almost instantaneous. Colonial officials realized the broad extent of Malay discontent and feared a general uprising. However, the leaders of the Tok Janggut rebellion were hunted down and killed by the Shropshire Light Infantry within a month, and a general uprising never occurred. Another major instance of resistance failed to materialize until the Ulu Trengganu incident of 1928.

European colonialism had affected traditional Malay social structure by weakening the military and commercial functions of the chiefs and by strengthening the symbolic and religious functions of the sultans. Many ordinary Malays did not join the rebellion because it did not have royal approval and was approved by a very weak territorial chief. Rebelling would have been almost traitorous.

British advisors had helped the sultans improve the centralizing institutions of government and had encouraged them to develop councils of religion and custom that maintained and embellished the ritual of Malay life. Moreover, the traditional ruling elite were given British education and high positions in the colonial administration. In this way, colonial rule encouraged a kind of cultural involution that produced political conservatism unmatched elsewhere in Southeast Asia.

Religion played a major role in Malay nationalist movements. By their own definitions of Malay ethnicity, Malays are necessarily Muslims. One of their duties as people of Islam is to make a pilgrimage to Mecca during their lifetime. There, in the nineteenth century and early twentieth century, Malays became familiar with the anticolonialist and antitraditionalist doctrines of the Islamic Renaissance. The reformist doctrines of the Renaissance emphasized the equality of all Muslims, thus undercutting the authority of rulers' councils of religion and custom. Although it failed in the long run to capture Malay loyalty, the reformist movement strengthened pan-Malay sentiments that had been introduced by Indonesian nationalists, and it was one of several factors that encouraged the development of Malay-language publications, which were a bulwark of nationalism.

Colonial officials encouraged publication of Malay-language newspapers, pamphlets, and books in the Roman alphabet. Many such publications were tedious translations of English-language publications, and most had no political content whatever. However, two anticolonial periodicals in Malay language were published by Islamic Reformists in Cairo and were generally available in Malaya. The anticolonial publications of the national language movement of Indonesia found their way to Malays, too. Intrigued with the possibilities but fearful of British repression, Malay authors usually expressed their nationalistic views in Jawi publications. Jawi is based on the Arabic syllabary but is slightly different. It appears to be an inefficient system of writing because it does not record most vowels, and vowels are very significant in Malay language. Writing and reading it requires a thorough knowledge of Malay syntax, vocabulary, and idiom. Very few non-Malays can read it; most Malays can because they are taught it in local Islamic schools. It was and is the perfect mode of publication for Malay nationalists. Nationalistic thoughts once expressed in Jawi were sometimes easier to express in Roman alphabet publications, but the function of the first was to inform and provoke constituents and the function of the latter was to inform and provoke the colonial regime.

Malay nationalists wanted to weaken British rule by downgrading the administrative institutions of the federation and upgrading those of the separate states. Also, they wanted to protect the political and economic rights of Malays against encroachment by foreign Asians. Late in the 1920s, Malays comprised only 34 percent of the population of Malaya, and the economic depression had forced many foreign Asians to seek civil service positions and to settle on lands previously reserved for Malays. British officials had begun to sponsor periodic gatherings of rulers as one means of increasing the power of the states. Rulers at these gatherings prevailed upon British officials to limit Chinese immigration and to increase Indonesian immigration. The elite had finally given effective expression to the basic concern of common Malays. Thereafter, Malay associations were formed in each state. In 1938 and 1939, some of the leaders attempted but failed to unite all of the associations into a single national organization. British officials did not interfere with the Malay associations. They were more concerned about another political association, the Kesatuan Melayu Muda (Malay Youth Union), which began about the same time and which combined pan-Malay interests with Marxist philosophy. Founded by a very small group of thoroughly westernized intellectuals, the KMM was not able to communicate its philosophy to ordinary Malays, and it failed as a political movement within a few years.

In the meantime (1930), Chinese Koumintang associations had been proscribed by the British. They continued as an underground movement, and some of them split from the Koumintang to form the Malayan Communist Party.

Japanese military forces effected a landing on the coast of Kelantan in December 1941. British army units, consisting mostly of Indian troops, fought and lost battle after battle. The Japanese conquered the whole of Malaya and Singapore before the end of February 1942.

At first, most of the population of the cities—Chinese, Indians, and Malays—fled to rural areas to avoid military control. Later, many returned. Except for the severe food shortages suffered by all during the occupation, Malays benefited from Japanese rule. Malaya was joined for a while with Sumatra in a single administrative unit, renewing the dream of a few Malay nationalists of a new empire that included all of the cities that formerly owed allegiance to Melaka, Melayu (Djambi), or even Sri Vijaya. The Japanese were as careful as the British had been in preserving the traditional Malay way of life. Additionally, they elevated many more Malays to high positions in the civil administration and favored them in business matters. Indians and Chinese received less favorable treatment. Indians who cooperated and especially those who joined the Indian National Army were treated equitably, but many others were imprisoned or conscripted as laborers for military engineering projects. Chinese were treated savagely because of their support of the war in China and because of their own fierce hatred of Japanese.

Guerilla forces began harassing the Japanese almost as soon as they arrived in Malaya. Almost all of the guerillas were Chinese, and at first there was no centralized command although many of the units had been organized just before the Japanese take-over by the Chinese Mobilization Committee (CMC). Later, a few Indians and a very few Malays joined Chinese-led guerilla units and all were organized into the Malayan Peoples' Anti-Japanese Army (MPAJA) under the leadership of the Malayan Communist Party. The MPAJA terrorized units of the Japanese army and committed many acts of sabotage. They also intimidated civilians, punishing those who collaborated with the Japanese and demanding food and supplies from all.

After Japan's surrender to the Allies and before the reoccupation by British forces in September of 1945, intimidators and collaborators settled old scores in a series of single and multiple murders that some Malayans remember as ethnic riots between Chinese and Malays. If nothing else, the Japanese occupation had increased the tension between the ethnic groups of Malaya. British policy after World War II increased it further.

Within a few months of returning, the British colonial regime forced the Malay sultans to sign treaties that ceded their sovereignty to George VI of England in order to form a Malayan Union in which all permanent residents of the Federated Malay States and the straits settlements of Penang and Melaka would be granted full rights of citizenship. Malays rose against their rulers, disclaiming the right of sultans to sign away the independence of Malay states. In Trengganu and Johore, the Malay masses went so far as to depose their rulers. The sultans reacted by explaining that they had been forced to sign as a necessary act of friendship to Britain or be replaced by successors who would sign. Malays forgave their rulers but demanded action to negate the treaties. The mass political movement became a political party, the United Malay Nationalist Organization (UMNO), which effectively denounced the formation of the Malayan Union and forced the British to recognize anew the sovereignty and prerogatives of Malay sultans and the special rights of their Malay subjects. Former colonial officials, Britishers, joined the sultans and UMNO in pressuring the British Parliament to release the sultans from the treaties that they had been forced to sign.

Representatives of the colonial administration, the sultans, and UMNO altered the charter of the Malayan Union. The new constitution reduced the power of the colonial regime, increased the authority of the sultans, and gave legislative powers to a Federal Legislative Council, whose official members were drawn from the councils of each of the nine states and two settlements and whose unofficial (advisory) members were a representative sample of the various ethnic communities. Special Malay rights to land and civil service positions were retained, and citizenship was defined more narrowly so as to restrict the number of Chinese who could qualify. The constitution of the new Federation of Malaya became effective in 1948.

Many former members of the Malayan Peoples' Anti-Japanese Army believed that they had earned more than the medals given to them by the British, and they rejected the new constitution on the grounds that it perpetuated the British colonial regime and that it gave unfair advantages to the Malays while discriminating against Chinese. Acting under the leadership of the Malayan Communist Party, they demonstrated their disenchantment in public parades and labor strikes that were repressed by the government. Failing to gain public support from a majority of the Chinese, the Malayan Communist Party began a campaign of terrorism. Government officials, prominent businessmen, and plantation owners were assassinated. Communication and transportation facilities were destroyed. Police and army units were ambushed. Ordinary people were forced to give food and supplies to the terrorist army.

The terrorist army was not very large, never at any time numbering more than five thousand persons. Recruits from the Min Yuen society, a communist-controlled association modeled after the traditional Heaven and Earth societies of the southern Chinese, replaced the dead and wounded. The terrorist army lived in the forest-covered mountains of central Malaya and ventured into the lowlands only for military purposes or to obtain food and supplies. Sympathizers who worked on plantations and in the towns committed many small acts of sabotage.

The government was never seriously endangered but, on the other hand, the terrorists were relatively secure, too. For 12 years (1948–1960), the civil war, or "Emergency," continued. However, the terrorists began to lose the war by 1953. British military tacticians developed helicopter warfare to the extent that terrorists had to remain hidden even in the mountain forests. Aborigines and Chinese squatters, who were most often coerced by the terrorists, were resettled into communities that could be more easily guarded by government forces. Communities that aided terrorists were "blacklisted" by the government, placed under curfew, and forced to set up central kitchens so that no food would fall into the hands of terrorists. As much as any of these tactics, an increase in the price of rubber on the world market deterred would-be recruits from joining the rebels. The price rise was brought about by increased American needs for their war effort in Korea. Temporarily it raised the living standards of rubber tappers and of other laborers in Malaya. Most effective in reducing the appeal of rebellion was the granting of full independence to the Federation of Malaya in 1957. An alliance of Malay, Chinese, and Indian political leaders talked the British government into taking this step.

The alliance had grown out of British-sponsored efforts in 1949 to reconcile the political and economic interests of Malays and noncommunist Chinese. British officials proposed that more of the Chinese be given full rights of citizenship in exchange for special economic assistance for Malays. These proposals were not accepted in 1949, but later they defined the basis of Malay-Chinese cooperation and conflict. Cooperation was first apparent in preparations for the first democratic elections under the constitution of the Federation of Malaya. The Malayan Chinese Association (MCA), a middle-class party founded by Western-educated millionaires, joined with UMNO against other political parties in the municipal elections in Kuala Lumpur. It was an extremely successful combination, and it was continued with excellent results in the municipal elections in Johore Bahru, Melaka, and Muar. The combination of MCA and UMNO was formalized as the National Alliance in 1953, and the Malayan Indian Congress (MIC) agreed to join it in 1954.

From the beginning, the alliance depended on Malay votes. Chinese enfranchisement had been increased through liberalized citizenship regulations in 1952, just before the elections; still, 80 percent of the electorate were Malays. MCA candidates depended heavily on Malay votes. This did not change as more Chinese gained the right to vote because the MCA was not especially popular in its own communal constituency. The MIC was even less self-sustaining than the MCA, but it served a purpose for the alliance as a token of Indian support.

UMNO profited from the modest successes of its junior partners. MCA and MIC followed the policies of UMNO and helped maintain a large enough majority in parliament (Dewan Ra'ayat) to prevent changes in the constitution. Malay support of UMNO was based on the maintenance of special rights for Malays that were guaranteed by the constitution—Malay as the only official language, Islam as the official religion of the state, a four to one ratio of Malays to others in the civil service, guaranteed access of Malays to agricultural land, and special programs to increase the numbers of Malays in business and the professions. In return for their support, the leaders of MCA and MIC expected help from UMNO in relaxing qualifications for citizenship and in protecting large capital investments.

Opposition parties that enjoyed support among Chinese and Indians tended to emphasize the need for noncommunal policies that would benefit the poor, whether Malay, Chinese, or Indian. Without Malay support, these parties had no chance in elections. They attempted to develop associations with Malay splinter parties. One such combination, the Socialist Front, consisted of the Indian- and Chinese-supported Labour Party and the Malay-supported Partai Rakyat (Peoples' Party). The Socialist Front eventually failed because the Partai Rakyat was not very popular among Malays. Malay-supported parties tended to be quite chauvinistic.

Even Partai Negara (State Party), which was founded by Datok Onn bin Jaafar (also the founder of UMNO), was less interested in establishing noncommunal policies than in guaranteeing the position of Malays by delaying independence from Britain and by returning the power of central government to the states. The Pan-Malayan Islamic Party (PMIP) was more chauvinistic than Partai Negara, and more Malays supported it. It frankly supported a return to the traditional Malay sultanate as the most appropriate form of government. PMIP never seriously threatened UMNO nationally, but it was powerful in two states in the northeast—Kelantan and Trengganu.

Viewed from another perspective, the politics of the new Federation of Malaya reflected differences of cultural homogeneity between the major communal groups. Malays dominated the political scene, not only because it was their right as *bumiputera* (subjects of Malay royalty), but also because they were culturally more homogeneous than the Chinese. There are dozens of subethnic identities among Malays, but the differences between subethnic identities are minor. Differences in language, for example, are mostly at the level of mutually intelligible dialects. Even where this difference is at the level of closely related but mutually unintelligible languages (for example, Javanese and any dialect of Malay), most persons are fluent in a second dialect, the Johore Riau dialect of Malay. Moreover, Malays are homogeneous in their religious beliefs. Chinese are more diverse linguistically than Malays. The most important dialects, which are mutually unintelligible, are Foochow, Hokkien, Teochew, Hakka, Cantonese, Hailam, and Southern Mandarin. Kuo-yu, a northern Mandarin dialect that is the national language of China, serves as a lingua franca. Chinese have various religions—Taoism, Mahayana Buddhism; Catholicism, Protestantism, and Islam. Indians are even more culturally diverse than Chinese. The most important languages, some of which belong to different language families, include Tamil, Telegu, Malayalam, Punjabi, Maharatti, Bengali, Marawari, Pushtu, and Sindhi. The religions of Malayan Indians include various sects of Hinduism, Islam, Catholicism, and Protestantism. These differing degrees of cultural homogeneity are reflected in communal politics, producing an unusual situation (from the perspective of theory in sociology and political science) in which the most threatened ethnic group (Indian) is least homogeneous and the least threatened ethnic group (Malay) is most homogeneous politically. Culture affects politics very strongly in Malaya.

As Malaya moved toward independence, popular leaders in the Crown Colony of Singapore approached the British government with the view of obtaining independence for Singapore, too. At first, Britain refused. Singapore differed from Malaya in being a purely colonial creation. The colony was founded by Stamford Raffles in 1819 and settled mostly by overseas Chinese. Singapore was developed as a free port by private entrepreneurs—Europeans, Chinese, Indonesians, and Malays—who depended upon the colonial economy of Great Britain. Moreover, Britain had established a huge naval base in Singapore. Singapore owed its very existence to Great Britain. And its large Chinese population might fall under the influence of Communist China.

In spite of the fears of losing an expensive investment and of promoting expansion of communist influence, the British government granted a greater measure of representative government to Singaporeans in 1954. Twenty-five of the thirty-two voting members of the parliament were to be elected, and the leader of the majority party would be chief minister. No party won a majority of the parliamentary seats in the elections of 1955, but the Socialist Front, headed by Donald Marshall, formed a coalition government with UMNO and MCA members. Marshall requested independence for Singapore but was refused. School and labor riots forced his resignation, and Lim Yew Hock, a labor union leader, became chief minister. By 1959, the British government had grudgingly promised independence for Singapore. Their worst fears seemed to be confirmed by the elections that year in which the Socialist Front was defeated and the more radical Peoples' Action Party of Lee Kuan Yew won a clear majority.

Fearing that Singapore was about to become communist and recognizing that the economy of his country was dependent upon Singapore, the prime minister of the Federation of Malaya, Tengku Abdul Rahman, proposed federation of Malaya with Singapore. Knowing that Malays would object to increasing the proportion of Chinese in the population, he also proposed federation with the British colonies of Sarawak, Sabah, and Brunei in northern Borneo. Brunei refused to join the new federation, but otherwise the proposal became a fact in September of 1963.

The new Federation of Malaysia was plunged into conflict immediately with Indonesia and the Philippines. President Sukarno of Indonesia viewed the federation of Britain's old colonies as a neo-colonialist plot, despaired the division of Borneo (or rather, Kalimantan), suspected that unfair treatment of Indonesian entrepreneurs would ensue in the port of Singapore, and feared that the White Prince (Tengku Abdul Rahman) would defeat the reincarnation of heroic Gaja Mada (Sukarno) as foretold in legend. For their part, Philippine leaders contested Malaysia's right to Sabah, a territory that they claimed for the Republic of the Philippines. They pursued their claim in the World Court and lost.

Indonesian leaders chose war, or as Sukarno termed it, "Konfrontasi." Some military units invaded Sabah and Sarawak from bordering areas in Kalimantan. Others invaded Malaya by parachute and by coastal landing craft. Assassins and saboteurs attempted to disrupt Malaysian politics and the economy. Indonesian leaders expected the rural Malays to join forces with Indonesian military units and rise up against their neo-colonialist masters. Instead, they turned in their Indonesian brothers to Malaysian military units. Konfrontasi failed. It was a low-budget war that never seriously threatened the Federation of Malaysia. In fact, it aided the establishment of the federation by providing a unifying issue. The Alliance Party drew an overwhelming victory from its pleas for loyalty and national unity in the national elections of 1964.

As Konfrontasi cooled, so did relations between Singapore's Peoples' Action Party and Malaya's Alliance Party. The PAP attempted to expand into Malaya as a balance to alliance participation in the politics of Singapore. At the same time, Malay voters began to understand that the Kadazans and Ibans of Sarawak and Sabah were not an adequate political counterbalance to the Chinese of Singapore. They began to fear that the Chinese would win political control of the federation. Such a possibility was repugnant to them and to their leaders. Singapore was forced out of the Federation of Malaysia in August of 1965, and it became an independent republic again. Shortly thereafter, Sukarno's government fell in a bloody coup and counter coup that ended Indonesia's policy of Konfrontasi.

Malaysia's major problem in foreign policy, Konfrontasi with Indonesia and the Philippines, was essentially resolved by 1965. Another problem—guerillas in the areas bordering southern Thailand—continued. Officially described as remnants of the defeated army of the Malayan Communist Party, at least some of the guerillas belonged to Malay nationalist organizations that opposed cultural conformity programs of the Thai government. The alliance government has signed several treaties with Thailand that were supposed to limit the guerillas' use of border areas as a refuge. But Malay voters in the federation continue to empathize with the plight of Malay nationalists in southern Thailand.

Domestic politics became more problematic. The MCA and MIC continued to lose popularity in their communal constituencies. Chinese and Indians turned more and more to noncommunal parties with socialist philosophies such as the Democratic Action Party (DAP) and Gerakan. Some Malays drifted away from UMNO toward the more communalistic PMIP. The old problem—Malay control of the political structure and Chinese control of the economic structure—had not been resolved.

Noncommunal parties gained the overwhelming support of Chinese and Indian voters in the national elections of 1969. MCA and MIC failed utterly. UMNO gained a majority of the Malay voters, but with its partners' failure, control of the alliance was meaningless. Just as it appeared that the alliance had lost its right to name the governor (Mentri Besar) of the State of Selangor (traditionally a Malay) and after ill-mannered supporters of other parties had staged victory parades through Malay neighborhoods in Kuala Lumpur, Malays rioted against Chinese and Indians. Hundreds lost their lives; thousands lost their homes and other property. The alliance government suspended the constitution and retired Tengku Abdul Rahman, architect of the alliance, from his long tenure as prime minister. A less politically and more technically oriented Malay, Tun Abdul Razak, became prime minister. Except for the privilege of free speech, the constitution was restored to assuage the fears of the non-Malays. New programs to speed increased Malay participation in the economy were announced. Still, the problem of political and economic equity between Chinese and Malays remained.

NEW AND OLD NATIONALISMS: THE PROBLEM

Nationalism is a very old problem in Southeast Asia. Before Europeans arrived, various states were discomfited by older or more recent loyalties. Burma struggled to keep Mon and Arakanese nationalism from reemerging and Shan nationalism from taking form. Vietnam had to control Cham and Khmer nationalism. Cambodia and Laos faced nationalistic expansion by Vietnam and Thailand. Thailand warred with neighboring Burma and Melaka, gaining their territories but not the loyalty of their former subjects.

Europeans added to the problem. They fostered the devolution of states. Burma was destroyed, her territories given to colonial India, and her minorities given special (quasi-national) status. Vietnam was cut into three pieces, which only approximately coincided with the three traditional provinces, and joined with Cambodia and the Lao principalities. The empire of Melaka was dismembered. Sumatran sultanates became part of the Dutch colonial regime of Indonesia. Malayan sultanates became separate regimes again, some of which fell under British colonial administration and others of which became part of Thailand. Colonial regimes encouraged the immigration of millions of Chinese and Indians into Southeast Asia, adding to the problem of too many nationalisms. Differences in the culture of the Europeans contributed other elements of philosophic, linguistic, and religious diversity.

Forced to recognize the independence of Southeast Asian peoples, Western officials reinforced old diversities and created new dimensions of diversity even as they left. British officials sponsored the idea of semi-autonomous states of Arakanese, Mons, Shans, Karens, Kachins, Chins, and Burmese bound into a federation or union against the idea of a unitary state controlled mostly by the Burmese. In Vietnam, the French and then the Americans sponsored a new division of the Vietnamese into two states—one communist and the other noncommunist. Americans sponsored a similar division between communists and noncommunists in Laos and Cambodia and remained oblivious to the sheer fantasy of their classificatory scheme. But perhaps the most fantastic development was one of synthesis rather than division. For the first time, northern Borneo and the Malay Peninsula were incorporated into a single state—the Federation of Malaysia. Malays received credit, but surely the idea was British.

One can blame Europeans for only a small part in developing the diversity of national loyalties in Southeast Asia. Most of the viable national loyalties are based on old cultural identities just as they are in the West. Ethnic diversity is the basic problem. The extent of ethnic diversity in Southeast Asia is too large to treat fully in a single volume. I will describe it too briefly, here.

REFERENCES

[1] See, for example, chapters 23–31 and 33 of Steinberg et al, *In Search of Southeast Asia: A Modern History* (London: Praeger Publishers, 1971).

[2] For a history of the evolution of cities in Southeast Asia see T. G. McGee, *The Southeast Asian City* (New York: Praeger Publishers, 1967).

[3] The standard work on nationalism in Southeast Asia is G. McT. Kahin, ed., *Government and Politics of Southeast Asia*, 2nd ed. (Ithaca, N.Y.: Cornell University Press, 1964). See J. Silverstein's chapters on Burma.

[4] J. Buttinger, *The Smaller Dragon* (New York: Praeger Publishers, 1958); and J. F. Cady, *The Roots of French Imperialism in Eastern Asia* (Ithaca, N.Y.: Cornell University Press, 1954), are especially instructive.

[5] See P. Le Boulanger, *Histoire du Lois française: Essai d'une étude chronologique des principautés Laotiennes* (Paris: Plon, 1931); and T. R. Stanley, "Establishment of the French Protectorate over Cambodia," *Far Eastern Quarterly 4*, no. 4 (1945): 313–340.

[6] See chapters 5–6 of J. F. Cady, *Thailand, Burma, Laos, and Cambodia* (Englewood Cliffs, N.J.: Prentice-Hall, 1966).

[7] See R. Emerson, *Malaysia: A Study in Direct and Indirect Rule* (Kuala Lumpur: University of Malaya Press, 1964); and C. H. Enloe, *Multi-Ethnic Politics: The Case of Malaysia* (Berkeley: Center for South and Southeast Asia Studies, 1970).

FIVE

ETHNIC DIVERSITY

No area of comparable size is as diverse ethnically as mainland Southeast Asia.[1] The kinds of differences between societies of mainland Southeast Asia—linguistic, religious, organizational, and technological—reflect the long and eventful history of human occupation of the area. Adaptation to particular environmental niches spawned some differences. Immigration and cultural diffusion from China, India, Indonesia, and the West account for others. Political and religious movements that might have led to greater unity never reached fruition, and there were many such movements. The overall result is a complex mosaic of unique societies and cultures. This diversity may be viewed in several ways.

LINGUISTIC DIVERSITY

Malay is the most important of the Malayo-Polynesian languages. It is the national language of Malaysia and the predominant language of the four most southern provinces of Thailand. Other important members of this language family that are spoken in Southeast Asia include Javanese in western Malaysia; Kadazan, Bajau, Iban, Kayan, Kenyah, Klemantan, Melanau, and Murut in eastern Malaysia; and Cham, Jarai, and Rhade in South Vietnam and Cambodia.

Khmer, the national language of Cambodia and an important language in the lower delta of the Mekong River in South Vietnam, is the most famous of the Mon-Khmer languages. Others include Bahnar, Mnong, Sedang, and Stieng of Cambodia, Vietnam, Laos, and Thailand; Lawa and Chaobon of Thailand; Palaung and Wa of northwestern Burma; and Mon of southern Burma. Semang and Senoi of western Malaysia are related to Mon-Khmer.

The dominant languages of Thailand and of Laos, respectively Thai (Siamese) and Laotian, are Tai languages. Others include Shan of Burma; Black and White Tai of Laos and North Vietnam; and Tai languages of southern China and Hainan. Kadai languages of North Vietnam appear to be related to both Tai and Tibeto-Burmese languages.

Burmese is the most familiar of the Tibeto-Burmese languages. It is dominant in the central dry zone of Burma, lower Burma, and parts of the Tenasserim Coast. Arakanese, which is closely allied to it, is a common language along the western coast and in the intervening highlands. Other Tibeto-Burman languages such as Bodo, Garo, Kachari, Jingpaw, Kuki-Chin, and Naga are spoken in the north and along the border with Assam. Lolo-Muso, Kaw, Kachin, Lisu, and Lahu are spoken in the north, along the border with Yunnan, and in northern Thailand, Laos, and North Vietnam. The Karen languages of northwestern and central-western Thailand and southern Burma are only distantly related to Tibeto-Burmese languages. They may comprise a separate language family.

Vietnamese of the coastal areas of North and South Vietnam and Muong of the interior highlands of North Vietnam comprise a distinctive language family. And the Miao and Yao languages of northern Thailand, Laos, and North Vietnam constitute still another language family.

All of these language families may be distantly related.[2] Maspero (1912) noted similarities between Vietnamese and Tai. Schmidt (1919) suggested that Vietnamese, Mon-Khmer, and Malayo-Polynesian all belong to a super-family, Austric. Benedict (1946) believes that Tai, Kadai, and Malayo-Polynesian languages are related. In addition, Tai is similar to Tibeto-Burman and Miao-Yao somewhat resembles Mon-Khmer. However, most of this is based on very slim evidence.

None of these language families is confined to Southeast Asia. Malayo-Polynesian languages are spread as far as Madagascar and Easter Island. Mon-Khmer languages are closely related to the Munda languages of India. Tai, Tibeto-Burmese, Vietnamese-Muong, and Miao-Yao languages are spoken in southern China.

This listing of indigenous languages is overly simple, of course, but it does illustrate the linguistic diversity of Southeast Asia. The languages of foreign Asians add even greater diversity. Important Chinese languages include Yunnanese, Hokkien, Cantonese, Hakka or Kheh, Tiechiu, Kwongsai, Hokchiu, Hokchia, Henghua, and Hainanese. Common Indian languages include Tamil, Telegu, Malayalam, Punjabi, Maharatti, Bengali, Marwari, Pushtu, and Sindhi.

Linguistic diversity hinders, but does not prevent, communication. In most countries, the national language is the native tongue of at least half of the population (South Vietnam, 88 percent; North Vietnam, 85 percent; Cambodia, 85 percent; Thailand, 80 percent; Burma, 55 percent; Laos, 50 percent; and Malaysia, 48 percent).

Members of ethnic minorities often know the national language as well as the languages of neighboring minority groups. Moreover, English has been an important medium of higher education for the urban elite in Malaysia, Burma, and Thailand. French has served the same purpose in North and South Vietnam, Laos, and Cambodia. These European languages, like the languages of the foreign Asians and of the indigenous people, mark the boundaries between different lifeways and world views—between the various national, ethnic, and "class" identities.[3]

RELIGIOUS DIVERSITY

Religion contributes almost as much as language to problems of ethnic diversity and national identity. Theravada Buddhism has the most adherents of any religion in Southeast Asia. It is the state religion in Laos, Cambodia, and Thailand, the religion of the majority and of important minorities in Burma, and the religion of a minority in South Vietnam. However, each country, indeed, each ethnic group, has its own religious bureaucracy. Mahayana Buddhism is important among the Chinese of every country in Southeast Asia and among the Vietnamese. But nowhere is it the religion of the state. Islam, the state religion of Malaysia, unites all of the Malays and a few Indians but separates them from the non-Muslim half of the population. Muslims are an overwhelming majority in Thailand's four southern provinces and are a visible minority in some central and northeastern areas although they comprise less than four percent of that country's total population. In Cambodia and South Vietnam, Muslims are an even smaller minority. Christians form distinct factions among the Karen and the Kachin of Burma, among the Vietnamese, and among the Chinese and Indians in all countries of Southeast Asia. Indians account for much religious diversity, including Hindus, Sikhs, and Jains as well as Muslims and Christians.

The civilized states of Southeast Asia have always been closely associated with universal or "world" religions. However, local sects and ethnic religions have been numerous, and sometimes, they have affected the policies of states. For example, the sects of Hoa Hao, Cao Dai, and Binh Xuyen among the Vietnamese have contributed much to the political and military problems of South Vietnam, but they have no significant following in other countries. The religions of villages in the hills are as specific. Although similarities between different ethnic groups abound, each has a distinctive configuration of rites and animistic beliefs. Sometimes the hill groups relate themselves to states through religious symbolism. The Sadat of Fire, a powerful sorcerer who is the paramount spiritual leader of the Jarai of the highlands of Cambodia, South Vietnam, and Laos, exchanges ceremonial gifts with

Cambodian (Khmer) royalty, and it is said that he is the guardian of their sacred saber. At one time or another, in virtually every country, ethnic groups of the hills have linked themselves with civilized states of the lowlands through myth and ceremonial exchange.

Religion has been as important as language in marking the boundaries of ethnic and national identities. In Malaysia, non-Malays who convert to Islam are said to have "become Malay," and some hill people of Thailand who become Buddhists conceive of their religious conversion as "becoming Thai." Probaby, some of the Karen and Kachin were attracted to Christianity because of their interest in being recognized as equally "civilized" but distinct from the Buddhist Burmese.

ORGANIZATIONAL AND TECHNOLOGICAL DIVERSITY

Differences of social organization—rules of inheritance, choice of spouse, place of residence after marriage, courtesies of rank, and rights and obligations of leadership—vary from group to group, often cutting across linguistic and religious affiliations. In a few instances, a difference in social form is the major distinction between otherwise identical ethnic identities. Minangkabaus and Malays of western Malaysia differ mostly because the former have matrilineal and the latter have nonlineal (cognatic) forms of social organization. In the highlands of Burma, whole villages sometimes shift from one ethnic identity to another by adopting social forms that harmonize better with changed requirements for subsistence.

Diversity frustrates attempts to synthesize. However, a few generalizations can be made. The easiest, from the perspective of Western culture, derives from contrasts between subsistence techniques such as hunting and gathering, fishing, shifting cultivation, wet-rice farming, and trade. Most anthropologists who specialize in the study of Southeast Asian societies prefer this sort of oversimplification—one that allows an emphasis on the functional relationships between different types of ethnic groups.

From this perspective, Southeast Asia consists of a number of states, each of which is dominated by a major people, who farm its lowland agricultural regions, fish its lakes and coastal waters, and control its political and religious institutions. Several types of ethnic groups relate to this core in different ways. Other lowland peoples, remnant populations of ancient states or overflows of population from adjacent states, constitute minorities who compete for lowland agricultural land, fishing waters, and small-scale entrepreneurial positions. Foreign Asians often control most of the medium to large businesses that import and export goods and arrange the sale of goods in the various territories of the state. They

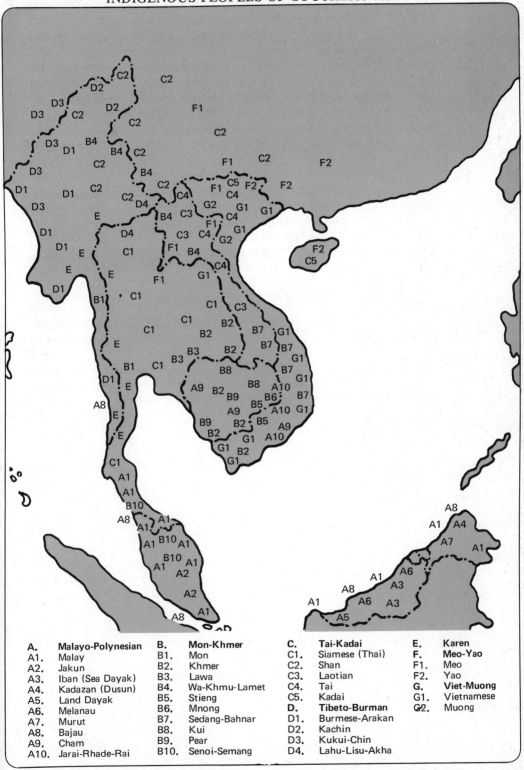

LANGUAGES AND DIALECTS OF INDIGENOUS PEOPLES OF SOUTHEAT ASIA

A.	**Malayo-Polynesian**	B.	**Mon-Khmer**	C.	**Tai-Kadai**	E.	**Karen**
A1.	Malay	B1.	Mon	C1.	Siamese (Thai)	F.	**Meo-Yao**
A2.	Jakun	B2.	Khmer	C2.	Shan	F1.	Meo
A3.	Iban (Sea Dayak)	B3.	Lawa	C3.	Laotian	F2.	Yao
A4.	Kadazan (Dusun)	B4.	Wa-Khmu-Lamet	C4.	Tai	G.	**Viet-Muong**
A5.	Land Dayak	B5.	Stieng	C5.	Kadai	G1.	Vietnamese
A6.	Melanau	B6.	Mnong			G2.	Muong
A7.	Murut	B7.	Sedang-Bahnar	D.	**Tibeto-Burman**		
A8.	Bajau	B8.	Kui	D1.	Burmese-Arakan		
A9.	Cham	B9.	Pear	D2.	Kachin		
A10.	Jarai-Rhade-Rai	B10.	Senoi-Semang	D3.	Kukui-Chin		
				D4.	Lahu-Lisu-Akha		

Sources: F.M. Lebar et al., Ethnic Groups of Mainland Southeast Asia (New Haven, Conn.: HRAF Press, 1964); and F.C. Cole, The Peoples of Malaysia (Princeton, N.J.: D. Van Nostrand Co., 1945).

may also have professional occupations in urban centers or work in commercial agricultural estates and extractive industries. Some of them are fishermen. Slash-and-burn farmers and hunter-gatherers live in the marginal territories of the state. Some grow special crops such as cotton, tobacco, or opium for sale to foreign Asians or major peoples. Others gather forest products—jungle fruits, rattan, wood oil, or resins—for sale in urban centers. A few of them are fishermen. It is among these hill farmers and hunter-gatherers, who comprise less than one percent of the population of Southeast Asia, that linguistic and religious differences are greatest.

REFERENCES

[1] There are more than three hundred ethnic groups and about twelve hundred names that have been used to refer to them. The standard compilation of data on ethnic groups of Southeast Asia is F. M. LeBar, G. C. Hickey, and J. K. Musgrave, eds., *Ethnic Groups of Mainland Southeast Asia* (New Haven, Conn.: Human Relations Area Files Press, 1964). Also, see P. Kunstadter, ed., *Southeast Asian Tribes, Minorities and Nations*, 2 vols. (Princeton, N.J.: Princeton University Press, 1967). There are HRAF monographs and U.S. Army handbooks for each Southeast Asian nation.

[2] See the appendix of Robbins Burling, *Hill Farms and Padi Fields: Life in Mainland Southeast Asia* (Englewood Cliffs, N.J.: Prentice-Hall, 1965).

[3] L. Sharp, "Cultural Continuities and Discontinuities in Southeast Asia," *The Journal of Asian Studies* 22 (1962): 3–11, is a classic statement of the dimensions of ethnic diversity in Southeast Asia.

SIX

MALAY STATES

MALAYS

Malay is the English version of the Malay word *melayu*. Malays speak of themselves as *orang melayu* ("Malay persons"). Probably the term refers to the ancient kingdom of Melayu in southern Sumatra. Its original meaning, the theme of several jokes told by Malays, is not known for certain because the root, *layu*, has different meanings in different dialects. Possibly, *layu (layo)* is an old Minangkabau cognate of modern Malay *layar* ("sail"), and *orang melayu* means "persons who sail ships." *Malay* should not be confused with *Malayan*, which includes all permanent residents of Malaya whatever their ethnic identity. *Malay*, on the other hand, includes only those who habitually speak a Malay language, follow Malay customs, and accept Islam.[1] From the Malay perspective, one's identity is much more a matter of behavior than of descent. An individual's subethnic and ethnic identities derive from adherence to a particular variety of customary law, *adat*, that regulates virtually every aspect of behavior from property rights and inheritance of high office to marriage and the formal courtesy of feasts. A Malay is simply someone who behaves as a Malay should.

Malays are the major people of the Malay Peninsula, where their five and a half millions comprise about fifty percent of the population. Most live in West Malaysia, but more than a half million of them, a remnant of the former Malay kingdom of Patani, comprise a large majority of the population of the southern provinces of Thailand (Pattani, Yala, Narathiwat, and Satun). They are outnumbered by other peoples in the west coast states of West Malaysia (Penang, Perak, Selangor, Negri Sembilan, Melaka, and Johore) and in Sarawak and Sabah. Only about twenty percent of the population of urban places (towns with more than a thousand persons) is Malay. And only two urban centers with more than twenty thousand population, Kota Bharu and Kuala Trengganu, have Malay majorities. Malays are predominantly rural in residence, but they are surprisingly urban in their religious and political attitudes. They control the government and civil administration of Malaysia.

Most of the states in the Federation of Malaysia are Malay kingdoms. The exceptions are Penang (formerly part of the kingdom of Kedah), Melaka (formerly center of the Malay empire), and Sarawak and Sabah (formerly territories of the kingdom of Brunei). Political and religious institutions of these exceptional states have been made to conform to those of Malay states.

Almost every urban place that has served as the principal residence of a Malay king, under-king, prince, or chief-minister has a large Malay community. The community *(kampong)* is usually rectangular in form and was founded on the edge of the royal compound. It became a major residential area for Malays in the town, and it became the site of a mosque *(mesjid)* and a market *(pasar)*. Very large *kampongs* are usually divided into hamlets each of which has a prayer house and marketing shops.

A traditional house, whether in town or village, rests on stilts or pilings that raise its floor from three to six feet above the ground. Typically, there is an open verandah at the front of the house, a large front room, and several sleeping rooms towards the back. This is the sacred and major part of the house. One must be barefooted to enter it. The kitchen is attached to the back of the house. It is profane and rests directly on the ground. Modern apartments in towns that have been built for use by Malays maintain the symbolism of upraised house and profane kitchen by having a kitchen floor that is 8 to 10 inches lower than the rest of the apartment.

Most houses in rural villages are occupied by a single nuclear family or a stem family. In towns, houses are often divided with partitions and inhabited by several families. Many such apartments are rented out. Some of the renter households consist of families who ordinarily reside in town; others are only temporary residents. Often several bachelor boys or several unmarried girls pool their household expense in a single apartment.

The form of rural settlements varies somewhat according to local topography but usually follows the line of a waterway, highway, or railway that allows easy communication with the outside world. Often, settlement continues for miles without any visually distinct breaks. From the perspective of Malay inhabitants, however, such a ribbon of settlement is divided into many communities, which vary in size from fifty to a thousand persons and which are defined more by focal points than by territories. Each of these hamlets *(wilayah)* consists of the house compounds of members of a prayerhouse congregation. Members of prayerhouse congregations also belong to a wider community or village *(kampong)*, which is the congregation of a mosque.

In the west coast states, where immigration has been common, hamlets within the same village often have different subethnic identities based on regional differences of language and custom. Such differences are important in some, but not all, situations. Malays of Javanese ancestry, for example, sometimes maintain separate prayer houses and celebrate ritual feasts in slightly different ways, but they attend the same mosques as other Malays and they participate in feasts with other Malays. Some Malays of Minangkabau descent in Negri Sembilan follow the customary laws associated with matrilineal descent *(adat perpateh)*; others in Negri Sembilan who claim descent from Minangkabaus follow the customary laws associated with the cognatic kinship system of other Malays *(adat temenggong)*. Malays of Achehnese, Boyanese, Bugis, Korinchi, and Mandiling ancestry sometimes refer to this fact, or their acquaintances call attention to it. The same is true of those from different states in Malaysia. These different subethnic identities are ranked in most *kampongs*, and the rankings vary somewhat from *kampong* to *kampong*. Javanese have assimilated least thoroughly to Malay culture and usually are ranked lowest. The highest rank is given to the subethnic identity of the founders of the *kampong*. Later immigrants have lower rank.[2]

Individual rank or scalar status is a very traditional aspect of social structure that continues to overshadow the slow development of class consciousness in Malay society. The same terminology that is used to address relatives serves to rank the seniority of nonrelatives whom one addresses in everyday situations. Other terminologies accord different ranks to members of royalty, aristocrats, government officials, descendants of Arabs, religious pilgrims, teachers, traditional curers, and successful businessmen. Behaviors of all sorts—greeting gestures, postures, vocabulary, and topics of conversation—vary according to the ranks of social participants and according to the systems of courtesy that are appropriate in different kinds of settings.[3] Different kinds of settings are not equally accessible to males and females, but females enjoy equal rights to own and manage property.

Kampong leadership is of several types. Members of a congregation usually ask a few devout men, a committee, to look after the affairs of the prayerhouse, organize the celebration of the Prophet's birthday, arrange funerals, and collect the annual tithe *(zakat fitrah)*. Members of the congregation or of the prayerhouse committee select a representative who serves on a committee that manages the affairs of the mosque and selects religious specialists. Members of prayerhouse committees and mosque committees, especially the chairmen of such committees, serve as leaders in secular matters, too.

Many *kampongs* have a ruling committee that is composed of representatives of the various *wilayahs* in the *kampong*. In some instances they are elected, in others they are selected by a government official *(penghulu,* district officer, or *mentri besar)* from a list prepared by *kampong* elders. Political parties sometimes form "shadow" committees, which replicate the structure of secular *kampong* leadership.

Certain kinds of individuals tend to be leaders whether they occupy formal positions of leadership or not. Teachers, senior government clerks, men who have made the pilgrimage to Mecca, curers, and successful shopkeepers are natural opinion leaders who merely confirm their role by accepting formal positions. Frequently, those who actually hold formal positions in the *kampong* are closely related consanguineally or affinally, and they usually belong to families that founded the *kampong.*

Leaders are patrons to other villagers who depend on them for advice, mediation of disputes, favorable treatment from governmental officials, and even small loans. Being a good leader requires tremendous sacrifice. Leaders avoid the appearance of seeking their role lest they be accused of seeking illicit rewards for themselves. The best appearance is that of having the role of leadership thrust upon one by others.[4]

A break in the formal structure of traditional leadership occurs just above the *kampong* level. *Kampongs* are integrated into a parish *(mukim),* which in turn is part of a district *(daerah),* and districts combine to form the state territory *(negri).* The head of the *mukim (penghulu)* and the head of the district *(pegawai daerah)* are civil servants. Traditional leadership reemerges at the state level. Formerly, of course, Malay chiefs filled this structural break between *kampong* and state. Now, representatives to state and national parliaments vie with civil servants for patronage in parishes and districts.

The nature of leadership is different among Minangkabau Malays of Negri Sembilan.[5] There, leadership is part of the framework of matrilineal organization that reaches from village virtually to state. Each village is a sublineage *(perut)* headed by a chief *(ibubapa).* He is the unanimous choice of members of the subclan, or failing that, he is appointed by the clan chief *(lembaga).* The office of clan chief rotates from one subclan to another in a set order that is abrogated only by unusual circumstances. Although the clan *(suku)* appoints its own chief, the choice must not be opposed by the council of eight clan chiefs *(orang delapan)* or by the chief *(undang)* of the district *(luak).* The office of *undang* passes from one founder clan to another in a strict order of rotation except for special circumstances as judged by the council of clan leaders. (This feature, rotation of an office which may be modified by judgment of a council of leaders from among whom the office holder is chosen, has been incorporated into the national constitution as the means by which the king of the Federation of Malaysia is chosen.) Clans of later immigrants are not allowed a turn in the rotation. Different moieties of clans distinguish not only founders versus immigrants, but also wet lands versus dry lands and low-lands versus mountains.

The system of Minangkabau kinship terminology is practically identical to that of Malays. It is a generational type of terminology in which the birth order of siblings is important. Basically, terms for persons older than oneself are differentiated according to gener-ation, seniority, and sex, and terms for younger persons are dif-ferentiated only by generation. The terminology serves equally as kinship terminology and as seniority terminology. Minangkabau terminology has a special term for one's mother's brother—the only terminological evidence of a strongly matrilineal system.

The fact that Minangkabau and Malay cultures are practically identical except for social structure and the fact of very close rela-tions between Pagar Ruyong (capital of Minangkabau) and Melayu in Sumatran history, as well as the fact of close relations between Melaka and Negri Sembilan in Malayan history, suggest that Malays and Minangkabaus are the same people living in different but complementary ecological niches. Briefly stated, at some not-too-distant time in the past, Minangkabau social structure may have been a correlate of wet-rice horticulture, and Malay social structure may have been a correlate of trade and commerce. Minangkabau customary law *(adat perpateh)* vests ownership of land in corporate groups so that agricultural land is not fragmented through inheritance. Moreover, membership in the corporate groups is inherited through females who do most of the work and who in a very real sense are the owners of the land. Males have rights to the produce of their sisters' lands, they are honored guests on their wives' lands, and they hold the positions of leadership of the corporate groups; but they are not really owners of the soil. Traditionally, young males without any prospect of holding office have left the rice fields to find their fortunes as traders in distant towns. This kind of migration still occurs. Those who fail in urban places return to their maternal villages. Others succeed and return only to get wives. They and their wives, being separated from the rice fields and the matriclans, have no occasion to follow ma-trilineal law. Instead, they follow the customary law of cognatic (bilateral with a slight patrilineal bias) inheritance *(adat temeng-gong)*. It is better suited to the interests of males who are con-cerned with personal control of property and in commercial trans-actions. *Adat perpateh* is usually too fragile for transplanting. It was successfully transplanted to Negri Sembilan from Minang-kabau at a very early time. But in the late nineteenth and early twentieth centuries, when many Minangkabaus migrated to the rural areas of Selangor and Perak, matrilineal law was dropped in favor of *adat temenggong*. Probably, not enough members of the right clans migrated to the same areas for the system to function properly.

At the present time, most Malays are lowland farmers. But many of them do not grow enough rice for their own needs. From the end of the fourteenth century until the sixth decade of the twentieth century, Malaya was a rice-deficient area that depended on imports from the Indonesian islands, Burma, and Thailand. At mid-twentieth century, the government introduced more productive varieties of rice and began to open large areas for wet-rice agriculture. A small surplus resulted.

Most wet-rice farmers who are not commercial producers have less than two hectares (about five acres) of paddy land. Formerly they planted one crop of rice each year. Traditional varieties of rice mature in six or seven months, and several months are required to prepare the fields. Now many farmers plant new hybrid varieties of rice that mature in less than four months, and they plant two crops a year in west coast states where there is no marked dry season.

Ritual is not wasted on the new varieties of rice. Traditional varieties of rice are protected and nourished with prayers and offerings. Divination guides the selection of new fields and the timing of each phase of cultivation. Prayers and offerings and chants persuade evil spirits to leave the fields. A special ceremony places the seed in the care of spirits of the soil.

Usually, an old man of the household prepares a small fertile corner of the field as a seedbed. The soil is soaked and worked into a fine mud. Soaked in water overnight and sown broadcast, the rice seeds sprout within a few days producing a thick lawn of seedlings. The old man tends them carefully. Others prepare the fields for transplanting. Softened by irrigation water, the soil is broken with hoes wielded by women or with plows pulled by water buffalo and guided by men. More water, hoeing, plowing, and treading reduces the soil to a fine silty mud. Old men pull up the seedlings that are 44 days old (44 is a magical number), trim the roots and tops, place the seedlings in small bundles on a hod, and carry them to convenient places in the muddy fields. Women pull seedlings several at a time from the bundles and insinuate the roots into the soft mud with their hands or with a special implement called a *kuku gambing* (goat's hoof). The clumps of young rice plants are about a foot apart across the whole field when the transplanting has been completed. Immediately, the field is flooded again. In a month or two, underground stems develop and interlace the spaces between the clumps of transplanted rice. Other rice plants sprout from the stems and fill the empty spaces.

Few weeds inhabit a good rice field. The ever-present water and the thick stand of rice discourage growth of weeds. Rice farmers have plenty of free time between the time of transplanting and harvesting. They tend the irrigation system so that the flow of water in the field is slow enough to encourage growth of some bottom algae (which provides fixed nitrogen for the rice plants) and fast enough so that the water does not become stagnant (depriving the roots of oxygen). And they pull the few weeds that grow.

The rice plants bloom and their panicles fill with seeds and the seeds grow large. Rice finches begin to harvest the crop, and children have a duty to frighten the birds. Twigs and leaves may be tied to strings that crisscross the field so that an old woman can sit in the shade, pull the strings, and drive away the birds.

The grain ripens after the fields have been drained. Boys and men go fishing the day that the fields are drained. Deep holes in the field and specially constructed weirs ease the task of harvesting fish that have grown fat in the lush environment of the rice paddy.

When traditional varieties of rice ripen, they must be treated with ceremony and care. One ceremony drives away evil spirits. Another, directed by a traditional midwife, placates the soul of the rice. The midwife harvests several panicles of rice with a semicircular knife that is set in a handle shaped like a bird. She does this in such a way that the spirit of the rice cannot see the cutting and be frightened. The panicles of rice are bundled and taken to the house, where the bundle is treated exactly as if it were a newborn baby. It becomes the core of rice that is saved as seed for the next crop.

Fields of traditional varieties of rice ripen unevenly. Panicles are cut as they ripen so that a single field is harvested again and again over a period of several weeks. Traditional rice-harvesting knives (tuai) that cut one panicle at a time are used, and they serve better than sickles for harvesting panicles that mature unevenly and shatter easily. The new varieties of rice mature evenly, deserve no ceremonial respect, and are harvested with sickles.

Harvest time requires extra hands, and they are usually available. Persons who live in distant places and have a claim to the products of the land return to help with the harvest and claim their share. Others work for wages. The grain is threshed and winnowed as it is cut. It may be stored as padi, with the hull and bran intact, in large burlap sacks. As padi is needed for food, the hulls and bran layers are pounded off in a large wooden mortar. The pounded rice is beras which will become nasi when cooked. More often, farmers send their padi to a rice mill and store the beras in burlap sacks.

Some Malay rice farmers do not own their fields. They pay half their crop to Malay landlords who have extra land. Since 1913, the land of Malays has been protected by law from non-Malay ownership. Sharecropping is becoming less common. Governmental land development schemes are giving sharecroppers fresh opportunity to own land, and government agencies also have sponsored the use of tractors by larger land owners and by members of agricultural cooperatives.

Many rice-farming families also tap latex from rubber trees. Often, members of the same family become specialized as rice farmers or rubber tappers. Older persons tend to be more interested in rice growing while the young prefer rubber tapping. Rubber holdings tend to be larger than rice fields. Sharecropping is more common and more remunerative than in rice farming. A sharetapper usually keeps about four-fifths of the latex, and the owner is entitled to only one-fifth. Possibly, the tapper's share is large because of the large amount of labor required in latex production. But the owner's investment is large, too. The best varieties of budded rubber seedlings are expensive. Trees cannot be tapped until they are 6 years old, and they are not very productive after 30 years of age.

Tappers begin working early in the morning because the latex stops flowing in the heat of the afternoon. They cut diagonal grooves into the bark and attach a spout and cup at the lower end of the groove. Usually, alternate trees are tapped so that each "rests" for a day between taps. Tappers cannot work in wet weather because the latex flows too easily on the wet bark and will not follow the groove. A tapper works until late morning or noon, trimming bark and setting cups until he (or she) reaches the end of the trail that runs back and forth through the grove of rubber trees. Then he returns to the beginning and in turn empties the cups of tapped trees into five-gallon tins. Usually, he fills only one tin. Sometimes he fills two.

Formerly, tappers added formic acid to their latex, and after it coagulated they formed it into sheets that they pressed with a mangle. They even dried their own sheets of rubber before selling them to a rubber trader. Now, most tappers sell the latex directly to a rubber trader who sells it to a modern processing plant. The latex is transported to the processing plant in tanker trucks. There, scientifically designed equipment coagulates and dries the latex, producing rubber of very high quality. This more recent pattern of rubber production is a direct result of governmental research, standards, and controls that are supposed to enhance the competitive position of natural rubber versus that of synthetic rubber in the world market.

Some Malay farmers produce other commercial crops such as copra, palm olives, pineapples, coffee, ginger, and tobacco. The Malaysian government has encouraged diversification of agricultural products so that the economy will be less dependent on the fluctuating market for natural rubber. In addition, the government has attempted to develop methods for international marketing of the tropical fruits that Malays grow for local markets. Durian, perhaps the most delicious fruit in the world, is the most valuable crop for local markets, but it is an unlikely export because foreigners usually cannot tolerate its odor. Jackfruit, another important fruit in local markets, has a particular taste that many foreigners cannot abide. Other fruits that many foreigners like, such as rambutan and mangosteen, are too perishable for long-distance shipment and too delicate for canning. As an alternative measure, the government has encouraged development of local fruit markets and has discouraged importing of fruit. Fruit is an important source of income for Malay farmers.

Many coastal Malays are fishermen.[6] They fish for small fry with throw nets that are cast into the surf and for mackerel and prawns with gill nets that are lowered from boats into the depths of the sea. Their traditional fishing techniques are effective in shallow coastal waters. Several boats, each with a crew of four to eight men, cooperate in finding and surrounding the schools of crayfish or mackerel with the gill nets. Having surrounded a school, several boats within the perimeter of the net splash the water and pound the sides of the boats, driving the frightened fish in all directions and into the net where many become entangled. The net is pulled into the boats, and the catch is harvested. This is the most dangerous part because small sharks and deadly sea snakes are often caught in the net, too. As the men pull the fish free from the net they store them under the floorboards of the boats. When the space below the floorboards is filled, the boats return to shore where old men, women, and boys lay tracks of boards on the beach and drag the boats above the high-tide mark. As the fish are unloaded, wives select fish for the next meal and buyers arrive and purchase the rest of the catch. Fishermen's wives bargain the price with the fish merchants.

Fishing tends to be a seasonal or a migratory occupation among Malays. Prawn fishing begins on the east coast after the end of the northeastern monsoon, in January. Mackerel fishing begins about three months later and lasts until August. Fishing becomes less productive and more dangerous as October and the northeastern monsoon approach. However, the most productive season of the west coast begins in September, following the southwestern monsoon. Many fishermen migrate back and forth across the Malay Peninsula in order to take advantage of seasonal differences. Others become rice farmers during the rainy season. And a few go into towns or cities to find temporary employment.

Unemployment and underemployment are common problems for urban Malays. Of course, these problems derive in part from the large number of transients from rural areas who are trying to find urban employment. Those who find permanent jobs remain in town. Those who fail return to their villages. In a few months or years, after having saved another stake, they may try again to find employment in an urban center. Relatives, friends, or acquaintances who live in town often support their quest by providing low-cost room and board.

Rural immigrants usually have had only four or five years of formal education and cannot qualify for government jobs. Like many other urbanites, they work as servants, gardeners, truck attendants, laborers, drivers, factory workers, and small-scale entrepreneurs. Other urban Malays, with somewhat better education, are office clerks or school teachers. The few with higher school certificates or college degrees usually do not reside in the traditional urban *kampongs* but in special government quarters or in prestigious residential areas.

Malays, like most Arabs and Egyptians, belong to the Shafi'i school of the Sunnis tradition of Islam. They honor the five pillars of Islam, which are: (1) acceptance of the Unity of God whose Prophet is Mohammed; (2) five daily prayers; (3) fasting during the daylight hours of the month of Ramadan; (4) pilgrimage to Mecca; and (5) annual payment of tithe and of alms *(zakat fitrah)*. Also, they observe Koranic injunctions against drinking alcohol, against eating the flesh of pigs or of improperly slaughtered animals, and against gambling and usury. Many Malays sin, of course, but their Islamic doctrines are orthodox. In addition, they have beliefs and rituals which are not Islamic.

Malays begin and end their ritual with Koranic prayer, but the symbolism of their ritual is mostly Hindu. Hindu symbolism is important in royal traditions, in wedding ceremonies, and in curing rituals. It blends imperceptibly with ancient Southeast Asian beliefs and practices that are an inexorable part of Malay culture.

The number and hierarchial arrangement of important officials in traditional Malay kingdoms conform to the numerology of Hindu cosmology—4 ministers, 8 chiefs, 16 subchiefs, and 32 *penghulus*. Palaces and royal compounds are designed to fit the same cosmology. The elements of architecture that symbolize Hindu numerology are so sacred and magically powerful that their use in secular buildings is forbidden by customary law. Their identification with Hinduism is explicit. The natural hill or artificial mound that is usually behind the palace, for example, is called Indra's Mountain or Mount Meru. Although Brahmin priests do not direct royal ceremonies, the court magicians who do are steeped in Hindu lore.

A Malay wedding consists of several ceremonies, two of which enact the coronation of a divine king and queen. Throughout, the bride and bridegroom are costumed in the royal style, and they are attended by "servants." The first ceremony is the giving of the male dowry of which red and white flowers (made of $10 bills) comprise a major part and are a proper offering to a Hindu deity. A complete costume for the bride (an appropriate gift of commission by a king) is often bundled into the shape of a bird (*Garuda*—the mount of Vishnu) and forms the other major part of the male dowry. After the betrothal, relatives and friends make obeisance to the bride and bridegroom whose hands and feet are stained red with henna. It is a sign of divinity. Guests lustrate the divine and royal couple, seated separately on a throne, with oil and offerings of rice. Islamic ceremonies follow—a Koranic recital by the bride and the signing and witnessing of the marriage contract. Then the groom and his bride sit together on the throne. People call him *raja sahari*, literally "king for a day." The royal couple sit motionless, occasionally receiving and sharing small portions of yellow cooked rice that are offered by close relatives and honored guests. And they sit in state, stiffly watching various entertainments such as saucer dancing and exhibitions of stylized self-defense *(bersilat)*. A buffalo or goat and many chickens are slaughtered, and a great feast is given for the whole community. Later, three days and again seven days after the "sitting in state" *(bersanding)*, the bride and groom are bathed ceremonially, and their marriage rituals are complete.

Other life crises—birth, first hair cutting, clitorectomy, circumcision, pregnancy, and death—have Hindu elements of ritual. But they are less obvious than Islamic and indigenous elements. One kind of ritual, *khenduri*, closely resembles the *slamatan* feasts of Javanese. A *khenduri* is a vital part of most life-crisis ceremonies, and sometimes, as in celebrating a death anniversary or a change in social status, it comprises the whole ceremony. Close relatives, friends, and the immediate neighbors are invited, and they often help by providing some of the food and labor. Women help in the preparations but do not participate in the ritual, which consists of chanting Koranic prayers and eating a formal dinner of rice and various fancy flavorings. One ought to give a *khenduri* on any major occasion that threatens to change one's life because change may cause loss of *semangat*, "vital spiritual force" (as a primitive root, *-mangat*, it is probably a cognate of Melanesian and Polynesian *mana)*.

Loss of *semangat* is a common cause of illness and death. There are other causes, but most relate in some way to *semangat*. Imbalance, impurity, and intrusion cause loss of *semangat*. One must take care to keep hot and cold elements of the body in balance and not allow wind to enter the body. Food and water must be ritually pure. And one should try not to excite the envy or hatred of place spirits *(hantu)* or of persons who control spirits because illness and death can result from a spirit entering the body. People who control spirits are potentially evil. On the other hand, it is perfectly legitimate to try to win the affection of others (not only lovers, but customers and patrons) by magical means.[7]

Food and drink are a principal medium of sorcery and of affectional magic. Also, food and drink are a principal accompaniment of social relationships. At *khenduris*, for example, hosts must offer food and drink, guests must accept, and all must attend to their differences of rank. On such an occasion, a guest may be influenced by a host or another guest who flavors the food with words or substance. A guest may fear that others are committing sorcery against him. All except the most tenuous social relationships eventually require attending to differences of rank and exchanging of food and drink. Food and drink are symbolic of the ambivalence of social relationship. And many medical practitioners *(bomoh)* perform rituals that symbolize the connection between changing social rank and frustrating oral gratification.

Malay medicine is a complex system that claims mastery over the full range of human illness. There are traditional specializations that correspond more or less to midwifery, bone setting, chiropractic, pediatrics, pharmacology, and psychiatry. Additionally, some practitioners specialize in treating only one kind of illness. A few practitioners have received their training only from a spirit tutor, but most have served apprenticeships with experienced practitioners before beginning their own practices.

Malays, like other peoples of Southeast Asia, continue accumulating, selectively, bits and pieces of other cultures without suddenly casting aside the traditional order and content of their own culture. Acupuncture, aspirin, chloroquinine, antibiotics, and BCG have not totally replaced traditional medical remedies but have merely supplemented them. Motion-picture films from India and the United States and television shows produced in England, Australia, and the United States are very popular among Malays; still, many Malays travel miles to witness traditional shadow puppet plays *(wayang kulit)* that are sponsored by royal courts and educational institutions. At the same time, they enjoy modern Malay stories that have been filmed or videotaped in Malaysia. Excellence in reciting traditional poetry—internally rhymed quatrains called *pantun*—is rewarded at national contests and so is excellence in writing modern novels. Jawi script continues to be used although most publications are in the Roman alphabet. Airplanes, automobiles, bicycles, and railroads have become integral parts of everyday life without replacing traditional *perahu* (boats) and *kerbau* (water buffalo) which are still plentiful and useful. English manners and suits are appropriate in department stores and government offices; Malay manners and *sarongs* are appropriate in mosques and kitchens; and both styles are tolerated in traditional markets and on public highways. Old traits survive and new ones are easily accepted. New traits are added to traditional cognitive realms within which they are compatible, or else they are kept in new cognitive realms that do not compete with the old. Malay culture survives and changes.

Malays tend to avoid involvement in some modern cognitive realms such as science. But they do not have an inferiority complex about their culture. Malays are too proud from the perspective of other peoples of Malaysia who fear that under the guise of "Malaysianization" they are being recruited to Malay culture.

CHINESE

More than eighty percent of all Chinese living outside of China (Mainland China, Hainan, and Taiwan) reside in Southeast Asia, and more than twenty-five percent of the Southeast Asian Chinese population reside in Singapore and the Federation of Malaysia.[8] Chinese comprise more than seventy-five percent of the more than two million people of the Republic of Singapore (formerly a state in the Federation of Malaysia) and about forty percent of the almost twelve million residents of the Federation of Malaysia. They are spread unevenly through the different states of Malaysia, contributing most to the populations of the west coast and least to those of the east coast of the Malay Peninsula. Chinese in both nations are "naturalized" in the sense that they consider their nationality to be Malaysian or Singaporean rather than Chinese. Still, they strongly maintain their Chinese cultural identity. And Malays, of course, consider them to be foreigners.

Most Chinese reside in urban centers. Economic class is a much more important dimension of social organization among urban Chinese than among urban Malays, and more and less prestigious Chinese residential areas of cities are quite apparent. More so than wealthy Malays, wealthy Chinese have occupied formerly European residential areas in suburban fringes where houses, servants' quarters, and gardens are truly grand scale. The middle class occupy terrace houses and shophouses. Terrace houses resemble American townhouses, more or less. Shophouses stand side by side like the terrace houses but are smaller. Often, a family business occupies the front room on the ground floor, and the family resides in rooms in the back and on the floor above. Older shophouses, squatter shacks, and new highrise apartments house the urban poor.

Until 1947, about half of the Chinese population of the Malay states lived in rural areas. They were tin miners and farmers who built their wooden frame houses directly on the ground. Roofs were usually galvanized tin, and often floors were dirt. During the Emergency, Chinese farmers and miners were gathered into "new villages." The new villages were small towns that varied in size from several hundred to several thousand households. Their streets were organized in simple grid patterns. After the Emergency, new villages continued as a major form of settlement, but isolated rural homesteads of farmers and miners appeared again, too.

Residential association usually coincides with linguistic affiliation. Most of the major "dialects" of Chinese are mutually unintelligible, and each is the medium of a slightly different subculture. Dialect, or rather language, is a natural basis of association. Major dialects and their places of origin in China are, in the order of their predominance, as follows: Hokkien—Amoy and adjacent areas of the mainland; Cantonese—coastal area north and south of Canton; Hakka (Kheh)—northwestern Kwangtung and southwestern Fukien; Tiechiu—around Satow; and Hainanese (Hailam)—Hainan Island.

Speakers of different dialects are concentrated in different occupations in different areas. Hokkiens are primarily shopkeepers and traders in Melaka, Penang, and Singapore, and they are pineapple growers in Johore, Perak, and Selangor. Cantonese are primarily tin miners, but they are strongly represented in other occuptaions, too. Hakkas are tin miners and market gardeners. Tiechius have urban occupations. And Hailams are small-town shopkeepers, domestic servants, and rubber tappers.

Chinese dominate four occupations—shopkeeping, tin mining, pineapple growing, and market gardening. Their success in shopkeeping has been attributed, with some validity, to their long experience with a cash economy in China, their patrilineal kinship system, and their stark fear of poverty as immigrants. The corporateness of Chinese groups probably contributed most to success in business because capital credit was made available to enterprising persons, cheap labor was easily available, property was not fragmented through inheritance, and decisions concerning its use were made by a very few experienced and capable men. Additionally, the British preferred Chinese rather than Malays as the small businessmen of the colonies. Chinese success in tin mining may be attributed to the same factors. But here their competitors are British corporations, which own 20 percent of the mines and account for half of the production. British mining technique is very thorough and requires little labor, but it requires great capital investment. Huge dredges, floating in shallow ponds of their own making, sift through alluvial deposits and mechanically sort the ores of tin and other metals from gravel, sand, and clay. Traditional Chinese partnerships *(kongsi)* own most of the mines, employ the majority of miners, and produce about forty percent of the tin. Their technique requires less capital but more labor than that of the British. Water, jetted against the sides of a mining pit, carries alluvium to a gravel pump at the bottom of the pit. Steam or diesel pumps raise the mixture of alluvium and water through a large pipe to the top of a tall trestle built of timbers. The mixture flows down through a long line of sluice steps that catch the heavy metal-bearing ores while other materials are washed away. Workers collect the ore (cassiterite—SnO_2), wash it again, and put it in sacks. Like the production of British companies, it is shipped to Penang, Butterworth, or Singapore, mixed with limestone and anthracite, and smelted.

The pineapple industry began as a cottage industry and, in 40 years, became the third most important export industry in the Malay states. Then it practically disappeared during the Japanese occupation. Now it has recovered. Chinese farmers with small land holdings in Johore, Selangor, and Perak produce most of the crop. Chinese entrepreneurs own and manage the factories that can the fruit and the export companies that ship it to Britain, Europe, and the United States. Some pineapple growers are market gardeners, too. Market gardeners, of course, grow the vegetables and fruits that are consumed by large urban populations in Malaysia and Singapore.

Most fishermen of the west coast of West Malaysia are Chinese. Some are inshore fishermen who still use traditional methods, but others have invested in modern offshore trawlers. Trawlers have begun to fish along the east coast, too. Inshore fishermen resent the low labor requirements of trawlers, and claim that trawlers are depleting fish populations.

Chinese have organized formal dialect associations which are the most inclusive corporate groups except political parties. Other bases of association—occupational and consanguineal—cut across linguistic differences, forming subsections within dialect associations. Formal associations abound in Malayan Chinese social organization, reflecting both a penchant of Chinese culture for corporate groups and an ordinance of British colonial administration against informal associations. The ordinance, promulgated in 1934, required formal registration of the name and charter of all associations with more than ten members. Its purpose was to enlarge the basis for legal action against secret societies. Its result was an increase in the number of Chinese formal associations to more than two thousand.

Secret societies survived British colonial administration but they are less important now than formerly.[9] Virtually all of them developed from the Triad Society (Heaven and Earth Society, Hung League, Three United Society, or Three Dots Society) which was devoted to the task of overthrowing the Manchu Ch'ing dynasty (darkness) and restoring the Chinese Ming dynasty (light)—a popular cause in the poverty-ridden provinces of southern China whence Southeast Asian Chinese emigrated. Many of the immigrants to Southeast Asia were already members of the Triad Society. It was the first well-established formal association, and it served as the very bones of immigrant society, guaranteeing letters of credit, maintaining law and order, and paying funeral expenses. Invariably, the head of the local branch of the society was also the Kapitan China who answered for his community to a Malay sultan or British administrator. As other kinds of corporate groups began to serve economic needs and as colonial administration began to provide full protection of law, the society became less important. It survives as a loose confederation of gangs that profit from extortion, prostitution, drug traffic, and assassination. Names of gangs are sacred Triad numbers such as Three Times Eight, Twenty-Four, Twenty-One, One Hundred-Eight, or Ought Eight. The traditional hierarchy of office titles—Elder Brother, Incense Master, Teacher, Vanguard, Red Staff, Councillor, Treasurer, Cashier, Assistant Cashier, Agent, Messenger, and Recruiter—remains. Initiation rituals replicate traditional rites. And the disciplinary code of 36 oaths, 21 regulations, 10 rules, and 10 punishments has been retained.

Modern gangs differ from the traditional society in their purpose, of course, and also in their membership. Most of the Chinese gangs have special sections of Malay or Indian members. And Malays and Indians have founded their own gangs using Triad principles of organization, discipline, and ritual.

One of the old rites, that of assuming the surname Hung, has lost part of its meaning among Malay and Indian members. *Hung* means "red," which symbolizes a warrior. That much is understood. But *Hung* also represents the patrilineal surname of the Ming dynasty. The object of the rite is to guarantee the absolute loyalty of an initiate by making him a member of the same surname group.

Surnames are an important aspect of Chinese social organization, especially from the perspective of the major peoples of Southeast Asia among whom only the Vietnamese use surnames. Moreover, Chinese immigrants in Southeast Asia have placed more emphasis on surnames than when they resided in China. Immigrants assumed, conveniently, that all persons who used the same ideograph for their surname belonged to the same patriclan *(tsu)* and thereby must extend hospitality and aid. It was a reciprocal arrangement by which new immigrants received jobs and sometimes capital loans while established residents received cheap labor and high interest. Technically, of course, it is the *tsu* that controls property, adjudicates disputes, and arranges major ceremonies for the worship of ancestors. When an immigrant and resident could trace descent from a common ancestor and belonged to the same patrilineage *(fang)*, the immigrant could certainly expect hospitable treatment. A major function of the *fang* is to disburse funds for welfare and education that are collected from members. Leaders of the *fang* and *tsu* are simply the oldest and richest men of the lineage and the clan.

The family *(chia)* is the smallest of the corporate kin groups. Its form varies. It may be a nuclear family composed of a couple and their unmarried children; a stem family consisting of a couple, unmarried children, and one married son with his wife and children; an extended family comprised of a couple, unmarried children, married sons with their wives and children, and sometimes sons of sons with their wives and children; or a joint family of brothers and their wives and children.

Members of the family work together or at least contribute to a common budget. The oldest capable members preside in matters of family business and are given great respect. Chinese women are more dominated by their men than are Malay women, but they still exercise control over household budgets and sometimes manage small businesses. Much greater dominance is apparent in a father's relationships with his children and in a mother-in-law's relationship with her son's wife. Whereas a Malay woman prays that her first child will be a girl so that she will gain a helper and successor to her responsibilities as manager of the household, a Chinese woman prays for sons so that she will have daughters-in-law to dominate. Sons are very important to the Chinese. They will adopt a male child or even a daughter's husband rather than allow a patriline to end. Daughters are much less important. In the past, very poor families sold their daughters; now they put them up for adoption. Malay couples, only some of whom have had no children or no daughers and who admire the pale skin of Chinese babies, adopt them.

Marriages and funerals are the most celebrated life crises. Traditional marriage ceremonies consist of little more than the bride arriving at her future home and the groom honoring his guests and receiving their gifts. But marriage breakfasts are the most extravagant of all Chinese feasts. Funerals have lesser feasts but more elaborate ceremonies. Indeed, funerals represent the core of Chinese ritual symbolism in much the same way and to the same extent that marriages represent Malay ritual symbolism. The greatest shame is to be unable to give one's parents expensive funerals. One of the most common and important functions of associations is to help members meet funeral expenses. Some associations, the prototype of rotating credit societies, have no other purpose. Each member collects shares from other members when one of his parents dies, and he pays a share when the parent of another member dies.

A death is reported immediately to the deities of the local temple, and wailing begins. Taoist and Buddhist monks begin chanting prayers for the dead. Music rends the air throughout the day. Firecrackers frighten away malignant spirits and excite the interest of small boys. Mourners within five degrees of relationship (wu fu) wear white garments to show their grief. A day or two of feasting precedes burial. Sometimes the deceased lies in state in his place of business where the feast is held. The coffin and its supporting structure are huge. Commonly, the coffin is a hollowed and ornately carved log. Sixteen bearers raise the coffin into the van for the funeral parade. Loud gongs and music attract spectators who view the portrait of the deceased and his richly decorated coffin and perhaps share in a distribution of money, and they appreciate the deceased's importance and wealth. Burial is an anticlimax.

In Chinese society, religion very obviously supports the social order. Confucianism, with its doctrine of filial piety, is an important basis of social organization and together with ancestor worship it forms a base line of belief even for those who subscribe to other religions. Many Chinese are simultaneously Taoists and Mahayana Buddhists. Unlike the temples of Hindus and of Theravada Buddhists or the mosques of Muslims, their temples may be entered without removing footwear. The temples have few monks or none at all. Very few men become monks, and those who do tend to remain monks all their lives. They live entirely on the income of their temples, which is derived from rentals of temple property and offerings made in return for specific spiritual services. Some monks earn offerings by dispensing magical remedies and prognostications.

Not all Chinese temples are Buddhist or even temples. Some are the headquarters of occupational or dialect associations, which also house small shrines for patron deities. Others are "halls of virtue," which house charitable associations. Some temples are Taoist. And others are mixed temples in which Buddhist and Taoist deities are worshipped.

The most popular Mahayana Buddhist deities are the Goddess of Mercy *(Kwan Yin)* and the God of War *(Kwan Ti)*. Both were very popular in China. In Southeast Asia, the God of War has also become the tutelary deity of business enterprise and of literature. Moreover, local heroes *(shen, fu,* and *yao)* have become important deities. The most popular are Toh Peh Kong (pioneer spirit) and Sam Po Tai Shan (Admiral Cheng Ho of the Ming dynasty who helped Melaka in its struggle with Sukhothai). Both help those who are enterprising and adventurous. Other spirits include Shui Hsin Lao Yeh who protects joss-stick makers, Chiao Sheng Lao Yeh who looks after carpenters, and the Kew Ong Yeah Beoh (nine sibling spirits) who cure tin miners of their illnesses.

Traditional conceptions of illness and medical treatment have survived their transplantation to Southeast Asia. The Yin-Yang theory of health, an elaborate pharmacology, and acupuncture have flourished. Spirit mediumship as a curing technique has become more important than it was in China, and it has absorbed some of the content and concepts of Malay medicine concerning sorcery. Sometimes Chinese seek treatment from Malay practitioners, and sometimes Chinese practitioners treat Malay patients.

Malaysian Chinese face certain long-term problems. Their interest in politics is threatening to Malays. Their storied wealth is envied, but the vast majority of Malaysian Chinese are poor. Cultural chauvinists, they are a minority in a society dominated by

Malays who are equally chauvinistic. Only in Singapore are South-east Asian Chinese masters of their own fate. But the very existence of Singapore casts a shadow on the loyalty of Malaysian Chinese.

Good relations between Chinese and Malays are necessary for political stability in Malaysia. On a person-to-person basis, they usually get along well together. Blood has not been shed by friends or even close acquaintances but by strangers in communal riots. Ultracommunalism has been as much a phenomenon of social class as of ethnic identity. Poor and relatively powerless Malays have accepted political domination by elite Malay politicians but have objected to economic domination by elite Chinese business-men. Malaysia's first leader, Tengku Abdul Rahman, seemed to have resolved the problem through an alliance of Chinese and Malay elites until the elections and subsequent communal riots of 1969 proved otherwise. The problem, dormant between elections, continues.

INDIANS

Immigration of large numbers of Indians did not begin until the beginning of the twentieth century, when commercial rubber plantations were being established in the west coast states of West Malaysia.[10] They now comprise about nine percent of the total population, and the majority are southern Indians (Tamils, Telegus, Chetis, and Malayalis) who work as laborers on rubber, palm olive, and coconut estates. A few are Sinhalese from Sri Lanka or northern Indians from the Punjab. Northern Indians usually reside in towns or cities. The Indians of Malaysia are much more heterogeneous than the Chinese or the Malays.

The houses of Indians are not especially distinctive. Many plantation workers live in "coolie lines," rows of barracks that are divided into rooms for each family. Some are built on stilts with cooking areas underneath. Others are built on the ground with cooking areas in the back. A few plantations provide a separate house for each family. The communities of some estates bear a superficial resemblance to small Indian villages that have their own Hindu temples and primary schools. Such communities commonly have a large percentage of recent immigrants. In the cities, some itinerant entrepreneurs who sell goods on the five-foot-ways (porticos formed by shophouses and business buildings that overhang the sidewalks) spend their sleeping hours on the five-foot-ways, too. One or several residential areas of a town or city are likely to be primarily Indian even though Indians tend to be less exclusive than Chinese or Malays. Common features of urban Indian communities include a Hindu temple and a toddy shop. Toddy is a yeasty and fruity beer that is the fermented sap of the flower stalk of a coconut or nipah palm. Toddy shops are a sort of Tamil version of English pubs where men and old women gather for a relaxing drink, talk, and argument.

Tamils are the most numerous and ubiquitous of the various kinds of Indians. They are the most numerous among agricultural laborers, and most of the Indian cloth merchants, news venders, shopkeepers, moneylenders, and small restaurant owners are Tamils, too. Some of those who live in urban areas are common laborers, railway workers, and clerks. Others are teachers, lawyers, and doctors. Telegus are the next most numerous among agricultural laborers. They seem to be very concerned with preserving their language and culture, having formed voluntary associations for that purpose. Most Chetis are moneylenders. Malayalis work as clerks on estates or in urban offices. Northern Indians are very few in number and most of them live and work in urban places. They favor professional careers and careers as policemen or railway workers.

Caste distinctions are practically unknown among Malaysian Indians. One reason for this is that so many have lower-caste origins. Also, immigration disrupted the composition of local caste groups *(jati)*. Moreover, many are not Hindu but Muslim, Roman Catholic, Methodist, or Sikh. Tamils, Telegus, and Malayalis have even intermarried to some extent. Northern Indians have tended to be aloof vis-à-vis southern Indians. Muslim Tamils are well integrated into Malaysian society. Malays accept them because they are coreligionist and because of the strong historical relationships between Tamil and Malay kingdoms. Many Tamils have married into urban Malay families, especially in Penang.

Indians dominate the trade union movement in Malaysia despite several disadvantages. They did not form unions until the 1930s, several decades after the Chinese began, and Indian leaders of the trade union movement were detained by the British after World War II for collaborating with the Japanese. Unions are important to Indians as a means of improving political as well as economic conditions. More than seventy-five percent of Malaysian Indians belong to unions, and many national leaders of the union movement are Indian.

Indian businessmen have organized chambers of commerce that have some of the same economic functions as the dialect associations of the Chinese. Business loans and credit, supplies of retail goods, and pricing policies are arranged within the context of the chamber of commerce. Chambers of commerce are politically active, too. Most members are long-term Malaysian residents or even second- and third-generation Malaysians, and most of them are middle or upper class. Like the members of unions, most of whom are poor, members of chambers of commerce have a strong

interest in consolidating their community politically and in acting
as a pressure group for Indian interests vis-à-vis Malays and Chinese.

Malaysian Indians are both more and less concerned than Malays and Chinese about language and education. Malays speak mutually intelligible dialects that are very similar to the national language (Bahasa Kebangsaan or Bahasa Malaysia); Chinese who speak different languages can communicate through the common ideographic system of writing, by speaking the national language of China (Kuo-yu or Mandarin), or by speaking the lingua franca of southern China (Cantonese); and Indians with different native languages can usually speak Tamil. But Tamil is much less a lingua franca among Indians than Kuo-yu or Cantonese is among Chinese. Its status as a common language of Malaysian Indians reflects little more than the numerical predominance of its speakers. Transient agricultural laborers who spoke another language pretty much ignored the task of learning Tamil. Upwardly mobile urban residents concentrated on learning English because of its association with higher educational opportunities, government jobs, and professional occupations. Some of the Tamils themselves and some other rural Indians who are long-term residents of Malaysia have been the only supporters of Tamil language as a medium of instruction in schools. Such schools were established at the elementary level on agricultural estates, but they lead nowhere. Secondary schools and universities are taught only in the medium of Bahasa Malaysia (Malay), Kuo-yu (Mandarin), or English. Malaysian Indians have traditionally followed the English route to higher education and have thereby enjoyed the advantages of fluency in the most extensive world language. Some Chinese have followed the English medium, too, but many others were diverted into the Kuo-yu medium. Malays seeking high education seem to be abandoning the cosmopolitan advantages of English and turning more to ease of education in Bahasa Malaysia. Chinese and Indians have been pressured to abandon English in favor of Bahasa Malaysia, too.

Language hardly unites Malaysian Indians. Religion does not completely unite them either. But it is not divisive. Hindus, Muslims, Roman Catholics and Methodists mix together easily in labor unions and chambers of commerce. A majority are Hindus, and those who are not have some social and cognitive orientations that derive from Hinduism.

Brahman priests tend the temples of urban communities and agricultural estates. They perform all of the rituals. Members of the community observe and absorb the spiritual power generated by the deity. Temples are not houses of worship, but abodes of gods. Mere humans enter barefoot and with great decorum. Their requests and offerings pass through intermediaries, the Brahman priests. Vishnu, Siva, or Kali usually serves as patron deity of the temple and of its community. A deity that fails may be replaced by another. Transient individuals change their loyalty from one god to another, conforming to the loyalty of the community in which they are residing. Brahmans are very few in number, and as in the case of Chinese Buddhist monks, they are not leaders in the everyday affairs of their communities. Indeed, their influence is less. The gods they attend have become less socially relevant.

The direct interrelationship of religion and social organization has been broken. Castes no longer exist. All that remain are attitudes that weakly reflect that interrelationship—the importance of large and closely knit families and the necessity of tolerating social and cultural differences of other groups while conforming to the customs of one's own community. Gone are ritual observances for place spirits of family households and for patron deities of localized castes (jati). Gone is the intricate system of ritual, social, and economic reciprocity between local groups of Hindus. Most Malaysian Hindus have the same economic functions, belong to the same social level, and observe the same rituals. They are laborers in agricultural industries. Theirs is just a segment, not even a traditional economic segment, of a system that requires many interlocking segments of different kinds.

The Hinduism of modern Malaysian Indians is not easily appreciated by Malays or Chinese although both have cosmological notions that owe much to Hinduism of an earlier time. Asked which of the Hindu ceremonies is most interesting, Malays and Chinese reply that it is the celebration of the Birthday of Lord Subramaniam (Thaipusam) in which penitent devotees carry elaborate burdens (kavadi) that are secured to their bodies with skewers driven into the flesh. The kavadi bearers, dancing frantically and whirling crazily, accompany a highly decorated silver chariot that bears an effigy of the Lord Subramaniam (Skanda, son of Siva) in procession through the community to a large temple. Lord Subramaniam is an agricultural deity. Waterfall Temple in Penang, Batu Caves near Kuala Lumpur, and Gajah Berang in Melaka are the most important sites of this annual ceremony. Many Chinese and Malays, as well as Indians, travel miles to see it.

Chinese and Malays are fascinated with the open display of masochism. They have their own masochistic rites, but they are displays of mystical power by magicians rather than purifying displays of devotion. Malays, particularly, tend to interpret Thaipusam by their own lights and see it as a demonstration of mystical power.

Malays and Chinese sometimes seek help from Indian spirit mediums. Indians, of course, sometimes are treated by Malay or Chinese practitioners, too. In general the ritual routines of Malay,

Chinese, and Indian spirit mediums are similar. Only the details differ.

The medical systems of Indians, like those of Malays and Chinese, include much more than psychiatric exorcisms. The major systems of Indian medicine that are practiced in Malaysia—Ayurvedic, Siddha, and Unami—are homeopathic. All practitioners have received their training in India, Pakistan, or Sri Lanka. The usual course lasts three years. One must study another two years in order to qualify as a surgeon. Surgery is not very important in these systems, however. Herbal remedies and diets are very important modes of curing. Homeopathy owes much to traditional Arabic systems and seems vaguely familiar to Westerners. It reminds them of the medical systems of nineteenth-century Europeans although that is perhaps an unfair comparison.

Malaysian Indians are very much aware of the brilliance of Indian civilizations. They are as proud as the other foreign Asians, the Chinese. But they comprise such a small segment of the total population and command so little economic power that even they recognize their impotence as a communalistic force. At best, they can side with either the Malays or the Chinese to give one or the other a clear majority.

IBANS (SEA DAYAKS)

The Ibans are the largest ethnic group in East Malaysia.[11] They are primarily slash-and-burn horticulturists and they control about two-thirds (3,000 square miles) of the arable land (4,000–5,000 square miles) in Sarawak where they comprise about one-third of the total population (1,200,000). Originally from the Kapuas area of Kalimantan (Indonesian Borneo), the Iban had migrated into the Rajang area of the Second Division of Sarawak several centuries ago. During the last century, they have migrated to all parts of Sarawak but have remained linguistically and culturally homogeneous.

Recently, some Ibans have become cultivators of wet rice and rubber. And even in the past, they engaged in riverine and coastal trade (whence the name of "Sea Dayaks," misapplied to them by early European traders). But originally and still to a great extent, Ibans cultivate dry rice. Each family (bilek) needs about one hundred acres, only about five of which are cultivated each year and allowed to fallow for twenty years.

Each year, full climax forest is cut and allowed to dry. Before the northeast monsoon brings rain, the dried branches and bushes are set afire. Men poke holes with dibble sticks in the ash-covered soil, and women follow, planting the seeds. It rains, the seeds sprout, and the women pull weeds and protect the rice from vermin. In the meanwhile, men go down the rivers to the coast to trade or to find temporary employment. In the old days (until the end of World War II), the men often whiled away their free time hunting heads. The men return for the harvest.

Typically, Ibans live in raised longhouses *(rumah)* that are built of bamboo. A verandah runs the full length of the house, connecting the line of separate rooms, each of which houses a family *(bilek)*. The *bilek* usually consists of a couple and their unmarried children. Sometimes it consists of two siblings, their spouses, and children or an elderly couple or person with a married child and grandchildren. All children of a *bilek*, whether natural or adopted, have equal rights of inheritance of household goods and land. But usually all move out when they marry, except one. Those who move out gain rights in the *bileks* of their spouses, or they found new *bileks*. If two siblings remain in their natal *bilek* after both are married, it often happens that one will eventually move out after having been compensated for his loss. Females are as likely to inherit as males, and the last born of a sibling set is as likely to inherit as the first born.

The *bilek* is the primary social and economic unit in Iban society. *Bileks* of the same longhouse are usually related consanguineally and affinally, but each *bilek* is responsible for working its own land and its members are free to leave the longhouse if they choose. Help given by another *bilek* in the longhouse is carefully reciprocated. A new longhouse is founded by agreement among six or more *bileks* who wish to pioneer new areas. The new longhouse is in no way subordinate to old longhouses from which it drew its *bileks*. Each longhouse has a leader *(tuai rumah)*. Leaders have little actual authority. They achieve their positions as respected and wealthy men who own many bronze gongs, Chinese jars, and much land. Although respected, they have little authority and must lead by example and advice. A *penghulu* is the leader of several related longhouses, and the *temenggong* is the paramount leader.

Leaders have some religious duties. They must see that ceremonies are held properly and that taboos are observed. There are several hundred deities, each of which has a particular form and particular interests. As occasion demands, specialists built a shrine on the verandah of the longhouse. Each relevant deity is called by magical word formulas that describe its journey to the shrine. When all of the necessary deities have been called, they are propitiated and given a sacrificial meal. Such rituals may be held for the benefit of a single individual, a *bilek*, or the longhouse. Such a ritual is necessary when a new longhouse is founded.

Spirit mediums are important among the Iban, too. Most of them are women. They lead annual ceremonies that attract evil spirits from the longhouse and send them downriver on a model raft loaded with food for spirits. Spirit mediums also recover spiritual energy for people who have lost it and fallen ill. And they exorcize evil spirits that cause illnesses.

The Iban have a prominence in the affairs of Malaysia that springs directly from the ideals of parliamentary democracy and the realities of communal politics. Four hundred thousand people in a state (Sarawak) that has a population of 1,200,000 ought to be represented. But they form no significant part of the population of any other state. To which of the major communal blocks do they belong? Culturally, they are more like the Malays than the foreign Asians. However, they are non-Muslims and to some extent, thereby, natural allies of the Chinese and Indians who oppose further Islamization of Malaysia. Ibans are not especially sophisticated politically so their political choices are necessarily made by a very few of their leaders. That is a basis for political intrigue. The problem is all the more vexing because many Malays who originally acquiesced to federation with Sarawak assumed that the *bumiputras* were Muslim or that they were under the political control of coastal Malays (who comprise only about twenty percent of the population). Moreover, the Chinese of Sarawak are about as numerous as Ibans, are somewhat more experienced politically, and are economically much more powerful.

KADAZANS (IDAANS, OR DUSUNS)

Kadazans comprise the largest ethnic group in Sabah (240,000 of 600,000 total population).[12] They are better known in anthropological literature as "Dusun," which derives from a mildly pejorative term, *orang dusun* ("orchard people," connoting "yokels"), applied to them by Malays. "Kadazan" is now used to refer to themselves, but it once referred to only one subtribe. Other subtribes, each having a separate dialect, include Kivijan, Mangbok, and Minobok. Their place of origin is not as precisely known as that of the Iban, but they may have migrated to northern Borneo from the Malay Peninsula centuries ago. Now, they inhabit the west coast of Sabah and the interior plains.

Kadazans are much more heterogeneous culturally than Ibans. Differences of dialect were mentioned above. Other kinds of differences abound. For example, coastal and lowland people live in single-family houses like those of the Malays, but some inland and upland people have longhouses like the Ibans. Kadazans of the uplands inland areas are slash-and-burn horticulturists. Those of the coast and lowlands have orchards of rubber trees and are wet-rice farmers. Among wet-rice farmers, a newly married couple usually resides with the woman's family, while among slash-and-burn horticulturists, the couple usually resides with the man's family.

Probably, the latter differences result from the relative importance of cooperative labor among women in wet-rice farming and among men in slash-and-burn horticulture.

There is a tendency toward formation of corporate local groups among Kadazans that is lacking among other indigenous peoples of East Malaysia. Indications of this include the strongly developed patterns of marital residence already mentioned and the extension of exogamy beyond fifth cousins. Other indigenous people in East Malaysia, as well as Malays and Tamils of West Malaysia, extend exogamy only to first or second cousins and seem to prefer marriages between distant kin rather than between foreigners. Among Kadazans, as among Ibans, leaders do not inherit their positions, and they have little authority.

Kadazan settlements are often not near rivers or other means of easy transportation, but they are not isolated. Kadazans are very interested in markets. They have special market days and places for trade with coastal Malays, and they also have inland markets.

The God of the Kadazan, with his wife, is creator of the seven heavens, numerous minor deities, earth, and human beings. He has little interest in earthly affairs and leaves details in the control of his descendants who are spirit familiars of female mediums. The mediums oversee communal ceremonies and conduct agricultural and curing rites. They train others to become ceremonial specialists and curers. Each village has several mediums who have different familiar spirits. Familiar spirits give advice for controlling bad spirits, which steal spiritual energy and cause illnesses. The rice spirit and the water spirit are held in great respect and are the objects of special ceremonies.

Kadazans have about the same potentials and problems as Ibans. Chinese (170,000) comprise a slightly smaller proportion of the population of Sabah than of Sarawak. But their economic and political powers are as great as in Sarawak. Malays are very few in number and, except through extension of federal power from Kuala Lumpur, would have hardly any political power. Kadazans waver toward alignment with non-Muslim Chinese for some purposes and toward alignment with culturally more similar Malays for other purposes.

OTHER INDIGENOUS PEOPLES OF EAST MALAYSIA

Land Dayak, Bajau, Melanau, and Murut populations are each less numerous and less important economically and politically than either Iban or the Kadazan. Land Dayaks comprise about eight percent and Melanaus about seven percent of the total population of Sarawak. Bajaus constitute about ten percent and Muruts about four and a half percent of the total population of Sabah.

Land Dayaks are slash-and-burn horticulturists like their enemies, the Iban, who through headhunting and territorial expansion drove them into inland areas of the First Division.[13] Culturally, they are very similar to the Iban but are more heterogeneous. The name "Land Dayak" has been applied to them by Europeans. They identify themselves by the name of their village or locality.

Land Dayaks live in longhouses like the Ibans, but their villages differ by the addition of a central headhouse. It is circular, has a conical roof, and it is raised higher on its stilts than the longhouses. Primarily, the headhouse is a dormitory for unmarried males. Like the sleeping lofts for unmarried females that are over the verandah of an Iban longhouse, the Land Dayak headhouse is supposed to keep unmarried people of the opposite sex from sleeping together. The headhouse also serves as a guesthouse and as a museum for trophies.

Land Dayaks' horticulture closely resembles that of the Iban. However, the Land Dayak have less need for acquiring virgin land because their farming techniques are more sophisticated. Although a newly cleared piece of land is used only one year for dry-rice production, it is planted in other crops such as manioc, maize, and sugar cane the following year or two and perhaps in quick maturing fruit trees as the natural flora evolves towards full climax. This procedure helps to keep elephant grass (lalang) and bamboo from capturing the fields cleared by slash-and-burn techniques (ladang). Once lalang or bamboo has taken over a field, it will not return to the forest stage that is the necessary starting point for new fields.

Land Dayaks also differ from the Iban in religion. Many have become Christians, of course, but even the traditional religion differs. Land Dayaks worship ancestral spirits. Some of these spirits are actual ancestors, others are renown persons of yesteryear who were respected as great farmers, priests, or leaders. The specialists who invoke protective spirits on behalf of the village are men. They gain their position as priests of the ancestral cult by consanguineal or affinal inheritance. Other men and women are herbalists or spirit mediums who pull sickness out of or return spiritual energy to the bodies of the ill. The best of these practitioners are called manang, and their techniques are very similar to those of the Malay bomoh.

Melanaus

Melanaus are coastal people who resemble Malays both physically and culturally. They wear Malay dress, live in Malay-type houses and villages, and many of them are Muslim. A few are Roman Catholics, and a few others are traditionalists. Melanaus are farmers who grow wet rice and rubber trees. They are also the major producers of sago palm flour, which ranks third among Sarawak's agricultural exports, after rubber and rice.

Many Muslim Melanaus regard themselves as Malays. Others who are non-Muslim regard themselves as Borneans. All are much more a part of the modern Malay world than other indigenous communities of East Malaysia, except perhaps the Bajaus.

Bajaus (Samah)

The Bajaus of Sabah were formerly nomadic seafarers. Related groups include the Badjo of the coasts of Sumbawa, Flores, Sulawesi (Celebes), and Halmahera in Indonesia; the Illanun and Moro of the Sulu archipelago in the Philippines; the Orang Laut of Singapore and the west coast of West Malaysia; and the Moken of the Mergui archipelago of southern Burma. These related groups are all sea nomads who fish, trade, and smuggle, and occasionally hunt and gather, on islands and in coastal areas. They speak many different dialects, but all are closely related to Malay, and they live in communities of 10 to 40 boats, each of which houses a nuclear family. The oldest and best navigator is the leader of the boat group. There is a hierarchy of titled chiefs and officals. Spirit mediums direct ceremonies and treat the sick.

Very few of the Bajaus of Sabah are now sea nomads. Most have settled in the Kota Belud region of Sabah. A few are boat people, others are fishermen, but they live in villages on the shore. Many grow wet rice or tend cattle. Their skill at horse riding has made them famous in Malaysia. Most of them are Muslims.

Muruts

The Murut are slash-and-burn horticulturists who cultivate dry rice and manioc and supplement their diet with jungle foods and game. Their dialects are mutually intelligible with those of the Kadazans whom they resemble physically. They live in the high inland areas of Sabah and still use spears and blowpipes to hunt wild pig. Muruts are organized in patrilocal bands headed by an experienced man. Members of the local group work together in tasks that require a major effort such as clearing fields. In the past, they all lived in longhouses. Many now live in individual family houses.

Other, even smaller, tribal groups of East Malaysia include the Kayan, Kajang, Kenyah, Kelabit, Penan, and Punan.

The position of all of the small indigenous minorities depends a great deal on programs of the federal government to protect and aid them by preserving the traditional world for some and by helping others to move into new worlds.

Indigenous peoples other than Malays comprise a very small percentage (50,000–60,000 of almost 12,000,000, or less than one percent) of the total population of West Malaysia.[14] They are politically and economically much less significant than the indigenous peoples of East Malaysia. Moreover, they are linguistically and culturally heterogeneous. The classical categories are Senoi (Sakai), Jakun, and Semang.

Senoi (Sakai)

Senoi are the most numerous of the three, accounting for about half of the total. They have many localized names for themselves, and other peoples have given them different names. They include the Semai of northwestern Pahang and southern Perak, the Temiar (Temer, Seroq, and Ple) of northern Perak and southern Kelantan, the Jah Hut and Che Wong (Beri Chuba and Siwang) of eastern Selangor and western Pahang, and the Mah Meri (Besisi) of the Selangor coast. Malays refer to them as *orang bukit* ("hill people"), *orang darat* ("people of the land"), *orang asli* ("aborigine"), or *sakai* (a pejorative term, perhaps from Thai language, that means "slave") but do not distinguish them from Jakun or Semang.

Most Senoi inhabit the foothills and mountains of the Main Range of the lower Malay Peninsula. Their settlements and fields are semipermanent. Temiar communities consist of a single longhouse, with a central ceremonial space and family compartments on either side. Other Senoi communities consist of a dozen or so individual family houses that are small and a single large longhouse for ceremonies and lounging. Houses are built on stilts. Cooking hearths are inside rather than outside the houses.

A few Senoi, Mah Meri and Jah Hut, are becoming wet-rice farmers but most are slash-and-burn horticulturists. Their techniques are sophisticated. They clear new fields during the dry season with large machetes rather than with the axes or adzes that are used in East Malaysia. After trees and bushes are cut, the debris is chopped into small pieces. Large trees are allowed to remain or may be topped. Just before the heavy rains begin, they set fire to the field, and after it has cooled, they plant it, using dibble sticks. Traditionally, the first crop was millet. In the nineteenth century, it was replaced to a large extent by maize. Since the beginning of the twentieth century, dry rice has become more and more important and has largely replaced maize as a first crop in the southern and western areas. Fruit trees such as durian may be planted in good places in the field when the first crop is planted. After an initial crop of rice or maize, manioc will be planted as the staple. Within a year or two, bananas will replace the manioc. Greens, pumpkins, sweet potatoes, yams, taro, onions, and chili pepper are sometimes planted with other crops. Harvesting takes place the year around in fields of different age. A field may last as long as eight years. When the forest begins to reclaim it, durian or other fruit trees that were planted when the field was first opened may begin to bear.

Senoi are also hunters and gatherers. They catch fish in mountain brooks with weirs, basket traps, spears, and hooks, and for feasts they stupefy pools of fish with the pounded root of the tuba plant. Young animals that are captured alive, such as pig-tailed macques, gibbons, otters, and pigs, are kept as pets. Dogs and chickens are the usual domesticated animals. Many Senoi still use blowpipes with poisoned darts to hunt game such as monkeys, civets, bamboo rats, and porcupines. The poison is made with sap that is tapped from the ipoh tree. It is boiled and mixed with other ingredients and applied to the tip of the dart. Shotguns are used when available, but Malay officials confiscate them if they are used for hunting meat that is sold commercially. Collected foods include jungle fruit, bamboo shoots, mushrooms and other fungi (which are classified as flesh in Senoi languages), snails, and turtles. Senoi also collect forest products, such as rattan, petai (tree beans), camphor, and resin, for sale to Malay and Chinese traders.

People who live in the same valley are usually related. Marriages are between members of groups that live near each other. The rule of exogamy extends to first or second cousins, varying from group to group. In some groups, a simple ceremony marks the beginning of marriage. In others, sexual relationships simply mature into more or less permanent social and economic arrangements that constitute marriage. Taking the soul of the rice at harvest time, curing sick persons, and burying the dead are all more important ceremonial occasions than marriage.

Taking the soul of the rice is the only annual ceremony, and it is like the Malay ceremony. Probably it is viewed simply as a part of the technology of rice growing. Spirit mediums preside over all ceremonies, most of which are healing seances in which the spirits of disease are removed from the patient. Formerly, it is said, the Senoi had to abandon their villages after a death, and for this reason they would carry a dying person out into the jungle and place him in a small hut with a supply of food and water. Neither custom is observed now. Spirit mediums are often buried in hollow trees or wrapped in a bundle and placed in the branches of a large tree. Ordinary persons are buried in the ground, the foot of the grave being marked for a time by a small spirit house into which offerings of flowers may be placed. A large feast is held the sixth day after burial, and mourning continues until a medium's familiar announces an end to it. A six-night ceremony and feast ensue.

Leadership is not strongly developed in Senoi society. There are no corporate kin groups. A person's belongings are inherited by the spouse, siblings, and children according to their own agreement. A half dozen elders in a group may each claim a title or rank, but the titles are devoid of structural significance. There is usually one man in each local group who deals with foreigners, and he is, in effect, the headman.

Jakun (Aboriginal Malays)

The Jakun differ from the Senoi linguistically. Senoi speak languages that are very closely related to Mon-Khmer languages, and Jakun speak dialects of Malay language. In popular accounts, they are supposed to differ physically, too. The Senoi is supposed to be a wavy-haired Veddoid, and the Jakun is supposed to be a straight-haired Proto-Malay. But language and race are not so neatly organized in Senoi and Jakun villages. Perhaps some groups of Senoi have adopted Jakun dialects as their native language and vice versa. And, of course, intermarriage has occurred.

Like the Senoi, the Jakun have many local names. They include the Belandas (Biduanda) of eastern Selangor and Negri Sembilan, the Temuan (Mentera) of central Selangor and Negri Sembilan, the Semelai of western Pahang and northern Johore, the Temok of southern Pahang, the Jakun of Johore, and the Kanak of southeastern Johore. Except that these groups are not seafarers, they closely resemble the Moken, Orang Laut, and Bajau, culturally and linguistically. Also, they are culturally similar to the western and southern Senoi. The Jakun live in small single family houses built on low stilts. Typically, the house timbers are hardwood, the floor is bamboo, the walls are split and flattened bamboo that is woven, the gabled roof is of atap, and the hearth is inside the house. Jakun houses are like the smaller Senoi houses. A village consists of a half dozen or more houses.

Jakun usually inhabit lowland areas that have not been preempted by Malays and foothill areas that are not occupied by Senoi. In the foothills, they use slash-and-burn farming techniques, and in the lowlands, they grow wet rice. Many Jakun have small orchards of rubber trees and durian fruit. They fish and hunt, using the same techniques as the Senoi. In some areas, most of their economy is based on selling jungle products to Malay and Chinese traders. Their lands in areas that are transitional between the foothills of the Main Range and the coastal lowland often have rich alluvial deposits of tin ore. They pan the ore from the banks of streams and sell it to Chinese traders. Sometimes they work as laborers on agricultural estates, tapping rubber or cutting palm olives.

Many of the Jakun and lowland Senoi moved into towns during the Emergency. A few of them liked town life, converted to Islam, and became Malays. But most of them returned to their own areas when the Emergency was over, even though (or perhaps because) some of them had been living in towns for a decade. In any case, they are not strangers to town life. Most of their settlements are within walking or bicycling distance of small towns, and they visit the towns to sell jungle produce, to enjoy visiting in the coffee shops, and to purchase goods.

The kinship system is cognate like that of the Senoi. Each village has a headman (batin) who inherited his position either from his father, his older brother, his mother's father or his father-in-law. If others besides the headman have some claim to the position by right of inheritance, they may claim other positions such as executive officer or herald. Disputes over rights to headmanship are common and lead to establishment of new communities that may be more or less subordinate. Some leaders, as a result of this process of community fission, claim to be paramount leaders over several villages.

Jakun beliefs are similar to those of western and southern Senoi and to Malay beliefs that are not Islamic. Some of the Hindu-Buddhist elements of Malay ceremonies appear in Jakun ceremonies, too. Weddings, for example, are remarkably similar to the non-Islamic portions of Malay weddings. The same theme —coronation of a Hindu king and queen—is very apparent. Its meaning—acquisition of spiritual energy (semangat)—is the same. Jakun, like Malays, are concerned about malignant influences (badi) that appear during transitions and ghosts or spirits (hantu) that can cause destruction or illness if annoyed. There are fewer accusations of sorcery among Jakuns than among Malays, but Malays consider Jakuns to be the most powerful sorcerers.

Medicinemen are highly regarded by Jakuns. They are mediators between spirits and human beings who calm the angry thunder of storms, neutralize the deadly effects of yellow sunsets, exorcize the spirits of illness, and reverse the ebb of spiritual energy. Medicinemen are expert practitioners of herbal medicine, too. Jakun herbal medicine is highly developed and includes the use of more than a hundred plant species.

Semang (Negrito)

The Semang are culturally similar to the eastern Senoi. They speak closely related languages. Possibly, a different Semang language has been submerged through linguistic acculturation to Senoi, which is closely related to Mon-Khmer. Semang are typically less than five feet tall with deeply curled to kinky hair and dark skin. Mendi, Meni, Menik, and Monik are the names they use to refer to themselves. Others have used other names that are better known, and there are different local names. The geographical distribution of dialect communities is as follows: the Tonga or Mos (Chong) of southern Thailand; the Kensiu of southern Thailand and northeastern Kedah; the Kintak of southern Thailand, southern Kedah, and northern Perak; the Jehai of southern Thailand, northeastern Perak, and western Kelantan; the Lanoh of northern Perak; the Menrik of southeastern Kelantan; and the Batek (Batok, Kleb, Tomo, Nogn) of northern Pahang.

The Semang comprise three or four thousand nomadic gatherers and hunters who inhabit the high foothills of the Main Range. Only one group, the Jehai, lives in the mountains. Their staple foods are roots, jungle fruits, fungi, bamboo shoots, and larvae that are gathered by women. Men fish and hunt in the same fashion as the Senoi, and they gather jungle produce for sale to Malay traders. Food is cooked by stuffing it into bamboo tubes, which are leaned over the hearth. Senoi, Jakun, and Malays cook some of their food in the same manner.

The typical Semang band consists of three to twelve families. Its core members are brothers and their families or an old man and his married sons. Each nuclear family constructs its own shelter—a small wind screen shaped like an open-ended quonset hut that has the ground as its floor and leaves for its roof. Sometimes these simple huts are ranged around a central fire; sometimes they are placed end to end. The incest taboo extends only to parent, children, and siblings. Marriage is by sister exchange or traditional reciprocal exchanges between bands. Inheritance of fruit trees and personal property is bilateral. The leader of a band is the oldest capable man. A medicine man *(hala)* is commonly an important leader.

Semang beliefs comprise very complex systems that vary from one group to another. There are dozens of anthropomorphic deities, and chief among them may be thunder *(karei)*. During thunder storms, Semang make small blood offerings to *karei*. Senoi and Jakun make similar offerings. Many Semang *hala* receive their training from Senoi medicinemen. It must be assumed that there are many similarities between Semang and Senoi beliefs. Semang medicinemen are spirit mediums and herbalists.

MALAYSIAN MICROCOSM

Many small towns in Selangor and Perak are microcosms of multiethnic society in Malaysia and other Southeast Asian countries. Such towns usually have a main street several hundred feet long. Most have a police station and a school. Shophouses line both sides of the street. Most of the businesses are provision shops owned and operated by Chinese. Indian Muslims operate several of the eating shops, several others are Chinese, and there may be a Malay coffee shop. A tailor, Chinese or Malay, may have a shop in town. One of the Chinese businesses is a furniture store, and another is a hardware shop that sells new and used bicycles and repairs them. There may be a gasoline station. It may not have a pump. In that case, the gasoline is stored in closed tin containers.

A Malay *kampong* stretches along the road outside of town. Clusters of houses, rarely more than a mile from the road, peer out from behind clumps of fruit trees and coconut palms. Small irregularly shaped groves of rubber trees cover the rolling hills, and rice paddies occupy the flat and low places beside streams and irrigation ditches. A school and a mosque mark the midpoint of the Malay *kampong.*

A huge rubber estate, British-owned, stretches out along the road on the other side of town. Its coolie lines are near town so that it is an easy walk or bicycle ride for the Tamil laborers. An estate road leads towards the nearby hills. The rubber trees are in perfect rows, and the crowns of the trees join, blocking out the light and creating a huge cathedral of sorts.

Beyond the great grove of rubber trees, the estate road becomes a broad trail. It passes by the small farm of a Chinese vegetable and fruit gardener and into a small Chinese-owned estate. Chinese tappers ride along the trail on their bicycles, balancing equipment and tins of latex. The trail has become a footpath. A Jakun or Senoi village comes into view. Several fields at different stages of maturity and with different crops may be visible. Chinese and aborigines may be busy panning tin in the stream that runs through the village. And a Malay trader may be carrying a bundle of petai beans or rattan along the trail back into town.

REFERENCES

[1] I. T. Davies, "Malay—As Defined in the States Malay Reservation Enactments," *Intisari: The Research Quarterly of Malaysia 1,* no. 2 (1963): 26–28.

[2] J. M. Gullick, *Indigenous Political Systems of Western Malaya* (London: London School of Economics, 1958), p. 32. A serious need exists for studies of subethnicity among Malays.

[3] R. Provencher, "Comparisons of Social Interaction Styles: Urban and Rural Malay Culture," in T. Weaver and D. White, eds., *The Anthropology of Urban Environments,* The Society for Applied Anthropology Monograph Series No. 11, 1972.

[4] S. H. Ali, "Patterns of Rural Leadership in Malaya," *Journal of the Malayan Branch of the Royal Asiatic Society* 41 (1968): 95–145.

[5] M. G. Swift, *Malay Peasant Society in Jelebu* (London: Athlone Press, 1965), is the best source on Minangkabaus in the Malay Peninsula.

[6]T. M. Frazer, *Rusembilan: A Malay Village in Southern Thailand* (Ithaca, N.Y.: Cornell University Press, 1960); and R. Firth, *Housekeeping among Malay Peasants* (London: London School of Economics, 1943), are good references on Malay fishing villages.

[7]K. M. Endicott, *An Analysis of Malay Magic* (Oxford: Clarendon Press, 1970), is a good recent work on Malay magic.

[8]V. Purcell, *The Chinese in Southeast Asia* (London: Oxford University Press, 1951).

[9]L. Comber, *The Traditional Mysteries of Chinese Secret Societies in Malaya* (Singapore: Donald Moore, 1961).

[10]C. Kondapi, *Indians Overseas 1838–1949* (New Delhi: Indian Council of World Affairs, 1951).

[11]J. D. Freeman, *Report on the Iban* (London: Athlone, 1970); and chapter 5 of G. P. Murdock, ed., *Social Structure in Southeast Asia* (London: Tavistock, 1960).

[12]T. R. Williams, *The Dusun: A North Borneo Society* (New York: Holt, Rinehart & Winston, 1966). Past and recent traditions sometimes are confused.

[13]W. R. Geddes, *Nine Dayak Nights* (London: Oxford University Press, 1957).

[14]R. K. Dentan, *The Semai: A Nonviolent People of Malaya* (New York: Holt, Rinehart & Winston, 1968); and P. D. R. Williams-Hunt, *An Introduction to the Malayan Aborigines* (Kuala Lumpur: The Government Press, 1952).

SEVEN

TAI STATES

STATES, SUBSTATES, AND TRIBES

Thailand, Laos, and Shan State in Burma are all Tai states. There are Tai-speaking populations in southern China (Kwangsi, Kweichow, Kwantung, and southwestern Yunnan), Assam, North Vietnam, Cambodia, and the northern-most part of West Malaysia. Altogether, speakers of Tai languages number about fifty million of which forty million live in mainland Southeast Asia. They are the most numerous and, except for overseas Chinese and Malays, the most widespread of Southeast Asian peoples. In light of these facts, they are remarkably homogeneous physically, culturally, and linguistically. But there are differences that derive from influences of neighboring major peoples and from incomplete assimilation of subject peoples.

Thailand is now the principal Tai state, but before the thirteenth century, the center of Tai political power was in southern China where many Tai substates continued to exist until the 1920s when they began to be absorbed into the bureaucratic structures of China. Now, only the so-called Chinese Shan states of southwestern Yunnan continue as structural entities. Sukhothai, whence Thailand evolved, began as a small principality. Through assimilation of indigenous peoples, through expansion of the wet-rice lands of its own people, and through warfare with older states, it became the most powerful of Tai states. In the area that is now Laos, a similar Tai state evolved in similar ways and then was divided by its more powerful neighbors, Thailand and Vietnam. It became merely three Tai principalities which were reunited again, almost by chance, in the French colonial period. The Shan State comprises 33 Tai substates. It is a semiautonomous state in the Union of Burma that owes much of its existence to British colonialist scheming against the Burmese (see Chapter Eight, States of Burma).

Most Tais are lowland people—major peoples that form the core of states. However, some are not. There are Tai groups that live in the hills and practice slash-and-burn horticulture. Possibly, they are merely subject peoples who are not fully assimilated. Less likely, they are Tais who migrated into areas where wet-rice agriculture was not possible or where they partially assimilated to the ways of indigenous people. The overwhelming trend at present is for other people to become lowland Tais (that is, Thai, Lao, or Shan).

THE CENTRAL THAI STATE

Tai or *Thai* is an old indigenous term. "Siam" is mentioned in an early (1120 A.D.) inscription at Pagan, in Burma, and it was the European name for Thailand until after World War II, when European nations finally recognized the native term *Prathet Thai* or "Thailand." Siam is probably the old Chinese name for the country. Probably, the term was first encountered by the Portuguese and was passed on to other Europeans. In any case, the Thai have always called themselves "Thai" or "Tai." European scholars have used the terms "Siamese" and "Thai" variously to refer to all of the citizens of Thailand, the Buddhists of Thailand, or the Tais of central and southern Thailand. Here, the term "Siamese" or "Central Thai" refers specifically to the people of central and southern Thailand, and "Thai" is a broader term that includes, as well, the very closely allied Tai speakers in the Chiengmai area, the Korat Plateau, and the Malay Peninsula.

Central Thai (Siamese)

The Thai are the major people of Thailand.[1] Their thirty-two million comprise about eighty percent of the total population. They are an overwhelmingly rural people and include many that have been assimilated only recently or that have mixed with other people. For example, the Thai of the northern area around Chiengmai are a remnant population of a formerly autonomous Tai state, Lan Na, that was usually vassal to the Siamese but occasionally vassal to Laotians or Burmese. Sometimes referred to as Lannathai or Tai Yuan, these people of northern Thailand have many specific cultural traits in common with the Lu (Tai-speaking immigrants from southern Yunnan), with the Khun (of the Shan State in Burma), and with the Laotian Tai. However, the Tai Yuan are now almost completely assimilated. Tai-speaking people of the Khorat Plateau are an instance of Thai-Lao mixture with another people, mostly Khmers, the Pak Tai of the Malay Peninsula have mixed with Malays and Semang, and many urban Thai have Chinese ancestors and some Chinese customs. All of these variant types of Thai are not very different from Siamese peasants of the central plain, but they are under strong pressure to become more thoroughly assimilated—to speak the Central-Thai dialect, which is the national language, to conform to the Siamese version of Theravada Buddhism, and to focus their loyalty on Bangkok.

Thailand has a very low percentage of urban population (about fifteen percent compared to about forty-four percent in West Malaysia). Although the metropolitan area of Bangkok, the largest city of Southeast Asia, has a population of approximately three million, Chiengmai, the second largest town, has a population of less than one hundred thousand, and other provincial centers are much smaller. Some Thai nobles, officials, traders, artisans, and laborers live in the capital city and in provincial centers. Others live in suburban or nearby rural areas. In Bangkok, there is a special royal quarter in the center of the city that includes the palaces, government offices, and major temples. Some members of the nobility and high government officials reside there, but most of them reside in a special residential quarter across the river. Also across the river are some of the principal residential areas of Thai traders, artisans, and laborers. Formerly, they lived in rows of houses built on pontoons and stilts along the edges of canals (klong). In recent years, many canals have been filled and transformed into streets.

A commercial sector developed just outside the palace compound after Bangkok was founded in 1767. It grew rapidly after the middle of the nineteenth century, surpassing the royal compound in size. Almost all of the inhabitants of the commercial sector were Chinese, however. Then, during the 20 years following World War II, Bangkok absorbed surrounding villages and tripled its area from about fifty to one hundred fifty square kilometers. New areas are devoted largely to low-density housing for civil servants, merchants, and laborers, many of whom are Central Thai immigrants to the city. Still, the Chinese comprise about half of the population of Bangkok, and they dominate middle-status commercial occupations. Most Thai are laborers, artisans, and small-scale traders. They are predominant among the urban poor. But others have professional occupations or high governmental positions, and Central Thai are predominant among the urban elite.

The king held absolute power in old Siam. For several decades after the revolution in 1932, the monarchy was pushed into the background by various administrative and military leaders. But the monarchy remained a powerful political rallying point because of the deep respect and spiritual loyalty with which the Siamese regard their royal rulers. By the time that Marshal Sarit came to prominence in 1958, the king was mature and increasingly respected. Sarit publicly esteemed the king. Sarit's successor, General Thanom, publicly esteemed the king, too, and he asserted less autocratic power as premier, giving the king even greater prominence. Finally, the king emerged as an active influence in the October uprising of 1973. But this dramatic event involving the person of the king should not obscure the fact that other members of royalty, even beyond the family of the immediate ruler, are due great respect and sometimes hold important positions as clerics, scholars, and heads of enterprise. As the royal blood thins to beyond the fifth degree of relationship, it is royal no longer, but some of the benefits, such as capital, education, and opportunity for high government position, may linger.

The Buddhist clergy have a special position in Thai society because most adult males have been temporary novice monks under their tutelage and because everyone, even the king, makes obeisance to them. Abbots of monasteries, more than other local authorities, command respect and a following among Siamese peasants.

Respect is due the sacred, the powerful, the. wealthy, the talented, and the elderly. Thai expressions of respect, like those of Malays, are situationally determined and depend on such factors as the difference of rank (rather than different ranks) of social participants and the degree of familiarity of participants with each other and with their audience. Each person must strictly honor rules of courtesy that govern the expression of respect. Westerners misapprehend the function of this careful politeness, expecting that it symbolizes fixed rights and obligations of classes of people. European scholars who have tried to analyze Thai social structure as if it were merely a class system have failed to account for a large proportion of Thai social behavior.[2] Those who have assumed that the traditional Thai social system is a class system have suffered a distortion of perspective in which Thai social behavior seems overly individualistic and lacking in regularity, discipline, regimentation, binding filial piety, administrative regularity, and business ethics. A much less distorted and applicable generalization is that from the European perspective the Siamese appear to overconform while in the direct presence of others and that there is no certainty that conformity will be sustained once face-to-face contact has ended.[3] The major function of courtesy in Thai society is not to symbolize fixed rights and obligations that are part of a rigid social order, but rather to regulate emotional states of individuals whose spiritual equilibrium might be endangered by fear, humility, envy, anger, or contempt. Other major peoples of Southeast Asia have this so-called loosely structured kind of social system.

Members of the ruling elite in Bangkok and even the administrative officials who represent the various governmental departments down to the district level (amphoe) know and can perform Western modes of interaction vis-à-vis Westerners. They employ Thai modes of interaction vis-à-vis Thai peasants, but Western forms of bureaucratic structure have been added. In old Siam, most public works were accomplished by self-help, by corvée labor (a form of taxation), or by slaves. Now the district governments employ wage laborers to maintain irrigation works, highways, and public buildings. Government agencies affect the lives of ordinary Siamese peasants more than in the past by intervening in matters of law and order, education, health, and agricultural production. The same is true in other Southeast Asian countries.

Siamese are a rural people. Their villages range in size from several hundred to several thousand persons. Three types of villages are common: a ribbonlike arrangement of houses along the edges of roads and waterways; a cluster of houses in the midst of an orchard of fruit trees and coconut palms or in a wet-rice field; and a wide scattering of houses in orchards or rice fields. The scattered type of village is more usual in newly opened areas. Older villages are usually compact. Landless traders and laborers often inhabit ribbon-type villages. Whatever the type of settlement pattern, a temple marks the center of each village. Schools may be located near the temples or between the villages. Shops tend to be near temples or schools. And most villages have a large pond that provides water for household use during the dry season and supplies fish throughout the year.

The houses of reasonably affluent peasants are similar to those of Malays. They are rectangular houses built on pilings that have clapboard walls of mahogany or teak, floors of coconut-palm wood, and gabled roofs of galvanized tin, atap, or tile. The kitchen is usually a slightly separate structure with a shed roof that attaches to the back of the house. The floor of the kitchen is usually lower than the floor of the sleeping rooms but rarely more than a step lower, and unlike the Malay kitchen, it is almost never on the ground. A charcoal hearth or a kerosene stove rests on a small platform of clay. Siamese houses of this type differ from Malay houses in having a front porch at or near ground level that is roofed. Malay houses usually have verandahs. The houses of very poor Thai peasants, like those of the Jakun, have walls of woven split bamboo and roofs of atap. Sometimes this poorer type of Siamese house is built directly on the ground. Houses in the central plains usually rest on an artificial mound of earth that provides some protection from floods.

Most Thai are wet-rice farmers. To Western eyes, they seem much more expert than Malays. Also, except among the Pak Thai of the extreme south, they appear to have less ritual that is directly related to wet-rice agriculture. Pak Thai have the same rituals as Malays. Malays, Pak Thais, and Central Thais prefer nonglutinous rice for meals and glutinous varieties for desserts. Thais of the Chiengmai area and the Northeast, like the Lao, prefer glutinous rice as a staple and make desserts of nonglutinous rice. Nonglutinous long-grained rice is the major export crop of the central plains, but other cash crops such as maize, kenaf, tapioca, mung beans, and peanuts are becoming increasingly important.

Central Thais use draft animals, water buffalo and Indian bullocks, to a greater extent in rice production than do Malays. Where Malays would use hoes, Siamese use plows and harrows.

Siamese also use more water-lifting devices. In the more steeply graded Malay valleys, it is not even necessary to dam the streams. A ditch cut through the riverbank farther upstream serves perfectly. In the more flat plains of Thailand, a variety of devices—water shovels and paddles or buckets mounted on endless belts—raise irrigation water to the level of the seedbeds.

In some areas, rice is not transplanted but rather is sown broadcast. Several varieties of rice are specially adapted to deep flooding. Planted in alluvial areas along the edges of large rivers at the beginning of the rainy season, they grow as rapidly as the floodwaters deepen.

Thais harvest the rice with sickles, cutting the stalks off near the ground and by the handful. There is no concern about frightening the soul of the rice. In the northern and northeastern areas, threshing is accomplished by the usual beating of sheaves into large baskets. But in the central plains, they place the sheaves on threshing floors that are located on the house mounds. Bullocks and buffalos trample the grain, freeing it from its panicles, leaves, and stalks. Winnowing is done with hand-cranked machines in the central plains and with basket trays in the other areas. Thai peasants dry the harvested rice in the sun, put it into gunnysacks, and deliver it to Chinese owned and operated mills whence it finds its way into world commerce.

Peasants grow other commercial crops such as rubber, sugar cane, coconuts, tobacco, and cotton. None is as important as rice. They also grow fruits, yams, manioc, legumes, and chili for their own consumption and for sale in local markets. Women are more important than men as traders of local produce in the markets. This same pattern occurs among Malays in Kelantan and may be a result of Thai cultural influence.

Siamese men and women perform many of the same tasks. Both sexes fish, an important economic activity. Men generally work in the field, but during periods of excessive labor requirements, women work in the fields. In central Thailand, they sometimes help plow the fields. Men sometimes help women with cooking and housework. The chief cultural distinction between males and females is that females are not ordained into the Buddhist priesthood whereas most men (ideally all but actually about eighty-five percent) are ordained at the age of twenty. Females are spiritually less worthy. Perhaps that is why they do not hesitate to become traders.

One part of Siamese kinship terminology, the distinction between paternal and maternal grandparents, possibly indicates that descent was once ambilineal.[4] More likely it is merely an indication of extreme respect for members of ascending generations because there are no other evidences of ambilineality. Relative age and birth order are important in other portions of the terminology. A majority of Siamese households are nuclear families. Others are stem families or limited extended families that are enlarged by married children, grandchildren, and collateral relatives. Often, the youngest child inherits the property of the parents (ultimogeniture). Some household members may be nonrelatives—informally adopted children of poorer neighbors or friends. In fact, household composition varies a great deal because Siamese accept the importance of convenience in this matter. Members of the same household should have compatible personalities and contribute their fair share of work and wealth. Sometimes relatives that live in different households of a village cooperate. These multilocal extended families are fairly common. Except that members are related consanguineally or affinally, there are no regularities or customs that define membership in such groups, and they are usually temporary groups that eventually disintegrate because of arguments and loss of common interests.

Villagers usually say, as a matter of ideal values, that they are all related to each other (phi-nawng, "siblings"), and some ethnographers report a pattern of village endogamy. But village endogamy is probably not a dominant pattern. In remote villages and in areas dominated by other ethnic groups, endogamy is strong as a function of limited choices in other Thai villages. The incest taboo is extended to first cousins. Second cousins are preferred spouses in some areas. Patrilineal surnames were introduced by law in 1916, but very few people use them at all, and women ordinarily do not change their surnames upon marriage. In northern and northeastern areas premarital sexual relationships are allowed, but not in central and southern areas. Individuals make their own choices in marriage. Courting in the central plains consists largely of conversations and perhaps recital of poetry.

There are no Theravada Buddhist ceremonies for marriage, but as in Malaya, Hindu symbols and acts are part of a very widespread and common ritual. Bride and groom wear tiny crowns on their heads, connected by a white Brahmanic string, receive sacral water poured over their hands by guests from a small conch shell, offer guests a tray of betel and receive a blessing from each, seek blessings from relatives, and then announce their intentions to the house spirit and seek a blessing therefrom. The wedding procession from the groom's to the bride's house is a time of great fun as the procession has to bribe its way past the front gate and again past the entrance to the porch of the bride's house. Parents of the bride and groom furnish a feast to honor the couple and sometimes provide a dowry. Poor couples often elope, and upon returning to the village, the groom gives a gift to his wife's parents. Adults who have been married before become married by mutual consent. Divorce is by mutual consent. Children may accompany either parent except in the north where they accompany the mother.

Perhaps the most important ceremonies of Thai society are the initiation of religious novices and the ordination of priests. The initiation of novices symbolizes Buddha's renunciation of worldly riches. At the beginning, novices parade around the village showing off their jewels and costumes of silk. A very uproarious time with raucous music, fun, bawdy humor, and frenzied excitement almost hurls the candidate into the contrary calm of the sanctuary at the end of the parade. Then the novices' heads are shaved. They remove their rich clothing and are invested with simple saffron robes. New names are given them, and they eat from begging bowls. This final portion of the ordination of priests is a solemn affair throughout. All of the priests of the monastery, relatives of the new priests, other villagers, and guests witness the taking of vows. Three months is the ideal minimum time of enlistment as a priest, but a two-week leave from the office or store may be the only time available. Many men spend six months or more as a priest. Others spend their lifetime. The priesthood is sometimes used as a shelter from unemployment.

A Thai priest lives simply, but he meditates almost not at all, in considerable contrast to Burmese monks. Priests study in Dharma school during the period of their enlistment. Some advance to Pali studies. A very few take exams to go on to Bangkok Buddhist universities. Most young priests are basically in a moral finishing school and spend most of their time as students learning ethics.

A priest has a typical daily routine. In the morning, he walks his rounds accepting offerings of food from those who wish to gain merit. He fasts every afternoon and chants verses. Villagers sometimes ask him to recite sermons or sing chants at their ceremonies. The elaborate funerals and cremation ceremonies that begin the deceased's journey towards a new existence require especially large numbers of priests. If the priest has a skill or craft that he has learned at the temple, he practices it for the benefit of the villagers.

Theravada Buddhism, which is literally atheistic, blends well with the worship of many spirits. Some spirits are guardians of houses, fields, and villages. Small abodes are built for them, and they are given offerings of food and flowers. Even good spirits can cause illness if they are annoyed. And illnesses may be cured by propitiating them. Spirits can help find lost objects and give advice of any sort. Spirit mediums are in great demand.

Thai ideas about health and illness are like those of Malays. The basic strength of a person depends upon the amount of spiritual energy or soul substance *(khwan)* that he possesses. Loss of spiritual energy can cause serious illness. Its loss may result from a strong and unbalancing emotional experience or through theft by a spirit. The ritual of calling the *khwan* is a part of rites of passage and may be used as a curing ritual during times of psychic distress. Otherwise, health is maintained through careful balancing of air and earth elements and of heating and cooling substances in the body.

Like Malays, the Siamese have traditionally trained midwives who assist women giving birth and help them to regain their health afterwards. The midwife cuts the umbilical cord with a bamboo knife. She helps speed the drying out of birth fluids by "roasting" the mother on a fire-heated resting place for an odd number of days. After the mother's balance has been restored, the placenta, which is the baby's spiritual sibling, is planted beneath a tree. All of these customs and beliefs associated with birth are widespread in Southeast Asia.

Other Major Peoples (Malays, Khmers, Vietnamese, and Mon)

Malays (see Chapter Six, Malay States) are a majority in the four southern-most provinces of Thailand, and they have settlements in all of the coastal areas. Altogether there may be a million Malays in Thailand. They are wet-rice agriculturists, rubber growers, fishermen, and traders. None hold government positions. In the past, Thailand controlled the Malay states of Trengganu, Kelantan, Kedah, and Perlis. Most Siamese continue to view Malays as a subject people. There are avid Malay nationalists who resent Siamese efforts to increase their use of Thai language and their knowledge of Theravada Buddhism. The Malay nationalists of Thailand have gained no official sympathy from the Malaysian government, but there is widespread sympathy for their cause among Malays in Malaysia.

Khmers (see Chapter Nine, The Khmer State) inhabited large areas of Thailand before Siamese expansion in the thirteenth century. Presently there are about four hundred thousand in Thailand. Most of them are concentrated in the northeastern and southeastern provinces that border Cambodia. A few others, descendants of prisoners of war, have settlements in the central plains. Most Khmers are rice farmers. Usually they plant wet rice (glutinous varieties), but in some areas of the northeast, they grow dry rice in fields prepared by slash-and-burn techniques. Khmer farmers also grow fruit, raise livestock, fish, and manufacture charcoal, rattan mats, and pottery. They are skilled artisans. Khmers assimilate more readily than Malays because they are Theravada Buddhists like the Siamese.

There are about two hundred thousand Vietnamese (see Chapter Ten, Vietnamese States) in Thailand. Somewhat less than one-fourth of them live in the area around Bangkok. They are descendants of Roman Catholics who fled their homeland more than a hundred years ago to avoid religious persecution. Almost all of them are citizens of Thailand, and they present no special problems. More recent immigrants in the northeastern provinces comprise a majority of Vietnamese in Thailand, and they are regarded with suspicion by the Siamese who view them as forerunners of Vietnamese imperialism. Some of them immigrated as early as the end of the nineteenth century, but most have arrived since the end of World War II. They were regularly repatriated to North Vietnam from 1959 to 1964. Most of the Vietnamese in Thailand live in or near towns, and many have urban occupations.

The Mon (see Chapter Eight, States of Burma) in Thailand number about seventy-five thousand. Their villages are scattered throughout the central plains and along the southwestern border with Burma. Their ancient states occupied portions of the area before the arrival of the Siamese. Other Mon immigrated during the last several centuries to avoid political persecution by the Burmese. They are wet-rice farmers and noted scholar-priests of Theravada Buddhism. Virtually all Mon in Thailand are fluent Thai speakers. Many of them no longer speak Mon languages and are practically Siamese.

Other Rice Farmers (Karen and Lawa)

The Karen (see Chapter Eight, States of Burma) of Thailand number about one hundred thousand. Most Karen live in Burma, where they have their own semiautonomous state. Some of them are still slash-and-burn horticulturists, but in the last hundred years, most of them have become wet-rice farmers. Karen in Thailand have assimilated most Siamese cultural patterns except language and religion. The Lawa were lowland people who became hill farmers when first Mons and then Siamese forced them out of the lowlands and into the hills around Chiengmai. Their language is closely related to that of the Palaung-Wa of Shan State in Burma. Lawa assimilation into Thai society has been rapid. At the end of the nineteenth century there were about eighty thousand and now there are about nine thousand Lawa.

Foreign Asians (Chinese and Indians)

The outline of customs of Singaporean and Malaysian Chinese (see Chapter Six, Malay States) serves generally as a report of the customs of Southeast Asian Chinese. Thailand has a large Chinese population of about four million. Most of them live in Bangkok and the provincial centers where they work in the full range of urban occupations but especially in commerce and banking. The major dialect groups, from largest to smallest, are Teochiu, Hakka,

Hainanese, Cantonese, and Hokkien. Chinese have immigrated to Thailand since the thirteenth century, and they had gained control of royal Thai trading and business monopolies by the seventeenth century. But by far the largest numbers came in the nineteenth and twentieth centuries as Europeans gained overall control of the economies of Southeast Asian countries. Early immigrants were usually men who married into Siamese families and were rapidly assimilated into Thai society. Their mixed descendants were called *Lukjin* and became especially important members of the Thai business community. They were partners in the royal trading monopolies and were granted titles of nobility. They served as tax collectors, port officials, and provincial governors. One of their number, General Taksin, rallied the Siamese to drive the Burmese army out of Thailand in 1767. He became king and founded Bangkok. Taksin favored the Teochius, to whom he was related, and encouraged them to immigrate. He was deposed in 1782, but his son-in-law succeeded and founded the present Chakri dynasty, which continued to sponsor Chinese, especially Teochiu, immigration and enterprise. In the early twentieth century, female immigrants increased in number, and China regained control of its destiny. Chinese assimilation into Thai society slowed and practically ceased. Some Chinese have resisted Thailand's assimilation policies. But recently, mutual accommodations have been worked out in higher education and in joint private business ventures. *Lukjin* are now a very large portion of college graduates, and Thais have moved more into private business with Chinese. Thais supply government connections and influence, and Chinese supply experience and capital.

Indians (see Indians in Chapter Six, Malay States) comprise a tiny percentage of Thailand's total population and they are not very important economically or politically. There are perhaps ten thousand of them in Thailand, including refugees from Burma. They are Tamils, Malayalis, Telegus, Hindustanis, Gujaratis, Bengalis, Sikhs, Pathans, and Sinhalese. Most of them live in or near urban centers and are small businessmen (especially textile sales), moneylenders, artisans, drivers, and guards. Dairying is the one activity in which they do not compete with the Chinese.

Meo-Yao Hill Farmers

The Meo (Mong) are the largest hill tribe in Thailand. There are about seventy-five thousand of them in the northern hills. They are more numerous elsewhere—about three million in southern China, two hundred thousand in North Vietnam, and sixty thousand in Laos.[5] *Meo* or *Miau* is the name applied to them by Tai and Chinese speakers. It may refer to "cat" or "rice shoot."

Meo and Yao dialects are closely related. There is little agreement about their affiliation with other languages. They have been variously classified with Mon-Khmer, Tai, Sinitic, and Tibeto-Burman languages. Meo dialects are many. Names of dialects refer to clothing color of subgroups—Red, Flowered, Striped, Black, Blue, and White Meo. Blue Meo and White Meo are the most numerous in Thailand.

The Meo are remarkably short in stature. Men are often less than five feet tall. They also have fairly light skin color. Head hair is straight, and occasionally it is brown rather than black. The forward part of the skull is often shaved, giving the impression of partial baldness. Eyes usually have pronounced epicanthic folds.

Meos are famous for their stories and legends. Creation myths are a common theme. A summary of one such story follows.[6] Two brothers plowed a field one day and returned the next morning to find the furrows smoothed and covered with grass. They plowed the field several more times with the same result. Suspecting foul play they hid near the field at night and discovered an old lady smoothing the furrows and replanting the grass. The older brother was furious and tried to kill the old lady, but the younger one stopped him and asked the old lady why she interfered with their work. She said it was useless work because a great flood was coming. They asked how they might be spared. She instructed the older brother to make an iron drum and the younger brother to make a drum from a tree. Each was to get into his drum and would be saved. The flood began and the younger brother asked his sister to join him and be saved, also. The iron drum of the elder brother sank, and he was drowned, thereby avenging his threat to the life of the old lady. After 20 days, the flood receded, and the drum made from the tree came to rest on the side of a cliff. Two eagles began to use it as a nest. Eaglets hatched, and the man bound their wings with cord made from his hair so that they could not fly. Troubled because their children could not fly, the eagle parents consulted a spirit. The spirit told them to consult the base of the tree in which their nest was built. After the eagles agreed to fly the man and sister to the ground, the man released the wings of the eaglets. The man and his sister had many other problems, and their solutions led to the invention of many important culture traits. They found no other people, and after a series of tests, the sister finally agreed to marry her brother. Their child was deformed. Consulting the spirits, they were told to cut it up into a hundred pieces and to plant each piece in a different area. The next day each piece had grown into a complete human being. And that is the way that the world was repopulated.

The Meo have a saying that "As fish are to water, and birds are to air, so Meo are to mountains." They avoid the tropic heat of the lowlands, building their villages near small streams just below the summits of mountains. Every ten to twenty years, they move their villages to new areas and build new houses and outbuildings. The site for a new house is carefully selected after consulting spirits and studying omens. A simple hut is constructed first so that future tenants of the house can dream in it to discover more omens. If there are no bad omens such as bird dung, black squirrels, deer, or snakes, the site is enlarged and a regular house is built. The rectangular house is built directly on the ground except for the sleeping area, and it has a gabled roof that is thatched. Most houses have two fireplaces—one in the kitchen and the other in the living room.

Outbuildings include sties for pigs, coops for chickens, stables for cattle and horses, and storehouses. The storehouses are built on pilings to protect goods from ground moisture.

A village consists of three or four to several dozen houses. Each house is the abode of a nuclear family, stem family, joint family, or patrilocal extended family. The house grows as the family grows. In some instances, the households of a village are divided among several patriclans. In other villages everyone belongs to the same patriclan. Clansmen share the same surname. Persons with the same natal clan cannot marry. A woman becomes a member of her husband's clan after marriage. A rich man usually has several wives. It is possible for a man to become a member of another clan through blood brotherhood. The clan is the focus of most economic and ceremonial activities.

Women have lower status than men in Meo society. Their status improves as they grow older and have younger co-wives and daughters-in-law to boss around. After men have prepared the fields, women plant, weed, and harvest them. Women cook, keep house, and make clothing. Men perform all of the heavy agricultural work, care for animals, hunt, and make weapons.

Meo are slash-and-burn farmers. The most important crop is dry rice. Opium poppies are next. In areas where there is a land shortage, opium may be more important than rice because opium fields can be cultivated for as long as twenty years without fallowing whereas rice fields must be fallowed after three years.

The requirements and techniques of opium-poppy cultivation are fairly specialized. Poppies do not grow well in the lowlands. Poppies prefer a cool climate for healthy growth, and the weather must be dry during the harvest. The fields are planted at the end of the rainy season in October or November, and the harvest takes place in March or April, before the rainy season begins. Seed capsules must be incised ten to fifteen days before petals fall from the flowers. Juice flows and dries becoming a sticky brown gum that collects at the bases of the seed capsules. It is then scraped off and gathered into great lumps that, with further drying, enter commerce as raw opium. The seeds, which have no narcotic properties, are an important food crop.

Other important crops include maize, millet, sugar cane, yams, beans, onions, tobacco, hemp, and cotton. Many fields are under cultivation at the same time, and crops are planted at different times so that there is a more or less continuous harvest of food. Some fields are distant—as much as a day's walk from the village. The Meo build small houses in distant fields so that workers can remain overnight or for several days.

Hunting and fishing are important economically. Hunting consumes a great deal of a man's time. Formerly, the principal weapon was the crossbow with poisoned darts. Homemade muskets and modern firearms have been used more recently. Meo build clever traps and snares. Birds, wild pigs, deer, and even, occasionally, elephant are taken. The meat is smoked, salted, and dried for storage.

Most villages have a blacksmith. His equipment includes a piston bellows, and he manufactures most of the iron tools that villagers require. The Meo are skilled artisans. Women make linen and cotton cloth and dye it using the batik technique common among Malays. Silversmiths fashion jewelry from old silver coins.

The most elaborate ceremony consists of an annual sacrifice of buffalo, pigs, and chickens to the ancestral spirits of the patriclan. Marriages are elaborate. They are occasions of ceremonial exchange between patriclans. Funerals are important, too. After death, the soul is reborn in the next child born into the local section of the clan.

A very few of the Meo of Thailand are Christians. The others believe in spirits and practice ancestor worship. Guardian dog spirits protect houses. Other spirits inhabit various natural objects and places. Sacrifice of animals is the standard means of propitiating spirits, and to this end, there are small altars in the houses, along the trails, and in the fields.

Spirit mediums may be either males or females. Trance states are very stylized and serve as a mode of communicating with tutelary spirits. Mediums exorcize evil spirits and interpret omens. Apparently, they are rarely suspected of sorcery by other villagers. Thai sorcerers are feared.

The Meo have an extensive knowledge of herbal medicines. They treat certain kinds of snake bites, goiter, eye sores, burns, and diarrhea. They are skilled at child delivery and are accomplished in the art of setting and splinting broken bones.

The Yao (Kimmien) speak dialects that are closely related to Meo. There are about three million Yao in southern China and Southeast Asia. Most of them live in southern China, Burma, Laos, and Vietnam. They number about ten thousand in Thailand, and they are concentrated in the north. Their immigration into Thailand began in the nineteenth century. *Yao* is a Chinese term that means "wild dog." *Kimmien* is a Yao term for themselves that means "people of the mountain." The Chinese term does not miss the mark if we can believe the Yao origin myth in which they show themselves to be descendants of a marvelous dragon dog that slew a Meo and thereby won as his wife the daughter of a Chinese emperor.

Yao, like the Meo, are divided into dialect groups that are named after differences in clothing. Each dialect group has slightly different customs. They differ principally from the Meo in living in even more inaccessible mountain areas and in such details as house type (their houses are on pilings). Their social organization, economic technology, and religious belief are very similar to those of the Meo.

Tibeto-Burman Hill Farmers (Lisu, Lahu, and Akha)

The Lisu, Lahu, and Akha are subdivisions of the Lolo.[7] They are closely related culturally and linguistically. Except for linguistic differences, they are also very similar to the Meo and Yao. In Thailand, the Lisu number about nineteen thousand, the Lahu seventeen thousand, and the Akha twenty-eight thousand. They are much more numerous in southern China and Burma. All of them have immigrated to Thailand since the nineteenth century. Like the Meo, the Lisu, Lahu, and Akha are each divided into subgroups that are named according to characteristics of clothing color. These subgroups probably derive from groupings of particular patriclans into appropriate-sized structural fragments for patterned marital and ceremonial exchanges.

They are all mountaineers who practice slash-and-burn agriculture, grow dry rice, opium, maize, millet, and yams, keep horses, cattle, water buffalo, pigs, and chickens, and move their villages every ten to twenty years. The Lisu, Lahu, and Akha depend on hunting and fishing for part of their subsistence. Crossbows with poisoned darts are common weapons.

These hill tribes are not Buddhists, and their native religions have elements that seem almost Sinitic. Sacrifices of animals are important. Ancestor worship penetrates every niche of society. And they all fear the potency of Thai sorcerers. They avoid the lowland people. But they trade with Chinese, and Chinese traders are occasionally allowed to marry into their patriclans. In areas of southern China where Han Chinese, Meo-Yao, and Lolo groups live close together, it is commonplace that the Han are overlords of Lolo and that Lolo are overlords of Meo-Yao.

The most fascinating aspect of distinctions between the various hill tribes is that of triviality. Differences seem to be perpetuated for their own sake so that each local group, each village, maintains its integrity in spite of rapid changes in the external world.

THE LAO STATE

About half of the population of Laos is Lao. The Lao are the major people of Laos.[8] They number more than a million and a half and are a majority in only 3 of the 12 provinces. Their situation in relation to other people is like that of the Thai centuries ago, before they assimilated many of their neighbors. Lao social structure is practically identical with Central Thai social structure. Political structure differs because of the difference in scale of the Central Thai and Lao states and because of different innovations that the French introduced in Laos. One result of Laotian conservatism and French innovation was that the country came to have two capitals—Luang Prabang, the royal capital, and Vientiane, the administrative capital—each the apex of different hierarchies that embrace the whole country.

Lao (Phou Lao and Laotian Tai)

Lao are very similar to the Thai. Lao understand Central Thai, but Central Thai cannot (or will not) understand Lao. In other respects, their cultures are practically identical. The Lao have a greater preference than the Central Thai for glutinous rice, and they are more conservative. They look up to the Thai, who look down on them as country bumpkins.

Subsistence techniques differ some from those of the Central Thai. For example, some Lao farmers in northern areas use slash-and-burn methods and grow dry rice. Also, the Lao are more avid food collectors and gather larvae, crickets, snails, and frogs to supplement the comparatively large amounts of pork that they consume.

The state religion of Laos is Theravada Buddhism. Like the Central Thai, the Lao also worship a multitude of spirits (phi). Spirit worship is more important than it is among the Thai and details differ. For example, khwan is not a generalized spiritual energy but a particulate soul. Each individual has 32 khwan. The phi receive more attention than among the Central Thai. Small houses for offerings given to them are located under the eaves of houses, along trails, and in gardens. Lao sacrifice animals to the phi. Also, the Lao relate many of their phi-worshiping rituals to the cultivation of rice.

Foreign Asians (Chinese, Vietnamese, and
Indians)

There are perhaps fifty thousand Chinese, twenty thousand Vietnamese, and a thousand Indians in Laos. Most of these are concentrated in urban centers. Chinese and Indians are primarily merchants. In the past, the Vietnamese were brought in by the French
to fill administrative posts. Most of them returned to Vietnam
after the French left. But some Vietnamese stayed on as merchants
and artisans.

Mon-Khmer Hill Farmers (Kha Khmu and Kha Lamet)

There are about one hundred fifty thousand Khmu in Laos. They
are closely related to a better known, but smaller, group (about five
thousand) called the Lamet.[9] Linguistically and culturally, both are
related to the Lawa of Thailand and the Palaung-Wa of Burma and
more distantly to the Senoi of Malaysia. They have lived in Southeast Asia since ancient times. Lao refer to them as *Kha*, which
means "slave." *Khmu* means "people" in their own language.

They practice slash-and-burn agriculture and plant the usual
crops—dry rice (glutinous), millet, maize, manioc, bananas, beans,
chili, cabbage, tobacco, cotton, flax, and opium. They use some
fields for several years, rotating different crops, and they use other
fields for only one year, planting the different crops all at one time
in the same field. They move often and depend less on planting and
more on hunting, fishing, and gathering than other hill tribes.
Khmu and Lamet gather forest products such as rattan and resin for
trade. Their patron-trader *(lam)* is usually a Lao merchant.

Social structure is similar to that of other hill farmers. Patriclans that are exogamous are the major kin groups. Households are
usually patrilocal extended families, and villages consist of three or
four to several dozen households. There are no social classes. Village leaders are often spirit mediums.

Meo-Yao

There are about sixty thousand Meo and five thousand Yao in Laos
(see The Central Thai State in Chapter Seven, Tai States). The traditional culture of the Meo has been devastated during the long war
in Laos. Meo were divided between the two sides. Their villages
were invaded by both sides and bombed by the Americans.
Evacuated from their home villages in vast numbers, some of them
eventually returned, but others remained in the lowlands and became wet-rice cultivators. Many of the Meo suffered enormously.
A few profited materially.

The Tai-speaking hill farmers of Laos number more than thirty-five thousand.[10] Linguistically and culturally, the Black, White, and Red Tai are very similar. The color of their clothing differs. Linguistically, they are similar to the Lao, but in many other respects, they more closely resemble non-Tai speakers who are hill farmers.

Usually, Tai hill farmers grow wet rice if at all possible. They tend to farm small alluvial fans at altitudes just below slash-and-burn horticulturists. Where wet rice cannot be grown, they too use slash-and-burn techniques. Swidden fields are cultivated three years and allowed to fallow for ten. Rice is the major crop, but maize, millet, yams, and beans are important, too. They raise some opium poppies, and they keep livestock. Fishing, hunting, and gathering provide important supplements to the diet. They trade with Chinese and Vietnamese merchants.

Unlike the bilateral Central Thai and Lao, but like many hill tribes, the upland Tai are organized patrilineally. They have patri-clans and surnames. Certain food taboos are associated with some surnames, but people with the same surname can marry as long as they are not known to be otherwise closely related, and women do not change their surnames when they marry. Among the Black Tai, surname groups are divided into three classes—noble, priestly, and commoner.

Religion and beliefs about illness among Tai hill farmers are precisely the non-Buddhist beliefs of the Lao with the addition of ancestor worship.

Many upland Tai, especially the Black Tai, feel superior to the Lao. Khmu and Lamet are thought to be inferior by the other ethnic groups. The Meo-Yao rest uncomfortably, just above the Khmu and Lamet.

CENTRAL THAI AND LAO DILEMMAS

Thailand has a very strong policy of cultural assimilation of non-Thai ethnic groups. Serious problems with minorities relate directly to this policy. Malays in the south, Vietnamese in the northeast, hill people along the border with Burma, and Chinese in urban areas continue to resist the policy of Thai conformity. Laos is the other extreme. Numerous non-Lao dilute the political power of the Lao in most provinces. Internal political factions further dilute the capabilities of the Lao government. Non-Lao control extensive areas of the country.

In both Thailand and Laos, it is apparent that many hill tribes avoid contact with the major people of the country and even with other hill tribes. Chinese traders often provide the economic linkage among hill tribes and between the hill peoples and the major people of the lowlands.

REFERENCES

[1] L. Sharp et al., *Siamese Rice Village: A Preliminary Study of Ban Chan 1948–1949* (Bangkok: Cornell Research Center, 1953); and H. P. Phillips, *Thai Peasant Personality* (Berkeley and Los Angeles: University of California Press, 1965).

[2] J. F. Embree, "Thailand—A Loosely Structured Social System," *American Anthropologist* 52 (1950): 181–93.

[3] Phillips, *Thai Peasant Personality*, p. 79.

[4] See page 201 of L. M. Hanks and J. R. Hanks, "Siamese Tai," in F. M. LeBar et al., eds., *Ethnic Groups of Mainland Southeast Asia* (New Haven, Conn.: Human Relations Area Files Press, 1964).

[5] Chapters 10–11 of *Minority Groups in Thailand*, Ethnographic Study Series, Department of the Army Pamphlet No. 550-107, 1970.

[6] S. R. Clarke, *Among the Tribes in South-West China* (London: Morgan & Scott, 1911), pp. 50–54.

[7] Chapters 5–6 and 14 of *Minority Groups in Thailand*.

[8] F. M. LeBar and A. Suddard, eds., *Laos* (New Haven, Conn.: Human Relations Area Files Press, 1960).

[9] Chapter 8 of *Minority Groups of Thailand*; and K. G. Izikowitz, *Lamet: Hill Peasants in Indochina* (Gothenburg: Ethnografiska Museet, 1951).

[10] "Tai: Central Upland Groups," in LeBar et al., *Ethnic Groups of Mainland Southeast Asia*, pp. 220–28.

EIGHT

STATES OF BURMA

A PLETHORA OF MAJOR PEOPLES

The Union of Burma, in spite of its name and the federal political forms prescribed by its constitution, is a unitary state with a powerful central government which is Burmese. Moreover, several of its constituent states belong to non-Burmese minorities that have a strong sense of independence. Year after year since gaining its independence from Britain (1948), the Union of Burma has been tested by conflict between the Burmese central government and various of the minorities that desire independence from the Burmese. From a structural point of view the problem is that there are too many major peoples in Burma. Some of them—Arakanese, Mon, and Shan—controlled most of Burma at different times in the past; others—Karen, Kachin, and Chin—merely aspire to form their own states. The Burmese are about seventy percent of the total population of about thirty million, but almost all of them live in the central plains of upper and lower Burma, and they are surrounded by minority peoples.[1]

SHAN STATE

Shan State consists of several dozen small states, each of which is ruled by a hereditary prince *(saohpa)*. His rule is absolute. He maintains a court that is usually the core of a town. Offices of the court are held by other members of the noble class. The prince may have a harem. The regalia of his court are like those of Siamese and Lao royalty.

Several of the larger Shan states are further divided into dependencies, which like the provinces of Thailand and Laos are called *muong*. Chieftains, usually relatives of the prince and in any case members of the noble class, rule the various *muong* for the prince. Commoners are traders, silversmiths, and wet-rice farmers who pay taxes to court officials and perform corvée labor. Fishermen and butchers, because their occupations are offensive to Buddhists, belong to a lower (almost outcaste) class.

Shan states maintain relations with other ethnic groups. They trade with hill tribes. Some hill people assimilate to Shan culture. Some Shan drift away from their states and become hill people. Chinese are important in Shan states. They are large-scale merchants in the towns and sometimes marry into noble Shan families.[2]

Shan (Tai Yai, Tai Tau, Ngio, and Sam)

There are more than three million Shan in Burma. They refer to themselves as Tai; the Siamese and Lao call them Ngio; the Kachin call them Sam; and the Burmese call them Shan. Linguistically and culturally, they are very closely related to their Siamese and Lao neighbors. Their dialects are not quite mutually intelligible with Central Thai or Lao, but generally their script is similar, although it shows some Burmese influence.

Shan villages are located in high valleys and in small areas of flat land in the hills. Villages are nucleated and consist of a dozen to a hundred houses. Most villages have a temple that is tended by a single priest. Large villages have streets and a central market. Shans, Chinese, Kachins, and Palaungs attend the market every fifth day. Other villages have different market days so that there is no conflict. Towns that are the seats of princely or noble courts have shops in addition to the market and the grand residences of nobles and chieftains. The houses of commoners are built almost entirely of bamboo and are raised high above the ground on pilings. A ladder leads up to the front verandah. Cooking is done beneath the house or on the back verandah. A garden surrounds each house, supplying its inhabitants with peas, beans, tomatoes, okra, cucumbers, melons, papaya, bananas, oranges, and mangoes.

Wet rice is the most important agricultural crop. It is cultivated in the classical manner. Shan fertilize their fields with manure. They raise water into their fields with dams and waterwheels, and they dig irrigation canals. Domesticated animals include horses, water buffalo, pigs, and chickens. Like other major peoples of Southeast Asia, they prepare rice beer and wine. Like the Thai, they go a step further and distill liquor from the rice wine. They also chew betel nut and smoke tobacco.

Trade is almost as important as agriculture to Shan economy. They manufacture pottery, paper, lacquerware, silver jewelry, and cotton cloth for their own use and for trade. Traders follow the markets in different villages, make trips to visit hill tribes, and journey in cart caravans to the central plains to trade with Burmese.

Family organization among commoners is bilateral with strong patrilineal tendencies. Nobility are organized into patrilineages.

Noble marriages are usually for consolidating or extending political power. A few marriages between rich commoners and lesser nobility occur. Village endogamy is usual for commoner marriages. The incest taboo extends only to immediate family members, and cousin marriages are common. Marriage ceremonies are elaborate only among the very wealthy and powerful.

Most Shan are Theravada Buddhists. Additionally, they practice the same kind of spirit worship as the Thai and Lao. Their folk medicine is similar, too. Additionally, they are famous tattoo artists. Blue tattoos cover the chest, back, arms, and legs of adult males. The tattoos are a sign of manhood and a powerful protection against malevolent spirits.

Shan differ from Thai and Lao in disposal of the dead. Thai and Lao bury only persons who died violently or those who were extremely poor. Most are cremated. Among the Shan, most bodies are buried. Only the very wealthy and powerful are cremated.

Mon-Khmer Hill Farmers (Palaung and Wa)

The Palaung (Da-ang) of Burma number about one hundred fifty thousand.[3] Most of them live in the northwestern part of Shan State, near the Palaung state of Taungbaing. There, a Palaung prince rules in much the fashion of a Shan prince. Elsewhere, Palaung villages are usually attached to Shan states. Many Palaung are partially assimilated into Shan society. All of them speak Shan as a trade language, and their literature is written in Shan.

A village consists of two to fifty houses. Larger villages have a monastery, a temple, a rest house, and a market. As many as six families may live in a single house. Each family has its own apartment. Houses are raised on pilings and are constructed mostly of bamboo.

Palaungs cultivate wet rice and dry rice. They have large vegetable and fruit gardens. Tea is an important crop. They grow, prepare, transport, and sell it. Two forms are prepared—dry tea for making the beverage and pickled tea for eating.

Palaung trade with Shans, Chinese, and Kachins. Shan traders sell them cloth, silver jewelry, salt, lacquerware, and betel nut. Chinese supply them with iron tools, kerosene, sugar, canned milk, and biscuits. They trade with Kachins for preserved fish. Palaung sell their tea and horses and cattle.

Village endogamy is common. The Palaung extend the incest taboo to first cousins. Choice of spouse is an individual matter, and elopement is a common form of marriage. There are no corporate kin groups other than the nuclear family.

Palaungs are Theravada Buddhists and worshippers of many spirits. The folk medicine does not differ substantially from that of the Shan.

Wa language is closely related to Palaung, but otherwise there are many cultural differences. More than three hundred thousand Wa live in Shan State. Many are acculturated to the Shan way of life and are said to be "tame." Others are unacculturated. The "wild" Wa are called Wa Hai by Shans, and they are by far the more interesting.

Villages of the wild Wa are large, numbering several hundred houses. The houses are raised on pilings and are built of heavy timber and bamboo. Rows of posts, which record sacrifices of buffalo, stand in front of each house. The buffalo skulls are piled inside the house. Villages are surrounded by heavy walls of earth and poles and sometimes a moat. Several villages are usually united under a single chief.

Wa farmers use slash-and-burn techniques to grow dry rice, which they convert to rice liquor. Beans, maize, and millet are important food crops. Domestic animals include dogs, pigs, and chicken. They get their buffalo for sacrifices from the Shan. The Wa grow opium for trade.

Wa religion requires the taking of heads. Some Wa prefer to use the heads of people who are already dead; others prefer heads freshly cut from living bodies. In either case, the heads are cleaned of flesh, dried, and placed in specially made wickerwork baskets which are attached to long poles that are planted in a sacred grove near the village. The purpose is to capture the spiritual energy of the former owner of the skull so that crops will be abundant and illnesses will be avoided. Skulls of strangers are best because their spiritual energy, not being familiar with the countryside, is more likely to remain near the skull. Wa bury their own dead in narrow burial mounds.

Shan traders visit the villages of the wild Wa with great regularity, without losing their heads.

KACHIN STATE (JINGHPAW, ATSI, LASHI, AND MARU)

Kachin villages are often attached to Shan states.[4] They had no state organization of their own until the British granted independence to the Union of Burma. Kachin language belongs to the Tibeto-Burman group. Atsi, Lashi, and Maru are more closely related than Jinghpaw to Burmese. There are more than three hundred thousand Kachin in Burma. Most of them live in the Shan State and to the north in Kachin State.

Kachin villages are large and they are entered through a sacred grove planted with prayer poles and equipped with small spirit houses. Community sacrifices are conducted in the sacred grove. There are no public buildings. Sacrificial posts for cattle stand in front of each house. The houses are large and shelter several families. Long and rectangular, and raised on pilings, the house is divided lengthwise so that there is one long public room on one side and a series of apartments on the other. A garden surrounds the house.

Kachins are traditionally slash-and-burn farmers whose main crop is dry rice. Some of them have become wet-rice farmers in recent years. They also grow maize, millet, tobacco, cotton, and opium. Like most slash-and-burn farmers, Kachin do not consider land to be personal property. The village chief and elders allocate land to those who need it. Domestic animals are bred for sacrifices. Hunting with pellet bows, guns, and traps provides meat for the table. Fishing, with traps and poison, provides additional animal protein.

Kachins obtain salt in trade with Burmese, iron tools and pots from Chinese, and cloth from Shan. They have no markets of their own and visit the markets of other people.

Communities are organized in one of two forms—*gumlao* (egalitarian) or *gumsa* (stratified). *Gumlao* organization is associated with Kachin modes of social structure while *gumsa* is associated with Shan. As a Kachin chief gains political power, his community shifts towards *gumsa* organization. Eventually, a son-in-law, placed in the position of serf, breaks this trend by revolting and reestablishing *gumlao* organization. Kachin political organization never proceeds beyond the chiefdom level. The basis for this lies in the peculiarly strong development of patrisibs, combined with an asymmetrical system of marital exchange in which wife-givers have higher prestige than wife-takers. This asymmetry, based on affinal relationships, appears to be a basis for class structure like that of the Shan, but it is not because of the obligations of kinship. Overall, the result is that Shans remain the overlords of the Kachin; where there are no Shans, political shifts embroil villages in more or less constant conflict.

Christian missionaries and Buddhist evangelists have been trying to proselytize the Kachin for more than a century with little success. They continue to worship ancestors and spirits. Some of them became Shan in order to use wet-rice lands and, thereby, became Buddhists. There are several different kinds of religious specialists—spirit mediums, seers, and priests, who specialize in sacrificing animals.

CHIN DISTRICT

The Chin of Burma number approximately five hundred thousand.[5] About half live in the Chin District, which borders Assam. Almost a million Chin live in Assam and another forty thousand live in Bangladesh. The center of the Chin world is the Hinduized state of Manipur in Assam, which is inhabited by a Chin group, the Meithei.

Chin hill tribes in Burma tend to trade with the lowlanders in Manipur rather than with lowland peoples of Burma. The same is true of other hill tribes that live along the Burma-Assam border such as the Nagas and Garos.

Chins, Nagas, and Garos speak closely related Tibeto-Burman languages, and they are culturally very similar. They are typical hill tribes with houses raised on stilts, slash-and-burn farming techniques, patrilineal kin groups, and spirit worship. Religious diversity is great. The lowlanders of Manipur are Vaishnavite Hindus, many hill groups are Christian, and the few Chin that live in the central plains of Burma are Theravada Buddhists.

Lowland Chin in Burma have accepted most aspects of Burmese culture. They are wet-rice farmers, speak Burmese fluently as a second language, and are Buddhists. Possibly, the Chin inhabited the central plains of Burma at some time in the distant past but were pushed west during the wars between the Shan and the Burmese.

KAREN STATES

More than two million Karen live in Burma.[6] They live south of Shan State along the border between Burma and Thailand. Karen language is usually classified as Sino-Tibetan. It is distantly related to the Tibeto-Burman languages. Sgaw, Pwo, and Pa-O are the principal dialects.

Karens were all hill people until the early nineteenth century when some of them were converted to Christianity by American Baptist missionaries. Many of them joined the British in their wars against the Burmese. Britishers provided the Karen with good schools, and an educated elite of ministers, clerks, teachers, and doctors emerged. After independence Karens were given their own state, Karenni, and they were the majority in Karen State. Karenni became Kayah State and Karen State became Kawthule State after 1952, but local control of the states remained in Karen hands. Despite the antagonisms between the Burmese central government and the Karen states, Karens have assimilated rapidly to Burmese culture. About seventy-five percent of the Karen speak Burmese, practice Theravada Buddhism, live in Burmese-style houses, and farm wet-rice fields in the Burmese manner.

Traditional Karen still live in the hills. They build longhouses of wooden planks. The longhouse is set on stilts and is divided into as many as thirty separate family apartments, which open on a common hallway that runs the length of the building.

Dry rice, legumes, yams, sweet potatoes, chili, and cotton are grown by slash-and-burn techniques. Karen depend heavily on hunting. They organize group drives to trap pigs, deer, and rabbits, which they kill with spears or crossbows. Fishing gear includes weirs, nets, basket traps, spears, poison, and hook and line. Karens are famous mahouts. They catch and train their own elephants, and they use cattle as pack animals. Dogs, pigs, and chickens are kept.

In the past, the Karen had matrilineal kin groups, and residence after marriage was in the longhouse of the bride's family. However, chieftainship was inherited patrilineally. Chiefs held authority over several villages, led religious ceremonies, and conducted warfare and slave raids against other groups.

Tribal religion consisted of belief in spirits and impersonal spiritual energy and worship of the ancestral spirits of the major matrilineages.

MONS

Mons are also known as Talaing.[7] Mon is a Siamese term and Talaing is Burmese. The English term *Peguan* is now obsolete, but it remains in the older literature. They call themselves Mon or Raman.

Mons are among the most ancient of the civilized peoples of Southeast Asia. But like another anciently civilized people, the Cham of Vietnam and Cambodia, they no longer have their own state or even their own city. They lost their independence to the Burmese in 1757. Before the development of Burmese and Siamese principalities, however, Mon kingdoms dotted the plains and coastlines of lower Burma and central Thailand. A confederation of Mon kingdoms straddled the base of the Malay Peninsula, stretching from the area around present-day Rangoon to the western borders of present-day Cambodia. Their present homeland is on the eastern shore of the Gulf of Martaban, in the northern third of the Tenasserim panhandle, near the city of Moulmein. More than ninety percent of the Mon of Burma (or seventy-five percent of all Mon) live in this area. Probably, there are about four hundred thousand Mon in Burma. But all of them speak Burmese as well as Mon, and a few no longer speak Mon.

Mon language belongs to the same language family as Khmer and the languages of most of the hill tribes of Southeast Asia. Mon-Khmer languages are like Malayo-Polynesian languages and different from Sino-Tibetan (Sinitic, Tibeto-Burman, Karen, and Miau-Yao), Viet-Muong, and Tai languages in that they are nontonal. That is, different tonal levels of vowels have no significant effect on the meanings of words.

The houses and villages of Mons are very similar to those of Thais and Burmese. Mons are primarily wet-rice farmers. In a few areas where it is impossible to raise wet rice, they use slash-and-burn techniques to grow dry rice. Like the Thais and the Burmese, they harvest rice with sickles and use cattle and threshing floors to separate the grain from the straw. Horses, cattle, water buffalo, pigs, ducks, chickens, and dogs are kept by Mons. They are great fishermen who use all of the devices known to Southeast Asian fishermen, and they are famous as manufacturers of fermented fish paste, which is important in lowlander cuisines throughout Southeast Asia. Mons are clever hunters, too. They use crossbows, pellet bows, and guns, as well as an assortment of snares and traps.

The kinship system has a definite patrilineal bias. There are exogamous patrilineal kin groups whose manifest function is the worship of a spirit *(kalok)* that dwells in a special basket that is attached to the southeastern corner post of the oldest male's house. Upon marriage, a woman changes her membership from her father's to her husband's *kalok* group. Succession to leadership of a *kalok* group passes to sons, brothers, or brothers' sons. Kinship terminology does not have a patrilineal bias. It is a generational terminology that distinguishes elder and younger siblings. Moreover, initial marital residence is matrilocal, and the most common household group is the nuclear family.

Historically, the Mons have been the principal bearers and proselytizers of Theravada Buddhism in Southeast Asia. It was they who maintained contact with Buddhist centers in India and Sri Lanka and communicated Theravada traditions to the Burmese, Tai, and Khmer. In the case of the Tais and the Burmese, the Theravada Buddhism of the Mons was a civilizing tradition that provided them with a system of writing, a literature (the Pali Canon and Mon books such as the *Mula Muli* creation myth and the *Hokavidu* presentation of Indian cosmology), and a universalistic philosophy.

Theravada Buddhism is more important to Mon religion than it is to the religions of Khmers, Tais, and Burmese. Like Hindus and Southeast Asian animists, Theravada Buddhists view the universe of living forms as a cyclical system that is eternally in flux. An individual's present life is only one of many phases of consciousness, each of which is animated at birth and deanimated at death by the presence and absence of spiritual energy. The individual is one role player in a long sequence of forms that are related to each other by a common mass of spiritual energy that temporarily inhabits each of them. A very simplified distinction among the overall perspectives of animists, Hindus, and Buddhists follows: the intent of an animist is to delay the migration of his mass of spiritual energy to the next form; the ideal intention of a Hindu is to direct the migration of his mass of spiritual energy to a higher form; and the ideal intention of a Buddhist is to help his mass of spiritual energy avoid having to inhabit any form. According to the doctrine of Theravada Buddhism, all living forms suffer, and salvation cannot be achieved by migrating from one life form to another.

The principal doctrine of Buddha repudiates the extremes of pleasure and pain and enjoins followers to follow the middle path of the four noble truths that lead to sublime selflessness and deliverance from suffering. The first truth is suffering, which comes from the endless cycle of life. Second, the cause of suffering is desire. Third, suffering may be extinguished by extinguishing desire. And fourth, desire may be extinguished by following the eightfold path. The eightfold path consists of: (1) right views—believing in the four truths; (2) right intent—avoiding sinful and cruel thoughts; (3) right speech—avoiding triviality; (4) right conduct —avoiding the taking of life or property or sinful sexual pleasure; (5) right livelihood—avoiding work that deceives or harms others; (6) right effort—subduing intentions of incorrect behavior; (7) right contemplation—seeking detachment from one's senses, emotions, and attitudes; and (8) right concentration—searching for serenity and insight.[8]

Theravada Buddhists, like Hindus, believe that it is possible to raise one's spiritual worth in successive lives and thereby work gradually towards the sublime selflessness that is nirvana. This belief is the basis for making merit by giving food to monks and paying priests to give sermons or chant religious sayings. It would be useless to pray to Buddha because Buddha, having achieved nirvana, does not exist as an entity anymore. The point of Theravada Buddhism is to follow the founder's example, not to ask him for help. Mahayanists have added a totally different dimension by asserting that Buddha is a personification of universal divine power.

Theravadins can and do worship deities. These deities are minor spirits whose personalities are small and therefore not strongly contradictory to the idea of salvation as selflessness or nonentity. In Mon culture, many of these spirits (dewatau) are drawn from the Hindu pantheon and include formerly great Brahma (prem) and Indra (in). The dewatau are related to agriculture and buildings. Another class of spirits (pea thong) are similar to the phi of Tai speakers, the neak taa of Khmers, and the nats of the Burmese. They are local place spirits. Finally, there are the ancestral spirits (kalok).

Most Mon boys are initiated as religious novices while they are adolescent. Later, after they are 20, they are ordained as monks. Mons also have a monastic order for women (prea min).

Some monks are spiritual healers and astrologers. In addition, there are female spirit mediums and practitioners of folk medicine. The folk medicine is based on restoration of the balance of four humors or bodily elements through diet and use of herbal medicines.

Major ceremonies of the Mon include the usual Buddhist observances at the beginning and end of the fasting period, the new year, and the local temple festival. Funerals are fairly elaborate. The wake lasts seven days and features nightly refreshments and entertainment and a large meal on the seventh day. Placed in a wooden coffin, the corpse is cremated at the cemetery. People who died violently are buried without a funeral or cremation.

ARAKANESE AND BURMESE

Like the Mon, the Arakanese are an anciently civilized people without a state of their own.[9] But they are linguistically and culturally very similar to the Burmese, and their assimilation into Burmese society has been thorough. Ignoring the historical differences in favor of present similarities, here they shall be counted as Burmese. A similar circumstance exists for the Tavoyan of Tenasserim. They, too, are Burmese.

The Burmese refer to themselves as Bama. They are called Phama by the Siamese and Hamea by the Mons. Their present homeland consists of the lowland valleys of the Chindwin, Irrawaddy, and Sittang and the coasts of Arakan and Tenasserim. There are more than twenty million Burmese in Burma and about a hundred thousand, descendants of nineteenth century political refugees, in Bangladesh.

Burmese live in linear villages along roads and watercourses or in nuclear villages in the midst of rice fields. Each village has a monastery, which is temple and rest house, and several provision shops. Houses are raised on posts and are rectangular with gabled roofs. They are usually constructed of wooden planks and have thatched roofs. Gardens and fruit orchards surround the houses.

Wet-rice fields stretch out between the villages. Burmese, like Malays, prefer nonglutinous rice for their everyday meals and reserve glutinous varieties for desserts. Near towns, farmers tend to specialize in market gardens. In the dry zone of central Burma, farmers grow cotton, maize, millet, tobacco, and sesame in addition to wet rice. Farmers in Tenasserim specialize in tree crops such as coconuts and durians. Burmese do not keep many domesticated animals. Usually, a farmer has only a buffalo for plowing. Fish are an important food. Most farmers catch fresh fish but not enough for their needs. The rest, salted fish, is purchased in the market. Burmese do not hunt or gather. Many men work part-time as craftsmen, and the women are traders in the markets.

Burmese have no descent groups or surnames. Kinship terminology is generational with terminological distinctions between older and younger siblings. Marriage between immediate relatives is forbidden. Cousin marriage is fairly common. Individuals make their own choice of spouse but confer with their parents if it is a first marriage. Arranged marriages are fairly common among the wealthy and are arranged by intermediators. Marriage ceremonies vary in elaborateness depending on the wealth of the couple's families. No ceremony is required. Marriage is a matter of public knowledge of cohabitation. The most common household group is the nuclear family with extra relatives such as a cousin, parent, or niece. A wealthy family usually has many extra relatives living in the household, some of whom are servants. Matrilocal extended families are not unusual among the wealthy. Sons and daughters inherit equally after both parents have died.

Funerals are important ceremonies. The wakes are very similar to those of the Mon. Burmese do not cremate the dead anymore. A procession accompanies the coffin to the cemetery where monks recite religious sayings and receive offerings for the added merit of the deceased and where water is poured to show his generous sharing of merit with all creatures. As the body is buried, the soul is told to be on its way. Like most other Southeast Asians, the Burmese believe that the form of the soul (the substance of spiritual energy) is a butterfly.

Other ceremonies and celebrations include the water festival at the beginning of the lunar year, the beginning and ending of fasting (from the full moon of the fourth month until the full moon of the seventh month), Buddha's birthday and death anniversary, monks' day, harvest festival, and village temple day.

The Burmese are Theravada Buddhists and spirit worshippers or animists. They are good Buddhists, but they are most interested in spirit (nat) worship. Hundreds of nats exist, but the most commonly known are a group of 37 nats that includes an Indian deva, tutelary spirits of particular regions, guardian spirits of the household, and national heroes. Small shrines or houses for these and other spirits hang from trees and the eaves of houses in Burmese villages.

There are various kinds of spirit mediums and medical practitioners. Perhaps the most interesting are the transvestite spirit dancers who attract spirits so that they may be propitiated or so that they will give advice.

THE BURMAN STATE

The Shan State is composed of complete states that have economic and political existences of their own. The people of areas that border on the Shan State are drawn somewhat into its systems. Other special states, for one reason or another, are states only in the most limited sense. Their peoples are dependents of the Burman state and of the Burmese. But the Burmese do not have a traditional state.

Burma has not been a kingdom for almost a century. The old monarchial institutions are gone. Present political structure owes much to the forms of British colonial administration and Japanese military organization. When the forms of colonial parliament and civil service have failed, the forms of military organization have been imposed. The Burma Socialist Programme Party functions more or less as the information corps of the Burmese army.

The army has been a very effective apparatus of state. No other organization could have maintained order and kept the union together half so well. Ordinary peasants, traders, and workers have not suffered greatly during the transition towards Burmese socialism. Foreign Asians have suffered and many have emigrated because the government has taken over the economic functions of medium- and large-scale businesses. There are less than a hundred thousand Indians and less than four hundred thousand Chinese left in Burma. The only foreign Asians who are doing well and increasing in number are the Chinese Muslim (Panthay) traders and muleteers of Shan State. They number about ten thousand. The future of other Chinese and the Indians does not appear to be bright. More emigration seems probable. Those who remain will become citizens and assimilate.

REFERENCES

[1] H. Tinker, *The Union of Burma* (London: Oxford University Press, 1956).

[2] L. Milne and W. W. Cochrane, *Shans at Home* (London: John Murray, 1910); and E. R. Leach, *Political Systems of Highland Burma: A Study of Kachin Social Structure* (London: G. Bell and Sons, 1954).

[3] See "Palaungs" and "Wa" in F. M. LeBar et al., *Ethnic Groups of Mainland Southeast Asia* (New Haven, Conn.: Human Relations Area Files Press, 1964).

[4] Leach, *Political Systems of Highland Burma.*

[5] F. K. Lehman, *The Structure of Chin Society: A Tribal People of Burma Adapted to a Non-Western Civilization* (Urbana: University of Illinois Press, 1963).

[6] See "Karen" in LeBar et al., *Ethnic Groups of Mainland Southeast Asia.*

[7] R. Halliday, *The Talaings* (Rangoon: Government Printing, 1917).

[8] R. S. Copleston, *Buddhism, Primitive and Present in Magadha and in Ceylon* (London: Longmans, Green, 1908).

[9] Good sources on Burmese society include: M. M. Khaing, *Burmese Family* (Bombay: Longmans, Green, 1946); Shwey Yoe (J. G. Scott), *The Burman: His Life and Notions* (London: Macmillan & Company, 1910); and M. E. Spiro, *Burmese Supernaturalism* (Englewood Cliffs, N.J.: Prentice-Hall, 1967).

NINE

THE KHMER STATE

AN EMPTY AND BOUNTIFUL LAND

Cambodia, or more properly the Khmer Republic, is a rich and relatively empty agricultural land.[1] It is a very flat and low plain, almost at sea level, that is surrounded by low mountains. In area and density of population, it is similar to the state of Missouri. Only about twenty-five percent of its arable land is under cultivation. It is productive land that has helped feed the people of rice-deficient areas such as Malaysia and Indonesia. Other states, Vietnam and Thailand, have absorbed vast areas that it formerly controlled and in the future they may continue to expand into the territories of Cambodia.

The Mekong River and Tonle Sap lake comprise a natural irrigation system for wet rice and provide a fertile environment for fish. One of the longest rivers in the world (2,700 miles), the Mekong flows through parts of China, Burma, Thailand, and Laos before depositing the soils of these regions in Cambodia and the South China Sea. It cuts through the plain to the east of the Tonle Sap, which commands the center. Sometime in the past, the Tonle Sap was a long inland arm of the sea, but millions of tons of silt deposited by the Mekong River eventually blocked its communication with the sea. Tidal waters no longer entered the Tonle Sap, and it became a huge freshwater lake. Moreover, at full flood during the rainy season, the waters of the Mekong cannot empty freely into the sea, the floodwaters back up into Tonle Sap river, and the lake fills and spreads the silt-rich waters over more than seven hundred square miles. The flood waters are fairly gentle and easily managed with levees. Seeds sown before the flood sprout, and plants begin to grow as the water recedes. In the dry season, the lake shrinks to less than one-third of its greatest size and is no more than five feet deep. More than sixty-five thousand metric tons of fish are harvested from the lake during the dry season.

Cambodia's neighbors are envious. Cambodians distrust their neighbors.

KHMERS

Khmers are the major people of Cambodia.[2] They are a bit taller and darker than their Tai and Viet neighbors, and their black hair is more deeply waved. They are probably descendants of the people of ancient Chenla. Their language is closely related to Mon. Their most commonly used script is derived from Pali script. Another script that has cuneiform characters is derived from another Indian script. Khmer is their ancient and modern name. Cambodian refers to any citizen of Cambodia whether Khmer or not. It derives from the name of the ninth-century founder of the Khmer monarchy, Kambu Svayambhuva. Chinese referred to his people as Kambu-jadesa, "sons of Kambu," hence the European name of Cambodge or Cambodia.

There are more than seven million Khmer in Cambodia. They comprise about ninety percent of the total population. Most of them are wet-rice farmers, market gardeners, fishermen, and craftsmen. Village houses line the roads and waterways or form clusters in the middle of rice fields in the few densely populated areas, but otherwise they are scattered and distant from each other. The houses are rectangular and raised on stilts and have gabled roofs. Houses of comparatively wealthy families are made of wooden planks and have roofs of tile. Houses of the poor have walls and roofs of thatch. The kitchen is usually a ground-level shed attached to the rear of the house. Fruit trees and vegetable gardens fill the spaces between the houses. Each village has a more or less central compound for its temple, great hall, monastery, and bathing place.

Khmer farmers use the same techniques and plant the same crops as Burmese and Siamese farmers. Sugar palms are very abundant. They are to the Khmer as coconut palms are to Malays. The trees provide juice, sugar, fruit, thatch, and wood and are a national symbol. They grow better in Cambodia than in other places of Southeast Asia. Only in the southern coastal areas of India are they more abundant. Khmers keep oxen and buffalo for plowing, pigs and chickens for sale, and cats and dogs as pets. Khmers are not hunters or even meat eaters. They catch and consume fish—fresh, salted, and in the form of fermented paste (parhoc). Some men are excellent woodworkers and work part-time making craft goods such as musical instruments for sale. Others try to find employment in towns during the months when fields need little care.

Some women weave decorative cotton or silk cloth for *sampot,* traditional Khmer garments that are wrapped around the waist and tucked through the legs. Poor families manufacture palm sugar during periods when agricultural labor is not needed.

Khmer kinship organization is bilateral. Aunt and uncle terminology and reference terminology for cousins is lineal (as in English), but address terminology for cousins is generational. There are terminological distinctions between elder and younger siblings. The incest taboo extends only to immediate relatives. Village endogamy is preferred, and marriages between cousins are common. Some marriages are arranged by parents. The elaborateness of marriage celebrations varies. Neolocality is the preferred and most common mode of marital residence. Matrilocality is common, too. The household group is usually a nuclear family or a stem family consisting of a couple, their unmarried children, and a married child with spouse and children. There are no larger corporate kin groups. Children share inheritance of their parents' property more or less equally. Land is given away to children as they marry, and parents sometimes favor one child over others. Other kinds of property are shared after the parents die.

Social stratification of Khmer society resembles that of other lowland groups. There is little evidence of social class within villages although there are individual differences in wealth. Age, piety, and talent are respected. Rural villagers and urban laborers are about equally lower class. In the towns, small businessmen, government clerks, teachers, and priests comprise a sort of small middle class, and the royal family, nobles, and high-ranking military, government, and religious officials comprise the ruling elite. Foreign Asians, Chinese, and Vietnamese control the commerce of the country and are wealthy. Chinese have fairly high social status, but Vietnamese have no scalar status in Khmer society.

Khmers are Theravada Buddhists and spirit worshippers. Their major ceremonies are the usual Buddhist celebrations. Their means of treating illnesses are the same as those of other animists. Khmer funerals do not last long since cremation usually takes place the morning after death. But the wake is as entertaining as Thai or Burmese wakes. And except for their brevity, funerals are like those of other Theravada Buddhists.

CHAMS

Chams are a major people, but they have not had their own state since the fifteenth century.[3] Their original homeland, Champa, was in the coastal lowlands of central and southern Vietnam. Defeated in 1471 by the Vietnamese, most of the ruling elite and the remaining population of Champa fled to Cambodia. The Khmer king guaranteed their rights and safety, and he began a tradition of formally appointing their paramount chief to the rank of Khmer royalty. Meanwhile in Vietnam, the Cham who remained were driven into the hills or into the least fertile coastal regions. They have been forced to the margins of Vietnamese society to a very great extent. The result is that if the Chams have a home it is in Cambodia rather than Vietnam.

There are more than one hundred thousand Chams in Cambodia. There are a few Malays living among them. Cham language belongs to the Malayo-Polynesian language family. It is closely related to the dialects of some hill tribes in Vietnam and more distantly to Malay, which Chams use in Islamic contexts. A script derived from Arabic is widely used, and an older Indian script is still known.

Most Cham villages are north and east of Phnom Penh. The villages are virtually identical to those of the Khmer. Even the mosques have the same form as Khmer pagodas. Although Chams cultivate some wet rice, they are less oriented toward wet-rice cultivation than Khmers. Cham farmers cultivate commercial crops such as cotton, indigo, and sesame, and they are market gardeners. They tend cattle, fish, and work as boatmen. Some of them live in the towns where they are traders and craftsmen.

Cham kinship is matrilineal. In the past, the structure of Cham society was probably dominated by a few exogamous matriclans that were joined by affinal relationships with each other and with a royal patrilineage. The legends of the matriclans have survived. Perhaps they still exist, and perhaps a patriline of paramount chiefs has assumed the function of the former royal line. It is known that property is inherited through women in Cham society and that a man must move into the compound of his wife's family when he marries. Moreover, it is the woman's family rather than the man's family that initiates marriage proposals, and the man's family must furnish a dowry for the couple. The presentation of the dowry and the witnessing of the marriage contract by an imam comprise the marriage ceremony, which is followed by a large feast.

The Chams of Cambodia are Muslims. They are as orthodox as Malays and much more orthodox than the Muslim Chams of Vietnam. Some Cham of Vietnam are Hindu. The ritual and doctrine of Islam and Hinduism have both degenerated in the face of Vietnamese assimilationist policies.

Among Cambodian Chams, the greatest ceremonies are Islamic—celebrations that mark the end of fasting month, the month of pilgrimage, the Prophet's birthday, and newly gained competence in reading the Holy Koran. They also participate in national holidays such as the water festival, which celebrates the annual change in the direction of water flow of Tonle Sap (when it begins to drain back into the Mekong).

FOREIGN ASIANS: CHINESE AND VIETNAMESE

The Chinese of Cambodia number about four hundred thousand. Half of them live in Phnom Penh where they constitute about one-third of the population. Most of the rest of the Chinese live in other major towns. The major dialect groups in the order of their size are Tiechieu, Cantonese, Hokkien, Hakka, and Hailam. Dialect groups are further organized into occupational associations headed by leaders called *bang* who mediate relationships between the Chinese community and the government.

Chinese control most of the commerce of the country. The rice trade is in their hands. They are prevented by law from acquiring rice fields of Khmers so the fields are not used as collateral for loans. The rice crops are used as collateral. Of course the rice is under-valued, and interest rates are high. Loans can rarely be repaid. The farmer is allowed to keep enough of the crop for his own needs. The surplus is given as payment to reduce his loan. Chinese who lend money to Khmer rice farmers are also rice traders. They maintain a very high margin of profit. Most of the fishing industry is controlled by the Chinese, too. They own the boats and equipment and employ the Vietnamese, Cham, and Khmer fishermen. Most of the rubber industry is owned by French interests, but Chinese own the remainder through silent partnerships with Khmers. Finally, Chinese monopolize retail trade.

Khmer attitudes towards the Chinese are not entirely negative. Many Khmer fathers have married their daughters to Chinese because they are excellent sons-in-law, clever in business and generous to fathers-in-law. Children of mixed Chinese and Khmer marriages are regarded as having the best features of both, and Sino-Khmers have a great deal of pride.

Vietnamese are as numerous as Chinese in Cambodia, and like the Chinese, about half of them reside in the capital where they comprise about one-third of the population. In towns they are professionals, merchants, clerks, artisans, and servants. In rural areas they are fishermen and wet-rice farmers. Nowhere are they appreciated by Khmers.

HILL TRIBES (PHNONG)

Many different kinds of people live in the hills and low mountains that surround the Cambodian plain. In most instances the territories of these people extend into other states—Thailand, Laos, and Vietnam.

The Jarai speak a Malayo-Polynesian language that is related to Cham.[4] They are closely related to other Malayo-Polynesian-speaking groups such as the Rhade whose territories lie along the Cambodian-Vietnamese border. The Jarai are important to the Khmer and the Khmer to the Jarai in a symbolic way that can hardly be appreciated by Western minds. A great sorcerer, the Sadat of Fire, lives among the Jarai, and it is his prerogative, his duty, to protect the Khmer Sword of State. For centuries, sadats of the Jarai were probably invited to participate in royal coronations. Lowland kings believed that part of their right to rule derived from ownership of all the territory of the kingdom, which they inherited through distant kinship to leaders of aboriginal groups. Traditionally, coronations of Southeast Asian kings required the presence of leaders of aboriginal groups. By participating, the sadat fulfilled a cosmological requirement for the Khmer king. Possibly, by the same acts, he pledged the loyalty of the hill tribes to the Khmer monarchy. The Sadat of Fire is the leader and most powerful of all the sorcerers of the hill tribes. Like the legendary first Kaundinya, he is "King of the Mountain." The next most powerful are the Sadat of Wind and the Sadat of Water. These other sadats are less powerful because they cannot communicate with the Sacred Sword (Prah Khan), which is inhabited by many powerful spirits. It is said that the last real Sadat of Fire died in the nineteenth century and that those who have since succeeded to the office are merely caretakers of the office. Succession is not inherited. Warriors contend with each other to gain possession of a copper bracelet that is the insignia of office and with themselves to attract the spiritual essence of the previous sadat.

The Jarai are not otherwise remarkable. Only a small portion of the more than two hundred thousand Jarai actually live in Cambodia. They are slash-and-burn cultivators who live in villages of three to sixty longhouses. Dry rice is their main crop, and they grow root and fruit crops, too. They hunt and gather, and they are organized into totemic matrisibs. Their political organization does not seem to be sufficiently complex to support a Sadat of Fire. Each village has a headman and a council of elders.

Stieng (Budip)

The Stieng live south and west of the Jarai along the Cambodia-Vietnam border.[5] Probably there are fewer than a hundred thousand Stieng. They speak a Mon-Khmer language. They grow dry rice with slash-and-burn techniques, and they fish and hunt. Their villages consist of single-family houses, raised on stilts and thatched. Individual families sometimes shift from one village to another. Witches and sorcerers who eat the livers of their victims are greatly feared by the Stieng. They also fear individuals who anger the village spirits. Divination ceremonies to discover witches and violators of taboos are common rituals in Stieng villages. Guilty persons are severely punished, sometimes by death. Sons inherit the parents' property, and for a brief period after marriage, residence is usually patrilocal. If a bride-price was not paid, initial residence is usually matrilocal. There are no large corporate kin groups such as patrisibs.

Pear, Chong, Saoch, and Samre

Many anthropologists believe that the Pear and groups closely related to them are remnants of a formerly widespread Mon-Khmer-speaking population of Negritos that included the Semang of Malaysia.[6] Some of them have short stature, deeply curled or kinky hair, bulging foreheads, and skin color that is almost as dark as that of the Khmer. Presently, there are only a few thousand of them. They live in the mountains that border Thailand in the southwestern part of Cambodia and in hilly areas just east of the Tonle Sap.

Pear villages range in size from several houses to more than three hundred. They are small rectangular houses set on pilings. The walls are of split bamboo and the gabled roofs are thatched. Most villages are near streams. Their Khmer and Cham neighbors claim that they used to live in tree houses or in no houses at all.

The Pear are slash-and-burn farmers. Their main crop is dry rice. They also grow maize, millet, bananas, root crops, cotton, chili, and tobacco. Gathering and hunting (with crossbows) supplements their economy. Some groups trade very little, and they manufacture their own pottery and cotton cloth. Others sell rice and woven mats to Khmer traders in exchange for various manufactured goods. Sometimes they work as laborers for Khmers, and a few of the men have married Khmer women.

The Pear are strongly patrilineal. They are divided into three totemic patriclans, which are subdivided into patrilineages. Chiefs of the patriclans have ritual responsibilities that include driving away malignant spirits. Chiefs of the lineages adjudicate infractions of community rules.

Other leaders include chief sorcerers who claim descent from sorcerers employed by the Khmer king in ancient times. Their major responsibility is control of the weather. They also cure illnesses, make amulets, and lead the community in cult ceremonies that honor the ancestors. Pears bury their dead. The body is washed and dressed in formal clothing, its head is anointed with coconut oil, and it is placed for viewing on a board for one day. Then it is buried, and the earth and wild plants are replaced so that there is no evidence of the grave.

An extensive area in northern Cambodia along the border with
Thailand is inhabited by the Kui.[7] There are about a hundred
thousand of them who have retained their own language and some
of their own customs. Another hundred and fifty thousand are almost assimilated into Siamese or Khmer society. Kui belongs to
the Mon-Khmer language family, and its closest affiliation is with
Pear. There is tremendous variation in physical traits of persons
even within the same village. Tall and short, dark and very light
skin, straight and kinky hair, low and high nasal bridges—all in-
validate any statement about typical physical appearance.

In the past, Kui lived in longhouses. Recently they have
adopted the single-family house styles of Siamese and Khmers.
Their villages often intermingle with the villages of Khmers.

A majority of Kui are wet-rice farmers. They use the same
techniques as the Khmers, which they learned as a result of the
campaigns of French colonial officials against slash-and-burn farming. A few are still slash-and-burn farmers. They cultivate the
swiddens for only two years and allow a fallow of more than
twenty years, so there is very little damage to the environment,
and, probably, the availability of floral and faunal species that are
gathered and hunted is increased.

The Kui produce several commercial agricultural products
—sugar, cotton, and silk—which they trade to Khmers. They make
pottery and weave cotton cloth for sale. They also mine and smelt
iron ore and manufacture iron tools for trade. Their fame as makers
of high quality iron tools dates back at least to the sixteenth century when King Ang Chan granted them a piece of land near his
capital for their iron market.

Iron mining and smelting occurs in a small hilly area that has
a massive deposit of hematite just beneath the surface of the
ground. The whole operation is directed by one person. His son
inherits his position, or if he has no son, a new director is elected
from among the villages in the mining area. The insignia of his
office are a deerskin cape and a special hat.

Smelting furnaces are built of clay. Ore is placed in the furnace
and mixed with burning charcoal, which is fed a continuous
stream of air through bamboo tubing connected to a bellows. After
the iron cools, it is taken from the furnace and reheated in a forge
that is equipped with a piston bellows. Then it is hammered into
shape on an anvil.

In the past, the Kui were special wards of the Cambodian king.
Exempt from service and other kinds of taxes, villages were organized according to craft specialization and forced to pay taxes in
kind on the special goods that they produced. Possibly, these occu-
pationally delineated villages were the basis of later ill-defined

"clans." Very little is known of the present-day social organization of the Kui. Most of them are now Theravada Buddhists.

THE KHMER COSMOS

Cambodia, like the Shan and the Lao and the Malay states, may be characterized as a carefully orchestrated system of symbolic, economic, and political relationships among different kinds of people. Khmers have gradually and gently assimilated other peoples. They, like the Shan and the Lao, have avoided the militant assimilationist policies of the Siamese and the Burmese, which seem attractive to some Malays. Khmer relations with other peoples differ sharply from those of the Vietnamese, who seem to be continuing their ancient tradition of expanding into other peoples' territories.

Unfortunately, Cambodia lies between Thailand and Vietnam, the Southeast Asian states with the fullest reputations for imperialism. Its continued existence seems problematic at this time, depending more on the good will of enemies than on the strength of friends.

REFERENCES

[1]D. J. Steinberg et al., *Cambodia* (New Haven, Conn.: Human Relations Area Files Press, 1959).

[2]M. Ebihara, "Khmer" in F. M. LeBar et al., eds., *Ethnic Groups of Mainland Southeast Asia* (New Haven, Conn.: Human Relations Area Files Press, 1964).

[3]See "Cham" in LeBar et al., eds., *Ethnic Groups of Mainland Southeast Asia.*

[4]See "Jarai" in LeBar et al., eds., *Ethnic Groups of Mainland Southeast Asia;* and P. P. Guilleminet, *Coutumier de la tribu Bohnar des Sedang et des Jarai* (Paris: EFEO Publications, 1952).

[5]See "Stieng" in LeBar et al., eds., *Ethnic Groups of Mainland Southeast Asia.*

[6]See "Mon-Khmer—Southwest Upland Groups" in LeBar et al., eds., *Ethnic Groups of Mainland Southeast Asia.*

[7]Chapter 1 in *Minority Groups in Thailand*, Ethnographic Study Series, Department of the Army Pamphlet No. 550-107, 1970.

TEN

VIETNAMESE STATES

EXPANDING FRONTIERS

The most extraordinary fact about the Vietnamese is their gradual and sustained expansion into new territory for a period of more than two thousand years.[1] In the process their culture has been little affected by the people whose lands they occupied. More than any other Southeast Asian people, they have a strong sense of national identity and a strong interest in frontiers. During a thousand years of direct Chinese rule, they expanded their frontiers, not for the Chinese, but for themselves. During French rule, they continued to expand, immigrating by the thousands into the Mekong delta, crowding out the Khmer farmers, claiming and gaining all the delta lands that had belonged to Cambodia when the French established the colonial regime. After the French left and Vietnamese immigrants from the north crowded the plains of the south, the southern government opened the highlands, lands of the Rhade and Mnong, to Vietnamese immigration. Vietnamese have displaced other people rather than assimilate them. Perhaps they fear assimilation from any perspective because of their experiences with Chinese imperialism.

VIETNAMESE (ANNAMESE)

There are about thirty-six million Vietnamese in North and South Vietnam.[2] More than half of them live in North Vietnam. Vietnamese also comprise important minorities in Thailand, Laos, and Cambodia. Their language, closely related only to Muong, is not clearly allied to any one Asian language family but to several. Many of the root words appear to be Mon-Khmer, some of the vocabulary is Chinese, and characteristics of the tonal system are like Tai. There are three mutually intelligible dialects that are spoken in northern, central, and southern Vietnam.

Vietnamese houses are not built on stilts, but on low mounds of earth. Building materials and roof styles vary. Houses are rectangular and have attached kitchens. Villages contain from several to several thousand houses. In the north, villages and hamlets are surrounded by walls of bamboo or earth. Villages are more open in the central area and in the south.

Wet rice is the most important crop. There are many varieties. Vietnamese methods are very sophisticated and include double-cropping and the use of large amounts of fertilizer. In the lower reaches of the Red River valley, a very complex system of irrigation and drainage has been developed. Irrigation systems are well-developed elsewhere, too. Cash crops such as rubber, coconuts, pepper, tea, and coffee are common in the south. Jute production has been introduced into the Dalat highlands by northern immigrants, and fruit orchards and market gardens are common everywhere. Vietnamese grow virtually every crop grown by lowlanders in Southeast Asia, and they keep all kinds of livestock. Many Vietnamese are fishermen, especially in the central coastal area where the plains are very narrow. Forests are lumbered commercially for wood and charcoal. And in the north, Vietnamese mine coal, iron ore, and other metallic ores. Craft villages of the north produce shoes, cloth, paper, pottery, iron tools, and bronze artifacts. Commerce, industry, and government service provide jobs for urban dwellers throughout Vietnam. Typically, northern Vietnamese are employed in crafts and industry, central Vietnamese in fishing, and southern Vietnamese in agriculture.

Vietnamese kinship is patrilineal. Patrilineal institutions are more thoroughly developed in the north than in the south. This probably reflects the greater need for flexible social structure in the expanding frontier of the south, and it may also reflect the impact of colonial agricultural enterprises in the south. For example, the surname groups *(ho)* function as exogamous patrisibs in the north, while in the south, persons with the same surname can marry if they prove they are not related. Patrilineages *(toc)* have a depth of five generations in the north and are led by the senior male of the senior lineage segment. In the south, patrilineages have a depth of only three generations and are led by the most able male. Traditionally, in the north, the *toc* leader controlled profits from inalienable family lands, using them to finance ceremonies of the ancestral cult and to pay for the upkeep of ancestral tombs. Most lineages in the south do not have inalienable family lands, and heads of nuclear families are much more important than in the north.

Marriages are often arranged by parents. Parents of the prospective groom initiate negotiations with the family of the bride through an intermediary. The horoscopes of the couple must match, and a bride-price must be negotiated. Traditional marriage requires a number of separate ceremonies—meeting of parents, setting of bride-price, kowtowing to bride's ancestors, and kowtowing to groom's ancestors. Marital residence is usually virilocal.

Patterns of inheritance differ. Only sons can inherit in the northern and central areas, and primogeniture is the rule. In the south, daughters sometimes inherit and ultimogeniture is common.

Other social organizational features illustrate a much greater emphasis on closed corporate groups in the north than in the south. Chief among these are the traditional craft guilds (phuong) that continued to function through the colonial period. Phuongs guarded secret techniques, set standards, regulated supplies, and fixed prices. The phuongs were very similar to Chinese occupational associations except that the phuongs were more tightly organized and were closed to all except the patrilineal descendants of members. Nothing of this sort ever existed in the south, where men were free to enter or leave craft specializations according to their choice and capability. In the south, corporate groups tend to be open voluntary associations. An example would be rotating credit associations (hui). Anyone can form such a group. Members contribute a fixed sum periodically and take turns (prearranged or decided each time by lot) using the total amount. The right to the sum at any particular meeting may be sold to another member. An association may cease to exist after each member has had a turn, or new members may join by paying a bonus for previous dues. Capital loans are the major purpose of these associations. In the north, capital loans were traditionally arranged through the guild or through the village mutual-aid society (giap), which were permanent associations with closed memberships.

Vietnamese religious traditions and ceremonies are in some ways similar to those of the overseas Chinese. Ancestor worship is the common basis of religious practices of all Vietnamese. In addition, they are Mahayana Buddhists, Confucianists, Taoists, and Catholics. Catholics tend to be more exclusive than the others in their practice of religion. They comprise a very distinctive and comparatively well-educated minority in both South Vietnam and North Vietnam. The usual nonexclusive attitude of Vietnamese regarding religious beliefs is illustrated by the eight Cao Dai sects, which incorporate many different aspects of Catholicism, Buddhism, Taoism, Confucianism, Hinduism, and Humanism.

Indigenous cults are of some importance to all Vietnamese. In addition to the ancestor cult, there are spirit cults associated with villages, animals, trees, and stones. Vietnamese also honor the goddess of fortune and spirits of national heros, and they fear and propitiate the spirits of major diseases such as cholera. Spirit mediums, male and female, communicate with the spirit world,

curing illnesses and giving advice. Traditional Chinese medicine,
geomancy, and other sciences are well known and comprise a
major portion of traditional Vietnamese science.

FOREIGN ASIANS: CHAMS, KHMERS, AND CHINESE

Chams were once the major people of central and southern Vietnam, but now they are not even an important minority (see Chapter Nine, The Khmer State). The brick towers near Nha Trang and
Phan Rang and the ruins of My Son in Quang Nam province seem
an unlikely legacy of the ancestors of the fifty thousand poverty-
stricken Cham of Vietnam. Their villages are in the most desolate
parts of the southern coast, in arid areas and among coastal sand
dunes. Rice is not the most important crop for most farmers. They
are market gardeners, and they keep goats, ducks, and chickens.
Some of the Vietnamese Cham are Hindus; others are Muslims.
Neither have very orthodox ritual and doctrine because of their
long isolation from coreligionists.

There are about a half million Khmers in the Mekong delta
(see Chapter Nine, The Khmer State). They occupy land that was
claimed by Cambodia until 1954, and which was peacefully infil-
trated by Vietnamese farmers before and during the French colonial
period.

The overseas Chinese of Vietnam are unequally divided between north and south. There are only about two hundred thousand
Chinese in the north and more than a million in the south. In the
past they often intermarried with Vietnamese and their children
(Minh Huong) were allowed to compete for positions in the mandarin service. During French colonial times the Chinese remained
aloof from the Vietnamese and formed their own communities.
Vietnamese governments have since attempted to assimilate them
culturally by forcing them to use Vietnamese surnames and by re-
strictions on private Chinese schools. At this writing, the position
of Chinese in North Vietnam is not clear. Probably, they are artisans and market gardeners. In South Vietnam, they control most of
the private economy.

HILL TRIBES: MUONG, MON-KHMER, AND MALAYO-POLYNESIAN

Muong (Nguon, Sach, and Tho) are probably aboriginal Vietnamese
who were not subjected to the benefits of Chinese civilization.[3]
There are more than five hundred thousand Muong. Most of them
live in the highlands southwest of the Red River. The name by
which they are known in Western literature, Muong, is a mis-

nomer, but it is too common to replace. *Muong* is a Tai word for a territorial division, and it is used by Vietnamese to refer to Tai hill tribes. Muong language is closely related to Vietnamese.

Houses are single family dwellings built on pilings. Sometimes they are connected by covered walkways. The houses are rectangular with walls of split bamboo and roofs of thatch. Domesticated animals are kept beneath the houses, and the kitchen hearth is inside the house. House compounds are sometimes walled or surrounded by hedges. Granaries, also built on pilings, are within the house compound. Usually, the house of the village headman and the temple of the soil spirit are in the center of the village.

Most Muong are wet-rice farmers. They terrace their hillsides and route irrigation water through a system of bamboo pipes. Some areas produce two crops of wet rice each year. Where wet-rice farming is impracticable, or where they are pioneering new areas for wet-rice cultivation, they use slash-and-burn techniques. Swiddens are cultivated for several years before they are transformed into wet-rice paddies or allowed to fallow. Fertilizer is used. Other crops include maize, manioc, sesame, and tomatoes. Muong use the same tools as lowland people—plows, harrows, and sickles. They keep buffalo, cattle, pigs, ducks, and chickens. Some industrial and cash crops are grown such as cotton, kapok, sticklac, and benzoin. Traditionally, land belonged to the man who pioneered the farmstead. People who arrived later had to ask permission to farm land not in use. This gave some incentive to pioneering and also led to the development of a landed gentry *(tho lang)* in densely populated areas.

Fishing is an important activity. Hunting is more a sport and is done with crossbows. Women gather some wild roots and greens. Most large villages have several Vietnamese shops, and the Muong trade with Tai and Meo tribesmen in town markets.

Descent is patrilineal among all Muong. The eldest son inherits most of the property. Among the gentry *(tho lang)*, there are named patrisibs *(ho)*, which are exogamous. Other Muong have unnamed patrilineages. Marriage arrangements and ceremonies are practically identical to those of the Vietnamese.

Muong worship their ancestors and dozens of natural spirits. Every house has an altar in the front room. It is an elaborately carved table with bronze candlesticks, offering plates, and lacquered plaques that represent the ancestors. The guardian spirit of the village is an important deity. He is the spirit of the pioneer who founded the village and the ancestor of the local *tho lang*.

Ritual specialists undergo a long period of training—three to ten years. In addition, each has to acquire his own tutelary spirit. The ritual specialists conduct rituals, cure illnesses, and supervise funerals. Muong funerals like Muong weddings are very similar to those of the Vietnamese.

Brief outlines of the customs of the other hill tribes found in North Vietnam have been provided above (see The Tai States). They include Tai and Yao slash-and-burn farmers, who live at somewhat higher altitudes than the Muong, and Meo, who live at the highest altitudes. Tai speakers include the Black Tai, White Tai, and Tho. Tho is a name also applied to the Muong. The Yao of North Vietnam are called Man. Altogether these non-Muong hill tribes of North Vietnam include more than two million persons. The North Vietnamese government has organized them into two semiautonomous areas.

There are more than a dozen Mon-Khmer-speaking tribes in the highlands of South Vietnam.[4] They include about eight hundred thousand persons. The Sedang, Bahnar, and Mnong, as well as the Stieng (see Chapter Nine, The Khmer State), are illustrative of similarities and differences between these groups. Sedang and Bahnar have populations of about one hundred thousand each. The Mnong number about fifty thousand. The Sedang are farthest north, the Mnong are farthest south, and the Bahnar are in between. Sedang and Bahnar are very closely related languages, and Mnong is closely related to Stieng.

The houses of these groups are raised on stilts, are rectangular, and have gabled roofs. The walls are of split bamboo, and the roofs are thatch. But there are differences. Sedang and Mnong have longhouses; Bahnar have single-family houses. Bahnar and Sedang villages have a separate house for male bachelors; Mnong villages do not.

All of these groups are slash-and-burn rice farmers. They also grow millet, maize, manioc, yams, taro, vegetables, bananas, and fruit trees. They keep all sorts of livestock. Hunting and fishing and gathering are important. The tools that are used in these activities are like those of other hill people in Southeast Asia. The Sedang, like the Kui of Cambodia, mine iron ore, smelt it, and manufacture iron tools for trade.

The kinship systems of these Mon-Khmer groups vary a great deal. The Sedang system is bilateral, that of the Bahnar is patrilineal, and the Mnong are matrilineal. Matrilateral cross-cousin marriage is the preferred form among Mnong. Cousin marriage is thought to be almost incestuous by the Bahnar and Sedang. Marital residence is ambilocal among the Sedang and Bahnar, and it is matrilocal among the Mnong. Of these groups, only the Mnong have corporate kin groups (matrisibs) that extend beyond the village. The village is the major political unit. It forms alliances with other villages through marriage and trade. The Bahnar are allied symbolically to many tribes that recognize the sacredness of the Jarai Sadat of Fire.

Spirit worship, of course, is common to all hill farmers in Southeast Asia. Among Mon-Khmer-speaking tribes there is a common reverence for the spirit of thunder, ancestral ghosts, and place spirits. *Yang* is the usual term meaning "spirit," and the concept of "soul" is richly developed. Sacrifices, particularly of buffalo, are a common means of placating the spirits and redistributing wealth. Spirit mediums are curers, prognosticators, conductors of ceremonies, and commonly great leaders.

There are almost six hundred thousand Malayo-Polynesian speakers in the highlands of South Vietnam.[5] Some of them are probably descendants of Chams who fled into the hills. Others are probably hill groups that were partially assimilated to Cham culture during the time of the Cham Empire. They are divided into many groups. One of these, the Jarai, has been described above (see Chapter Nine, The Khmer State). Others include the Rai, Raglai, Rhade, Hroy, Churu, Krung, Noang, and Bih. Their territories center on the area of Darlat and the Darlac Plateau.

Most of the Malayo-Polynesian hill farmers live in nucleated villages of several to a dozen longhouses. They are mostly slash-and-burn farmers but practice wet-rice cultivation where possible. Maize, millet, and root crops are grown, and they have orchards of fruit trees. Hunting and fishing and gathering are important for subsistence. Their kinship systems are matrilineal. They have exogamous matrisibs. Among the Rhade, matrisibs are grouped into phratries, and the phratries are organized into a system of asymmetrical marital exchange. In all groups, inheritance of agricultural land is through females, and each longhouse is inhabited by females of a matrilineage and their spouses. A man gains positions of leadership in his sister's rather than his wife's group.

Most of the Malayo-Polynesian groups recognize the Jarai Sadat of Fire. There is only one Sadat of Fire. He lives in Plei Mtao, in South Vietnam. His recognition by most Malayo-Polynesian groups and Khmer royalty is an intriguing indication of a larger solidarity that perhaps was more powerful in the past. Malayo-Polynesian speakers of Cambodia and Vietnam worship spirits called *yang*, which are usually represented in human form. Special rituals honor the spirits concerned with agriculture. The spirit or soul of the rice is specially honored at planting time, and it is ritually retrieved from the field at harvest time and lured into the seed for the next rice crop. They also honor a spirit of the land, and special rituals are observed when a new longhouse is built. A priestess *(po-lan)* officiates at these ceremonies. Animal sacrifices are a common means of propitiating the spirits.

LOWLAND CIVILIZATION AND FOLK SOCIETIES

Nowhere else is the contrast between a major people of the lowlands and minority peoples of the hills so sharply drawn as in Vietnam. The topography, which is so much hills and so little plains, has given hill tribes a certain protection from Vietnamese expansion. French colonial officers probably enhanced the isolation of hill tribes from the Vietnamese through their policy of preserving the cultures of aboriginal peoples. However, the southern plains have been filled, and the relieving flow of Vietnamese into Thailand, Laos, and Cambodia has been slowed. The uplands are becoming more attractive to Vietnamese.

North Vietnamese have had better relationships with the hill people because of the proximity of Muongs, who are closely related to them, and because of their greater ease of communication with other hill groups through the Muongs. In South Vietnam, all of the hill people are very distinct from the Vietnamese. Some of them are similar to the lowly regarded Chams whom Vietnamese pushed aside five centuries ago. Moreover, the southern Vietnamese were discomfited by a sudden immigration of their fellows from the north, and it was they who had to find a new frontier. Hill tribes have objected to the expansion of southern Vietnamese into their lands. They have generally supported insurgency against the South Vietnamese government.

Perhaps the problem of the hill tribes would not be so great were the Vietnamese less technologically sophisticated, or less conscious of their capabilities, or less enamored of their sense of national destiny. The hill tribes seem to have little chance of long surviving as societies, and individual hill tribesmen seem to have little chance of assimilating effectively into Vietnamese society. The same problem faces all of the hill people of Southeast Asia, but elsewhere the problem seems less acute.

REFERENCES

[1] E. J. Hammer, *Vietnam Yesterday and Today* (New York: Holt, Rinehart & Winston, 1966).

[2] J. B. Hendry, *The Small World of Khanh Hau* (Chicago: Aldine Publishing, 1964); G. C. Hickey, *Village in Vietnam* (New Haven, Conn.: Yale University Press, 1964); and A. T. Rambo, "The Development of an Open Peasantry on the Lower Mekong Delta Frontier of Vietnam: A Case of Social Succession or Evolution," mimeographed (Honolulu: Department of Anthropology, University of Hawaii, 1973).

[3] "Muong" in F. M. LeBar et al., *Ethnic Groups of Mainland Southeast Asia* (New Haven, Conn.: Human Relations Area Files Press, 1964).

[4] G. Condominas, *Nous avons mangé la forêt* (Paris: Mercure de France, 1957).

[5] "Malayo-Polynesian—Upland Groups" in LeBar et al., *Ethnic Groups of Mainland Southeast Asia.*

ELEVEN

THE OLD AND THE NEW

DISCONTINUITIES

The cultures of mainland Southeast Asian peoples are old and new, strange and familiar, simple and sophisticated all at the same time. Successive periods of foreign influence have not obliterated older patterns of technology, cosmological belief, and social organization. Old patterns of culture have survived as new ones were being acquired. Old patterns have persisted in contexts where they did not compete with new patterns, or they have survived in blends with the new. Old contexts have transformed new artifacts and behaviors, and new contexts have transformed ancient traditions. The new has affected the old but has not replaced it.

Change at all times has been uneven. New elements and patterns have been added to some cultures and not to others, or they have been transformed differently by different cultures. Diversity has increased. Different combinations of persistence, addition, displacement, and transformation of different elements and patterns have produced many varieties of culture in Southeast Asia. Moreover, each variety embodies alternative philosophies, institutions, and behaviors that do not fit together neatly.[1]

No culture of Southeast Asia truly represents a particular stage of the past. None is entirely modern in the Western sense. Crops of the ancient horticultural Neolithic and crops brought to Southeast Asia by Europeans grow in the same fields. Medieval Hindu-Buddhist rituals and modern Western medicines cure the same patients. Water buffalo, bicycles, and buses transport the same little boys. Shadow plays of ancient Hindu epics, Chinese sword-fighting movies made in Hong Kong, and American television shows entertain the same audiences. Southeast Asians are much less interested in what is old or new than in what is appropriate in particular settings. Sometimes the appropriate is old.

Cities of Southeast Asia have very complex arrays of social settings which reflect cultural history. Before the beginning of the Industrial Revolution, cities were principally the abodes of native elites and wealthy foreign merchants who considered cities to be sacred centers of the universe and marketplaces of luxury goods. Between the sixteenth century and the middle of the nineteenth century, Europeans effected a decline of the marketplace function of traditional cities through the establishment of their own market towns.

The Industrial Revolution blossomed and bulk goods became more important than luxury goods. Market towns became "bulk and break" centers where raw materials from mines, forests, and agricultural estates were readied for transport to Europe and where shipments of cheap manufactured goods from Europe were distributed to wholesalers. Eventually, Europeans usurped the political power of native elites and gained better control of the production of raw materials and of the marketing of manufactured goods. This trade expanded rapidly. Labor was in short supply. Colonial governments and European enterprises subsidized the transportation costs of foreign Asian immigrants. Millions of them came to Southeast Asia. Many of them settled in the towns. The market towns acquired new political, administrative, and economic functions and became colonial cities. Each colonial regime, like the native regime that preceded it, developed a "primate" or great city that was several times the size of the next largest urban center. Traditional cities declined to the status of towns. Bangkok is the exception that proves the rule. The most traditional of the great cities of Southeast Asia, it is the capital of the only Southeast Asian country that did not become a European colony. Its growth kept pace with the growth of colonial cities, and it acquired many of the characteristics of colonial cities.[2]

Most residents of colonial cities were neither Europeans nor Southeast Asians but foreign Asians who owned small and medium-sized businesses or who were employed by colonial agencies and firms as business agents, clerks, craftsmen, laborers, or servants. A few Southeast Asians, members of the native elite and their followers, moved into colonial cities, too. But rural peoples of Southeast Asia did not begin to migrate to the cities in large numbers until the wars of independence that followed World War II. Many were refugees. Others foresaw an expansion of employment, business, and educational opportunities in the cities after independence. At first they moved into urban communities of major people that had been reserved for followers of the native elite during colonial times. Soon these traditional communities overflowed with rural migrants, many of whom began to build squatter communities in the unoccupied spaces of cities. Southeast Asians have continued to migrate to cities.

In some respects, Southeast Asian cities have become more traditional since the end of the period of European colonialism. The major people of each country have claimed the great colonial cities as capital cities and have added architectural and institutional embellishments that add to the image of cities as centers of the universe. Palaces, religious shrines, museums, universities, sports arenas, and international airports have been built on a grand scale in or near the capital cities. Burma's U Nu, a socialist, convened a world council (the sixth) of Theravada Buddhism in Rangoon. Malaysia's Tengku Abdul Rahman, certainly more a British gentleman than a religious fanatic, created an international Koran reading contest that is held annually in Kuala Lumpur. These were ways of affirming the sacred and central quality of cities—a quality that was lacking in colonial cities. The masses of major people have been appreciative.

The same elites that have tried to enhance the image of cities as being sacred have planned the building of factories in industrial parks just outside the cities. Only North Vietnam has succeeded in developing several industrial cities (Thai Nguyen, Nam Dinh, and Viet Tri) that are separate from the capital. In other countries, the capital is the center of manufacturing. Factories are concentrated in port areas or in industrial parks, and craft industries are scattered throughout the city. Between ten and twenty percent of all urban workers are employed in manufacturing, less than half the percentage employed by government and other service industries. But this does not reflect the great effort of high government officials to develop manufacturing industries so that they will no longer be dependent on Japan and the West, as they have been since colonial times.

Between the industrial park and city, a zone of vegetable gardens usually encircles the city. This zone supplies the city with fresh vegetables and fruit. It is usually divided into small plots worked by Chinese owners and their families, many of whom market their own produce in the city.

Traditional markets are located in residential areas throughout the city. Some portions of a market are devoted to wholesale transactions, such as those between garden farmers and owners of retail vegetable stands, but most portions are devoted to retail sales. Usually, a large part of the market is roofed. Stalls, rented from the municipality, are arranged in long rows with narrow passageways between them. Stalls with similar merchandise are in the same area of a market. Usually, there is an overflow into open areas of temporary stalls, which are dismantled at the end of every market day. The range of goods in the markets is tremendous, including fresh foods, canned foods, cloth, clothes, kitchen utensils, dishes, tools, fuel, small appliances, medicines, and jewelry. Individual sales are often very small. One can, for example, buy a single cigarette. Bargaining is the traditional mode of transaction, but for those who know the market, prices are not really flexible. However, prices vary a great deal. The prices of some goods increase while the prices of others decrease as the hours of the market day pass. The price varies according to the quality of the goods, and the standard price paid by regular customers is lower than that paid by strangers. One understands these pricing mechanisms and pays the proper price, or one does not understand and is cheated. Major peoples as well as foreign Asians are sellers and buyers in traditional markets. Small shopkeepers of nearby residential communities buy goods at the market for resale. They are of the same ethnic identity as other members of their residential community. Peddlers of different ethnic identity from other areas of the city may enter the community and sell goods during the day. All of these entrepreneurs are petty capitalists whose incomes are modest.

A very different kind of commerce takes place in the business firms located along major thoroughfares and in the business district that adjoins the central area of government offices. Goods are sold in larger amounts and at prices that do not change as quickly as in the traditional markets. This merchandising offers goods graded by quality and makes use of advertising displays, sales clerks, and cash registers. It is commerce in the Western style. Foreign Asians dominate this sector of commerce to the point of virtually excluding major peoples.

International firms have business offices near the center of the city. Banks, oil companies, insurance firms, import-export firms, automobile agencies, and travel agencies are about the same as in the West. Often, the managers are Europeans, but foreign Asians hold high positions in the firms. Major peoples are sometimes employees, but usually they have the lowest paying jobs.

Kinds of transportation in the city are as varied, from traditional to modern, as kinds of commerce. Boats are still an important means of transporting people and goods in Bangkok, although many of the canals have been filled to become highways for bicycles, motor scooters, and automobiles. In most cities, oxen carts are banned on the main thoroughfares but are commonplace in the suburbs. Bicycles abound. Bicycle trishaws transport people and goods. Motor scooters serve as family vehicles, transporting two or sometimes three passengers. Mini-taxis, three-wheeled motor scooters with small enclosed cabs, are common in some Southeast Asian cities. Then, of course, there are the various kinds of automobiles—Mercedes Benz limousines and taxicabs, Jaguars, Citroens, Toyotas, Datsuns, Volkswagens, Austins, Fiats, Fords, and Humbers. Public transportation is more efficient than in most American cities. Taxicabs are a relatively inexpensive means of traveling in the city or even between cities. Bus transportation is cheap. Service is frequent, and virtually all parts of the city are served. Buses have scheduled routes through many small towns that are distant from the city. Railroads and airlines connect cities and some of the larger towns. Modern Western modes of transportation are as much a part of the natural world of urban Southeast Asians as soda pop.

Riding through a Southeast Asian city in a limousine or trishaw, a visitor from the West is initially less aware of the diversity of people than of the diversity of architectural styles. Some of the recently built suburbs, although much smaller in area, resemble suburbs of American cities. Multiple-storied apartment and office buildings are modern Western in style. Government and business buildings of the colonial period are nineteenth-century European in style, as are some of the houses of the elite. Many dwellings are a blend of West and East, having elements of Southeast Asian architecture, such as wide overhanging roofs, slotted shutters, large verandahs, open eaves, and upper walls of lattice or wire screen —features that protect inhabitants from sun and rain and cool them with freely moving air. Classical Southeast Asian architecture is represented in the styles of ancient shrines and some recently constructed national monuments. The common Southeast Asian architectural styles are present in the communities and squatter settlements of major people. Galvanized sheets of iron have replaced roof thatch, wooden planks have replaced split bamboo, and the areas between the house pilings have been walled in. But the styles are basically traditional. Chinese and Indian communities are architecturally distinctive, too. Temples and the houses of wealthy persons, especially, retain the styles of the "old countries," India and China.

Elements of diverse styles of architecture often exist side by side, even in the same building, but overall architectural style makes quite visible the boundaries between different ethnic communities. This and other evidences of ethnic diversity such as the multilingual traffic and business signs—in Kuala Lumpur, Guinness Stout is good for you in four languages—often show a blending of old and new.

Few modern travelers from the West see the full spectrum of everyday life in Southeast Asian cities. Most remain within the narrow context of international upper-class culture, people who are transported by automobiles, housed in airconditioned buildings, pampered by human servants and electrical appliances, nourished with bland westernized foods, informed by European language media, and titillated by European kinds of entertainments and sports. A few Southeast Asians, including members of the ruling and administrative elites, medical doctors, university educators, and wealthy businessmen, spend a very large part of their lives in this same cultural context. They have Western or Western-style education. They speak European languages, understand Western perceptions of the universe, enjoy Western forms of entertainment, and can be appropriately critical of expressions of Western art, law, and science. Some have made creative contributions to Western systems of knowledge.

The urban elites of Southeast Asia have in common a knowledge of Western culture. But there are differences among them. Thais have had the broadest exposure to varieties of Western culture. Malaysians and Burmese see the Western world through British-colored glasses. Laotian, Khmer, and Vietnamese elites are best acquainted with the French version of Western culture, although they have had recent experience with the American version.

There are differences among the elites of each Southeast Asian country, too. University professors, medical doctors, and other professionals are more westernized than other elites, and they are more diverse ethnically. Overseas Chinese, overseas Indians, major peoples of Southeast Asia, and Eurasians are represented among the professional elite. A large majority of the ruling and administrative elite in each country is of that country's major people (Burmese, Khmer, Lao, Malay, Thai, or Vietnamese). They are strongly bicultural, critical of Western culture, and deeply interested in their own culture. The business elite consists principally of foreign Asians (overseas Chinese and overseas Indians). Many of them know large portions of three cultures—their own culture, Western culture, and the major culture of the country in which they live. Their cultural loyalties vary.

Western artifacts and products are everywhere in the cities, but Western philosophy, language, and courtesy tend to be confined to particular kinds of settings and social relationships such as those associated with offices and public facilities of functional and administrative agencies of government and of large-scale businesses. The elite are very westernized during business hours. They cease being Western when they participate in traditional rituals and when they relax in the privacy of their homes. Traditional rituals are not all derived from a homogeneous cultural fabric of the past, but rather from different cultural sources that were influential at different times. Attitudes and behaviors that are appropriate for one kind of ritual may be inappropriate for another. For example, some traditional Malay curing rituals are Arabic in origin, some are Hindu-Buddhist, and others are animistic. Malays recognize the differences between these three categories of curing rites, and they recognize Western curing rites as still another category. Each category of ritual requires of participants a particular decorum. There are overlaps, of course, but essentially each category of ritual is a separable universe. Like any other important problem, a serious illness may be treated in several ritual universes to insure that an appropriate universe is found. When Western medicine fails, members of the Malay elite have no qualms about seeking non-Western treatment. Neither do they see any contradictions among Western, Arabic, and Hindu-Buddhist rituals that accompany the installation of a new head of state. In the privacy of their homes, many of the westernized elite lounge in their native-style clothing, eat their native food, speak their native dialect, and observe the rules of their native systems of courtesy. They are not so much concerned with preserving their traditional culture from modern influences as with adjusting their attitudes and behaviors to conform with the significant characteristics of different settings.

The concern to fit into the particular setting or universe that they occupy is very important and common among Southeast Asians. Given positions in governmental administrative services, they quickly learned to behave like European clerks. Their intense devotion to fitting properly into the European-style bureaucracy of colonial regimes has been described by some Western scholars as evidence of "clerk mentality" or of "authoritarian personality."[3] As European colonial regimes became Japanese regimes, Southeast Asians adjusted to the new setting, and some Europeans accused them of treachery. Americans who attempted to thwart communist-led rebellions were similarly offended by the shifting "loyalties" of Laotians and Vietnamese, who merely conformed to shifts between communist and non-communist forms of local government. Members of the elite who change cultures from Western at the office to Southeast Asian at home conform similarly to a shift of setting.

The urban masses are predominantly descendants of foreign Asians who migrated to Southeast Asian cities during the colonial period. They are, of course, enmeshed in modern technology —using railroads, buses, trucks, automobiles, motorcycles, motor scooters, kerosene and propane stoves, electrical and electronic appliances, plastic utensils and bags and string, and canned foods. Many people are quite familiar with the details of modern Western technology because they work as machine operators, mechanics, and technicians. Many who work as teachers in government schools, or as clerks in government offices or large business firms, speak a European language and have read European books. But most habitually speak their native language even at places of work. They participate fully in traditional rituals, and they seek treatment from traditional healers more often than from doctors of Western medicine. Many of them attempt to help maintain private schools so that their children will learn their own traditional culture (Chinese or Indian) in addition to the culture of the major people and portions of Western culture that are taught in government schools.

An increasing proportion of the urban masses are major people (Malay, Burmese, Thai, Lao, Khmer, or Vietnamese). Most governments are attempting to increase the proportion of major people in urban occupations as a part of economic development schemes. Most of them are clerks, servants, unskilled laborers, elementary school teachers, or operators of small business enterprises. Many are unemployed or underemployed. But their situation is not hopeless. Some of the younger members of the modern ruling and administrative elites stem from this background. They compete successfully with members of the traditional elite for admission to secondary school and university. This new elite is more westernized and more alienated from the urban and rural masses than the traditional elite, who have a vested interest in the continuation of the culture of the past.

Major people who are of the urban masses live in cultural settings that are technologically westernized, but most of them do not understand the details of Western technology. Many are professional car and bus drivers, but few are mechanics. Most of the men are clerks. Some have small businesses that occupy front rooms, and many house owners rent out portions of their houses to others. Like rural villages, the urban communities have temples or mosques, religious schools, and prayer houses. Traditional attitudes, courtesies, and rituals are very important aspects of everyday life that overshadow Western technology. A few members of the elite who themselves cherish the traditional ways live in these communities.

There are many ties with rural villages. Individuals move back and forth between urban community and rural village, following the best economic opportunities and visiting friends and relatives. Young male adolescents, especially, move easily between rural and urban settings, gaining experience that is considered to be important in the transition to adult status. In the urban communities, they live with relatives or in groups of three or four in rented apartments. Increasingly, young women are finding employment with urban firms and government agencies and are moving to the cities. They, too, stay with relatives or live in groups in rented apartments. Traditionally young bachelors of rural areas have sojourned in cities, but young unmarried women have remained in the villages. Young women who migrate to cities have broken with tradition and probably will alter other traditions in urban communities. Like the bachelors of recent years, these young women tend to remain aloof from the traditional urban communities in which they live and to immerse their minds in movies, television shows, magazines, and books when they are not working at the office or doing household chores. They are very much interested in the modern world.

CHANGE AND PERSISTENCE IN RURAL AREAS

Culture change is less apparent in rural areas than in cities. But rural traditions have changed and are changing. Western scholars are often ignorant of rural lifeways in their own societies, and having no basis for comparison, they overstate the cultural conservatism of the rural communities of Southeast Asia. All of the plantation communities of foreign Asians and many of the lowland villages of major people owe their very existence to rapid culture change during the colonial period. Temples of plantation communities, for example, reflect the traditional architecture of foreign Asian workers who were imported by Europeans, and the "coolie lines" in which the workers live were built according to the architectural specifications of European managers. Many of the most important plantation crops—rubber (from Brazil), oil palms (from Africa), and pineapples (from Mexico)—were imported and first established as commercial crops by Europeans. Other crops such as rice, coconuts, and tea became commercially valuable because of a rapidly expanding world market that was developed by Europeans.

Many rural villages of major peoples were established because of the advantages of new systems of transportation, new crops, and new markets that were developed for commercial agriculture by Europeans. Europeans brought many new kinds of plants to Southeast Asia from their colonies in the New World. Those that did not become export crops entered the cuisines of Southeast Asians and became important crops for local markets. Examples include papaya, tapioca (manioc), sweet potato, maize, chili, tomato, peanut, potato, tobacco, seedy guava, and avocado. Together with rice, rubber, and palm oil, which are produced for international markets, these crops for local markets comprise a major source of income for Southeast Asian peasants. Economic relationships with cities are no longer characterized by tithes and corvée labor but by participation in markets as producers and consumers. Urban markets had existed before the Industrial Revolution, of course, but were then not developed to the present extent.

Consumer goods of the West and the modern westernized consumer goods of Japanese, Chinese, and Southeast Asian industries are ubiquitous in the rural communities of Southeast Asia. Bicycles, sewing machines, milled cloth, plastic or rubber sandals, tinned food, kerosene lanterns and stoves, sheets of galvanized iron, galvanized nails, flashlights, transistor radios, clocks and watches, cigarette lighters, sun glasses, reading glasses, patent medicines, soda pop, magazines, and newspapers are very common in lowland villages and are available in many communities of hill people. It is an unusual lowland village that is not served by a bus line and does not have at least one inhabitant who owns an automobile or motorbike. Hill people rarely own cars or motorbikes, but some have bicycles.

The technology of the West has entered every rural community of Southeast Asia, but it has not swept aside traditional technology. Palm leaf thatch and split bamboo are still acceptable alternatives to sheets of galvanized iron and mill-sawn planks of wood. Crops of the horticultural Neolithic—taro, yams, bananas, breadfruit, and citrus—have not been replaced by newer crops. Tobacco smoking has not entirely replaced betel chewing. Even bark cloth continues to be important in some ritual contexts. Blowguns and crossbows continue to be used by hill people who cannot afford guns, and even hunters who own guns continue to use snares for catching certain kinds of game. Western technology has added few alternatives to some aspects of traditional subsistence technology, such as freshwater fishing, and some products of Western technology, such as toilet paper, are regarded as bizarre.

In the rural areas, particularly, products of modern Western technology have acquired new meanings. For example, peasants of northern Thailand have used bottles of Coca Cola as religious offerings and cans of evaporated milk as ritual gifts to priests, and aboriginal hill peoples of Malaya reserve their canned sardines for great festive occasions such as marriages.[4] Among Malays, aspirin and injections of penicillin are acceptable medicines for illnesses that are believed to be caused by "cooling" influences. But many people believe that the same medicines cause great harm when prescribed for illnesses that are believed to be caused by "heating" influences. They believe that the curative properties of aspirin and penicillin derive from the fact that these are "heaty" substances. Thus Western medications are accepted in accordance with non-Western theories of medicine.

Many traditional beliefs have hardly been affected by Western influences. Even Hindu-Buddhist beliefs, which were introduced much earlier, have not replaced all earlier beliefs. Islam and Theravada Buddhism are still in the process of spreading among hill peoples. Among Malays and Chams, belief systems have at least four layers—animism, which was partially displaced by Hindu-Buddhism, which was partially displaced by Islam, which is being partially displaced by Western "rationalism." The belief systems of many other mainland Southeast Asian peoples that were not complicated by the addition of Islamic beliefs were complicated by the addition of Christian beliefs or Confucian and Taoist beliefs. But older beliefs did not disappear. In many rural communities each belief system is isolated within a particular ritual context as if to preserve it for special enjoyment.

Modern media of communication have exposed rural peoples to urban and foreign culture much more thoroughly than in the past. Nationalized radio and television stations and a carefully controlled press carry some aspects of Western culture, such as news items, entertainment, and product advertising, to most rural villages. The media encourage use of the national language, broadcast information concerning government policies, and otherwise spread the urban version of the culture of major peoples so that the residents of rural villages are increasingly involved in the culture of the capital city.

Hill peoples have some contact with the culture of the great cities. They listen to the programs of the national radio stations, and they occasionally speak with government officials who are supposed to protect their interests. Some of them have traveled to cities. But most of them only visit small towns where they participate in the markets, socialize in the coffee shops, and purchase a few goods from shopkeepers. Their relationships with government officials and others of the major peoples are ambivalent. Governments have attempted to provide them with modern medical care and with educational opportunities but have also confiscated their lands for rural development projects that benefit the major peoples. Most of the development projects that are supposed to benefit hill peoples focus on their conversion to the culture of the major peoples.

Hill peoples, never entirely isolated, are now more exposed to the culture of major people than ever before. It seems probable that most of them will be increasingly exposed to urban influences as advances in agricultural technology allow wet-rice agriculture and other kinds of commercial agriculture to replace slash-and-burn horticulture. The rapidly increasing populations of major peoples will force governments to discover and apply the new technology.

PROBLEMS AND PROSPECTS

Rapidly increasing population is a major problem. The populations of major peoples increase about three percent annually. Foreign Asian populations increase almost as rapidly. Only the populations of hill tribes are remaining the same or declining. Governments have sponsored agricultural development of "empty lands" in order to increase food supplies and earnings from exports. These rural development schemes have not slowed the flood of migrants to the cities.

Urban centers that have populations of more than twenty thousand persons continue to increase at a tremendous rate (5 to 12 percent annually). Shortages of housing have not been relieved entirely by government financing of low-cost housing projects. One of the most economical forms of mass housing, multistoried apartment buildings, has been popular with the Chinese of Singapore but has not been popular with the major peoples of other countries. They dislike living at great heights, in close proximity to people who have different customs, and without enough space for a small garden or a chicken coop. They prefer squatter settlements to high-rise apartments. Thus, squatter settlements have not been eliminated. Many of the older ones are developing into permanent communities that have city utilities. Squatters still build settlements on vacated land.

Employment and business opportunities in the cities increased after the wars of independence but not enough to fulfill the expectations of all immigrants. Unemployment and underemployment have been severe problems. In some urban communities of major peoples, unemployment has exceded twenty-five percent. Many who work are underemployed in the sense that their particular businesses or jobs are not really essential and produce very small incomes. Street hawkers, trishaw drivers, and proprietors of small stores, for example, are too numerous for any of them to prosper. In offices, three or four office boys do the work of one and share the salary of one. The same is true of sales clerks and family servants. Underemployment forces many individuals to work at several part-time jobs or to rely on rural relatives for part of their subsistence. Moreover, their economic relationships with foreign Asians have become important politically. In rural villages, they are symbiotically dependent upon foreign Asian entrepreneurs, but in the cities they compete with foreign Asians for jobs. On the one hand, foreign Asian businessmen control employment in private firms and they tend to hire persons of their own ethnic identity. On the other hand, major peoples control the government agencies. Government has granted major people the major proportion of government jobs and has pressured private firms to employ more of the major people. Moreover, Southeast Asian governments have increasingly entered the field of business in attempts to relieve the economic problems of major peoples and have come into conflict with the business interests of foreign Asians. Major people and foreign Asians continue to be annoyed with each other over this issue, which has its basis in the economic and political characteristics of European colonial regimes.

Demand for education has outpaced increases in educational opportunities. Secondary and university education are important qualifications for positions in government service. Prospective students must pass examinations for places in secondary schools, and they compete by examination for places in universities. Many students take the examinations several times before succeeding or deciding to accept failure. Private tutors, small private schools, and a few special government schools prepare those who previously failed their examinations. There are always large numbers of youths in cities who are engaged primarily in studying for examinations. University students are also judged by examination, and some spend many years gaining their degrees. These circumstances and increasing numbers of places in secondary schools and universities account for the large numbers of students in Southeast Asian cities. Students have been an important political force because of their large numbers in capital cities, their familiarity with international and national issues, and their willingness to express their views.

Education has been a divisive issue everywhere. Students and professors have rarely agreed with politicians. In several countries, especially Malaysia and Thailand, overseas Chinese have felt that politicians have interfered with legitimate efforts to maintain educational institutions in which Chinese is the language of instruction. Moreover, foreign Asian and native Southeast Asian students are concentrated in different academic disciplines. Foreign Asian students have excelled while native Southeast Asians have failed in the sciences. Native Southeast Asians dominate the humanities and social sciences. Examinations for entrance into universities emphasize the humanities and social sciences, and university degrees in these subjects have been required of aspirants to the highest positions of government administration. Some foreign Asians have felt that these circumstances discriminate against them. The politics of ethnicity are important even in university education.

Class consciousness, in the Western sense of consciousness of kind among persons of the same economic level, has not been an important factor in the political and economic behavior of the major peoples of Southeast Asia. Vietnamese, of course, are an exception. Otherwise, the few individuals of the major peoples who have cooperated with foreign Asians in labor movements and political parties are of the westernized elite. Ethnic identity rather than class consciousness has been the major factor in the politics of Southeast Asian countries.

Differences of social rank are very important in the social systems of major peoples but so far have not comprised an important basis of economic and political conflict. Among Theravada Buddhists, the wealthy are believed to be so blessed because of spiritual merit accumulated in the past, and they are expected to expend large sums to accumulate merit for the future. Moreover, the poorer one is, the more one should spend to accumulate merit for the future.[5] Malays, too, are required by their customs to expend their material wealth on charity, feasts, and a pilgrimage to Mecca. In their view, the wealthy of their own ethnic identity are blessed, and the wealthy are expected to be generous to a fault. Moreover, each person is responsible for his own spiritual (and economic) transitions. In such societies, where successful development of a cooperative movement is incredibly difficult, the development of an intraethnic class struggle is truly revolutionary. Even in North Vietnam, class struggle was stopped short of full fruition by the highest ranking mandarin, Ho Chi Minh, and the Vietnamese are not Theravada Buddhists or Muslims.

The greatest economic and political problem of mainland Southeast Asian countries is the lack of intraregional trade. Most of the countries continue to compete with each other as producers of raw materials for industrialized countries. They are still economically dependent upon the West and Japan. Dependency will decrease as their economies become more complementary. Some of the countries will develop their reserves of petroleum and natural gas and will increase their industrial capacities. The institutional forms that will be utilized to bring about these developments will not be purely Western.

The traditional economic and political institutions of mainland Southeast Asian government were not entirely forgotten during European rule. They remain like the patterns of old wallpaper under a thin coat of new paint. Overseas Chinese and Indians (foreign Asians) have long controlled the private sector of national economies of Southeast Asian countries, but major peoples, who control the national government, will reduce the importance of the private sector, and they will reduce foreign Asian domination of the private sector. North Vietnam and Burma have virtually eliminated private enterprise. Thailand has forced prominent overseas Chinese businessmen to become Thai. Malaysia has attempted to follow a more gentle course towards assimilation of foreign Asians. But the policy of assimilation exists and will continue. Also, the Malaysian government will continue to increase its participation in commerce through government corporations and will continue to increase its regulation of private enterprise. These policies derive from concern over the economic domination by overseas Chinese and Indians.

The trend toward nationalized economies and authoritarian forms of government may be little more than a return to the traditional forms of the precolonial period. PERNAS, the government trading corporation of Malaysia, for example, is similar in concept to the royal trading corporations of the Melaka sultanate. The form of rule by cadres of the Communist Party of North Vietnam is very similar to traditional rule by the mandarinate. Generals ruled in South Vietnam, Thailand, and Burma in precolonial times just as they have in modern times. Thailand's monarchy has reasserted its strength recently, and members of royal and chieftain families still rule in all the other Southeast Asian countries except Singapore.

Only Singapore, which was created by the British and populated by overseas Chinese, has maintained parliamentary democracy in a nearly Western form. Democracy was introduced by the West to all of the major peoples of Southeast Asia, but they have found it to be partially or entirely inadequate. Marxism, too, was introduced by the West. Similarly, it has been either changed or rejected. The association of capitalism, democracy, and Marxism with Western culture has tainted all three in the eyes of many Southeast Asians. But capitalism and democracy have had the misfortune of being sponsored by the former colonial powers, which proved themselves to be untrustworthy many times over. Anticolonialism still lives, and its dark suspicion clouds the prospects of political and economic development of the region.

Future leaders of Southeast Asian countries will have difficulty solving the problems associated with developing new nationalisms, restraining territorial expansion of other major peoples, increasing industrial capacity of national economies, and developing intraregional trade. If there are no more serious crises, the energy, mineral, and human resources of the region can be developed tremendously. However, such development awaits a restoration of balance or normalcy in which Southeast Asians are no longer reacting to the European colonialism of the past.

Southeast Asian countries are still recovering from the withdrawal of direct European rule. Lowland cultures are rebounding to some extent, dropping cultural traits almost acquired during colonial times. As lowland cultures reacquire their own balance, they will probably exert increasing acculturative pressure on foreign Asians and the hill tribes. New cultural traits will spread unevenly from elite to urban to rural populations. Perhaps new technologies will redefine the practical differences of life in the city, on the farm, and in the hills. But I suspect that the ancient bases of organizing experience and behavior—conceptions of spiritual energy, behavioral definitions of identity, integrative systems of courtesy and personal polity, and cosmological conceptions of leadership and state—will remain.

REFERENCES

[1]L. Sharp, "Cultural Continuities and Discontinuities in Southeast Asia," *The Journal of Asian Studies* 22 (1962): 3–11.

[2]The best general source on cities of Southeast Asia is T. G. McGee, *The Southeast Asian City* (New York and Washington: Praeger Publishers, 1969).

[3]J. F. Guyot, "The 'Clerk Mentality' in Burmese Education," in R. O. Tilman, ed., *Man, State, and Society in Contemporary Southeast Asia* (New York, Washington and London: Praeger Publishers, 1969); and J. C. Scott, *Political Ideology in Malaysia* (New Haven, Conn.: Yale University Press, 1969).

[4]M. Moerman, "Western Culture and the Thai Way of Life," in Tilman, ed., *Man, State, and Society in Contemporary Southeast Asia.*

[5]D. E. Pfanner and J. Ingersoll, "Theravada Buddhism and Village Economic Behavior, A Burmese and Thai Comparison," *The Journal of Asian Studies* 21 (1962): 341–61.

INDEX

210